BAY SORREL RANCH

Bay Sorrel Ranch

BAY SORREL RANCH

BY JUDE STRINGFELLOW

Bay Sorrel Ranch

Copyright © 2023 by Jude Stringfellow.

All rights reserved. No part of this book may be used or reproduced by any means, graphic, electronic, or mechanical, including photocopying, recording, taping or by any information storage retrieval system without the written permission of the publisher except in the case of brief quotations embodied in critical articles and reviews. No character in this book is to be considered real in any way, shape or form. This is a novel; it is a work of fiction.

Bay Sorrel Ranch

THANK YOU PAGE

Thank you, Yvonne Espinoza Ramirez for suggesting the word "*Harbinger*".

Thank you, Jeannie Clarke for suggesting the words "*Farrier*" and "*Abysmal*".

Thank you, Robin Hatt Moorhead for suggesting the word "*Realm*"

Thank you, Jedelle Givens for suggesting the word "*Equinophobia*".

Thank you, Gordon Dean Flick for suggesting the words "*Rough neck*"

Thank you, Barbara Hill for suggesting the words "*Cactus Rose*".

Thank you, Julie Szabolcsi-Anderson for suggesting the words "*Buckle bunnies*".

Thank you, Rita Miller McHann for suggesting the words "*Bull chips*".

Thank you, Caity Stringfellow for suggesting the word, "*Pantomime*"

Thank you, Laura Stringfellow for suggesting the word "*Paraphernalia*"

Thank you, Reuben Stringfellow for suggesting the word "*Bedlam*".

Thank you, Marty Kapp for suggesting the words "*Blue Ridge Mountains*"

Thank you, Bill McFarlin for suggesting the word "*Texas*".

Thank you, Tex for your humbled spirit and cute dimples.

Bay Sorrel Ranch

DEDICATION PAGE

It is my privilege as well as my pleasure, to dedicate this book to my long time and long-suffering friend Robin Hatt Moorhead. Robin will understand every word in the book, as she herself is a great horse lover. She and I met when we were way too young to ride solo, but over the years we both managed to make it happen as often as we possibly could. I was envious of her horse ownership as a kid, and she became envious of my family owning German Shepherd dogs. Since about the time we could run up a hill, we've been running, climbing, walking and hanging around hills and trails with our various kids and animals in tow. Though she rarely adorns her head with her once-signature pigtails, it is that Robin that I will always remember when I think of her; what's time got to do with it? We're both Christians, we'll see each other for eternity! I truly love you, friend.

Bay Sorrel Ranch

DISCLAIMER

Oh, the disclaimer! How I love my disclaimers. This one is a good one, because it deals with having to be sure that none of the really rude, nasty, mean, or callous characters we've run across during the years both in Oklahoma and Indiana will try to step up and sue me for pointing out their incredible inept mannerisms. I decided to write this book because we've had to put up with, deal with, tolerate, and ignore more than what anyone could consider a *"fair share"* of horse-people who think they know it all. In all the years I've owned or boarded horses, I've run across ONE person who I would say actually knew more than anyone should, and that would be a twelve-year-old we called *"Kenz"*.

This book will mention *near-names*, and it will draw conclusions, and I may even basically physically describe this or that person or horse; but those names, images, thoughts, and actions are strictly based on partial reality, not true reality. They are not themselves reflective in any way shape or form of the real people we met, or knew by reputation. There is NO ONE in this book who fully characterizes any real human (or animal for that matter). I wrote a book! It is a fiction book. Nothing in this book is real, nor should it be taken as being real. It may remind some of their past behavior, it may remind some of their present behavior, but I assure you, I am not pointing fingers at anyone in any specific way, but if it makes you feel better, there will be a few mistakes in the book that I missed during the editing process. That may even the score a bit.

If what I've said sounds really mean of me to say, it is mean. The horse world is by far the worst world I have ever been a part of. The lies, the actions, the reactions, the scams, the cover ups, and the out and out falsehoods would turn most people inside out. That being said, some of the best people in the world also own horses; and they have been both an inspiration to me, and a reason to continue hoping for the best.

I often said, and I still say it, that the best thing about horse-people is their dogs! I stand by that statement. The books *"Tartaned Soul"* and *"Tartaned Spirit"*, which are mentioned in the book, are my own books, my own creations. If there are another books by the same title, so be it. I'm talking about the manuscript I wrote and am tweaking to release it sometime soon. I got out of the horse world because of the people, and the expense of keeping a horse. Geez Louise! If you've never checked into it, just read on, my character Jule explains it to her friends.

ENJOY the read!!

Bay Sorrel Ranch

1

The thought occurred to her, that the first sip of her McDonald's unsweetened tea literally tasted like water from an outside rusty tap being poured over dried out hay that's been left in the Oklahoma sun a bit too long. It may be on ice, but it wasn't something most people would have chosen to cool themselves in the heat of another hot summer day. She assured herself that what she was tasting couldn't be better if she had made it at home herself; which was the one reason she found herself making the one-mile trek to Micky-D's nearly every day. Hay tasted pretty damn good to the woman; it had been simply too long since she had been around it for any real length of time. If she had to make a comparison to it and anything else she would say that the tea seemed like a harbinger of good things to come; earthy, real, not something fake or made to fool anyone.

Juliett Leigh Armstrong, "*Jule*" to most anyone who knew her, was the sort of woman who wasn't impressed with the fancy things in life; even now that her seventh published Highland romance book had somehow *"taken off"* and was as they say *"flying off the shelves"*. To be honest, and she usually was honest, Jule would be the first to tell you that she never wrote any of her books with the intention of actually selling even one of them. She did write them with the hope that they would be enjoyed, certainly, but if she and her kids were the only ones actually reading the books, she would have been content. When *"Tartaned Soul"* sold as quickly and as proficiently as it had over the past few months, Jule found herself searching the net to find not only a good publicist, but also another full-time promoter and manager who could bring about desired results not only in book sales, but also a meaningful tour which could allow her to travel at the same time. Clearly, a win-win for everyone.

Her new manager Michael Maguire lived in Las Vegas, having removed himself from the East Coast area for personal reasons. While the mountains outside of Vegas couldn't hold the same magic as did his wife's longstanding love for the Blue Ridge Mountains of Tennessee, Maguire knew that the wheels turned a little faster in the land of chance. His guidance for Jule, in just under a few months' time, had proven to be literally worth his weight in gold; and Maguire was a big man! Within weeks of their meeting online, Maguire had planned both a seventeen-city domestic book tour, along with an eleven-city international tour including Edinburgh, London, Dublin, Stockholm, Paris, Madrid, and Rome as well as a few more interesting venues. So many expectations, so many sites to explore. Due to his own personal passion and fascination with Europe, *"Mac"* made sure each and every date was spread out over at least a couple of days, giving them time to delve into the sites and history of each gloriously lavish and ancient city they set for venue.

Sixty-eight days abroad meant staying in expensive hotels, being trotted about by book sponsors; all of which were more than happy to bring the newly inspiring author into their stores and professional lives during each leg of her stay. However, as both she and Mac discovered, traipsing about Europe during the rainiest season of the year meant showing up at locations often covered in mud or less than Jule would have wanted to present herself while asking folks to buy one or more of her books. Experiences like this, she knew, weren't necessarily going to be an everyday event, and she absolutely tried all she could to bring about the positive in every solution. No doubt she had no problems finding those silver linings with Mac around, as the man simply oozed out the most upbeat demeanor known on the planet. No one, and she knew that to mean no one on Earth, could ever have accused Mr. Mike Maguire of being anything but confidently and decidedly positive. She told herself she wouldn't put it past Mike to have Type B-positive blood running through every vein in his body.

Mornings in Europe, as opposed to the mornings in the States when they were fetching their coffee, meant standing in queues and being patient about it most of the time. While in Berlin it wasn't necessarily the rudeness of the people that caught Jule's attention, but the fact that the locals literally considered themselves to have the right to push past a tourist to place an order before they headed off to train stations to push past tourists to get to work. She wondered if when they actually got to work if any of the Berliners were apt to push past their fellow co-workers to use the copiers, or to swipe their security badges before someone else could do so. It was just a thought; thoughts pass easily enough. Silver linings! She told herself, find one! While in Berlin the parks and greenways were as exquisite as she could possibly have imagined. *"There you go,"* her mind reminded her heart, *"...there's always something nice you can say."*

Though it had been a few months since her feet had returned to the States from her less-than-whirlwind adventures overseas, Jules hadn't forgotten the agonizing and senseless errand she had needed to take care of even before taking the afternoon to rest from the 18-hour flights including her two-hour lay over in Atlanta; one of busiest and most confusing airports in the world. Upon arriving at her final destination, Jule landed and found her car parked off campus of Oklahoma City's compact airport enthusiastically named Will Rogers World Airport. She came face-to-face with a bright yellowish green envelope dangling lacklusterously from the windshield of her car. The Oklahoma City Police had contacted her via email during her long trip to inform her that the sticky decal sticker on her back tag, the one with the written year on it, had been cut from the tag and was now probably hanging cockeyed on the tag of some illegally or ill-gained vehicle somewhere in the state.

The fact that anyone could just walk onto one of these off-site parking lots was upsetting enough; when she was told there hadn't been any night security at the place in over a month, Jule Armstrong thought seriously about holding the company itself responsible for the theft. After being told that the place had been abandoned, she all but felt that much luckier that only the decal of her tag had been taken, and not the entire car. The off-site parking garage had been the center of a divorce dispute that somehow ended up falling through various cracks in the court system. The gates had been locked, their new locks had been changed, but no one took the time to seal up the open corners of the fence. There were huge holes that gaped open allowing anyone to pass through.

She told herself that had she driven her adorable white fancy 1968 Volkswagen Beetle to the off-site parking facility, her luck may not have been so good. Not that many people gave her newer model Subaru Outback a second look. It had been painted a rather boring Cinnamon Brown Pearl. Why she put herself through that choice in color she couldn't remember; but at least she didn't have to look at the exterior of the car if she were driving it. She thought maybe the price had been lower, but the price of the car wasn't what she was mulling over in her brain at the moment. For a second she remembered that the Beetle was a stick-shift and no one under the age of fifty could probably drive it if they did steal it. Geez, she thought, has it come to this?

"My Bug is precious to me, but not necessarily to anyone else. I learned to drive on it. I've had it since, gosh, 1985 maybe? I was eighteen when I got it, that was November, of...damn, I'm old, I can't remember, but I can come up with it if I really want to. It was November. That much I am sure about."

She laughed, as the lonely younger attendant tried hard to walk away without carrying on anything resembling a real conversation, and not apologizing for any inconvenience.

Because she had agreed to take care of the matter as soon as she returned, Jule felt that it couldn't hurt to give it a good college try. Driving up Meridian Avenue from the airport she was all but guaranteed to find at least one open tag agency that afternoon. Her luck held; the Southside Tag Agency just a few minutes north of the runways was in fact open 24-hours a day, and because she had kept her registration with the little decal sticker's outline and receipt of purchase in the glove compartment, it wasn't hard to find the record of her purchase. She did notice that since she had been in Europe the tag had actually expired, so there were penalties to pay, but at least she didn't have to pay for an entire second year. Who does that, she wondered? Who steals the decals of the car if it's about to expire?

It made sense once she thought it through. In Oklahoma, there are two sticky decals for each tag. One, the one on the left, has the month highlighted, and the second decal, the one on the right, had the year. No one really ever took the sticker on the left; just the one on the right. Damn, just damn. They took the sticker, causing her a little trouble, but since the tag had already expired by the time she landed, maybe someone at the parking garage knew more than they were saying. Maybe they knew she wouldn't be back until after the start of the new year. It made her wonder if the owners or an attendant wasn't making a little something-something on the side; who knows?

Pulling up to her condo and parking the car under the carport still made her feel rather exposed. If they could do it once, they could do it again. Though she had been certain it was the transients or the workers at the park lot who had nicked the tag accessory, she didn't like leaving the butt end of her vehicle open to the public. From this day forward, she told herself, she would take the time to turn her car around and back it into the carport. Pursing her lips and squinting her eyes before finally deciding to do so, she backed the car as far back as it could go so that no one could squeeze themselves into the space and get any elbow room to cut through it again.

She had noticed on the tag itself, that the perp had left a rather large "*X*" where he or she had literally cut the decal from the little grove it sat in. She remembered her son had told her that once she bought the new decal, she needed to take a box-knife and do the same thing, so that if it happened again the crooks would see the "X" and know they couldn't get the decal off in one piece. Smart. Clever, and it made sense; but the sad thing was that people needed to protect themselves from theft. Jule Armstrong remembered a time when her younger self, little Juliett, could ride her bike for miles and miles on Halloween night collecting treats from anyone and everyone. Some of the treats weren't ever wrapped because they were handmade. Times had certainly changed; but not for the better. The tag situation was a few months back, but still, she thought about it every time she needed to park her car.

With Autumn creeping up on her, Jule had only two weeks to call the duplexed townhouse, the place she referred to as *the condo*, her home. In the next few days, she would need to hire people, probably a couple of college kids, to help her pack her belongings. She considered hiring students since she lived less than a mile from the Oklahoma University campus. Packing was never fun, but with a bunch of young hearts and good music blasting in the soon-to-be empty halls, she figured she could get the job done rather quickly. A call to the campus student union would secure names and bodies soon enough. Buying boxes at Lowe's and setting it up would be her job; let the kids do the rest.

Spending so many years in one spot left very few spaces in the condo that hadn't been taken up with some sort of memory; be it furniture, accessories, art, or some little thing one of her three kids had given her along her nearly fifty-four years. When she thought about it, she realized she had actually only been a mother for 34 of those years, so the first twenty wouldn't count unless she had been holding onto something from before she birthed her firstborn.

Thirty-seven boxes down and with a few more to go over the next few days, it was time to make good on her promise to herself not to miss the condo, but to make a list of all the things she really couldn't stand about the place so her transition to living in a rather large house on over a hundred acres of ranch land would make more sense and be a bit more comforting than she was feeling at the moment. Good times had taken place in the condo for sure; many with her family, some without. Countless stray kittens had been born just outside her door and in the hedges lining her storage unit. She had even rekindled a sort of howdy-do friendly relationship with the new maintenance man, a retired policeman whose idea of retirement was not to actually retire, but to work until he dropped. Jule could relate. The man had been quite helpful when the last round of the stray cats in her life decided to birth four new faces. It wasn't as if he was a mere stranger – this man was a blast from her past.

Mama cats would somehow manage to dig through the rough branches to find a missing board leading under the storage unit where Jule had placed a makeshift bed for any of them if they so desired to give up their feral ways to bring life into the world with at least a smidgeon of dignity. When the kitties were born Jule could give the mothers a bit of food laced with a slight sedative so she could remove them long enough to bring them all to the wildlife reserve in her city; the one that never asked questions, and never killed a live creature. She knew it was a long shot to do all that she did for the fur babies that considered her home theirs, but it was something she couldn't and wouldn't ever write down on that list of things she wasn't going to miss. About the only thing she would actually miss was the maintenance man; or the way she thought of him. Stephen Mueller had been a part of her life too many years ago. She had all but given up on ever seeing the man again; he had ridden off as it were into someone else's sunset. Here he was now, she wasn't sure she could trust herself not to make an utter fool of herself, so she only smiled when their paths crossed.

Retirement perhaps, had brought him to her homeowners association; even if it would have been early retirement, she knew the man as a youth. She had known of his successful and decorated career as a local law enforcer in the township near her old homestead. It could have been, she argued within herself, that he was the main reason she sought greener and different pastures for herself once she became aware that plowing through dirt on the back of a horse made more sense for a younger girl than it did as an adult. Growing up sent her into the College of Hard Knocks until she realized her pen was her best friend; when once perhaps Steve Mueller could have claimed that role.

2

Having looked her realtor in the eyes at least twice with disbelief concerning the all but unbelievably low price of the ranch up near the corners of both Canadian and Oklahoma counties, Jule had to give Alyse Bedford one more squinted-stare as if to ask if she was telling the full truth about the ranch.

"What's wrong with it, if it only costs $500,000? There's over 100 acres of land, two houses, two barns, fencing, and three water wells. Is it haunted, is it a former landfill? I don't get it? Tell me the truth, and give me the chance to figure out just exactly what's wrong with the place before I sink not only the downpayment but well over another fifty to sixty thousand in repairs to the barns and homes alone. My daughter Melora is out there now measuring the fencing, and deciding what we can keep or salvage. If it's bad Alyse, I can handle it; but I have to have the truth."

Her good friend stepped up from behind her desk to bring Jule the papers she had collected on the ranch to show her that as far as she could tell, and she had done quite a lot of due diligence on the matter, the ranch hadn't been surveyed by ghostbusters but there had been enough police reports over the years to fill up a few pages of negative documentation. What was now being called the "*BSO*" ranch, had been named quite a few things over the past one hundred years. In fact, the place had been part of the Oklahoma land run of the "*Unassigned Lands*" of 1889; the one where people lined up on literal border lines to run in from all sides in the middle of Indian Territory to claim free federal land that probably didn't belong to the government in the first place.

When the BSO had first been chartered as a ranch, long after it had been claimed in the land run, it had been done so by a woman whose initials were in fact, B.S.O. Her name was Barbara Susann Olsten (nee Miller); an aged woman who had become a rancher herself after a several decades-long stint with American Airlines. She had been one of the first young attendants to fly on board the more luxurious planes meant primarily for business men and the like. Barbara had married a man she had been acquainted with over the years, and through his connections she had opened up a modeling agency which doubled as a training facility for several airlines. Barbara, with her shrewd and sensual disposition, was the perfect overseer for such a unique and timely business venture. As the years waned on, and the need for beauty queens onboard the discreet flying gentlemen's clubs became less and less important, Barb took her money and bought something of equal or even greater beauty than women; she bought into horses. When her first husband passed leaving her without children, Barb set her mind to a more progressive means of leaving her mark on the world.

Barb had been a pageant queen in her home state of Indiana. She completed college there, but took her role as a flight attendant much more seriously than trying to use her Secondary Education degree to become a teacher. In 1936, when American Airlines began flying their Douglas DC-3 services between Chicago and New York, Barb Miller was their favorite hostess. Many men of means flew that particular route, and Barb made sure to develop relationships with as many as possible. One man in particular stood out; one Nathan Allen Olsten of Elgin, Illinois. Olsten ran numbers for agricultural companies. He knew every corn, soy bean, and wheat field in the country; he knew every barrel or peck they'd produce. It was his job to keep them in check, to keep them controlled. Barb liked the fact that he kept track of the money, she knew she could keep track of Nathan.

Barb and Nate had an understanding if not a shared agreement, and within months of their first drinks at the Admiral's Club in Chicago one snowy morning, the two were married. Barb married Nate when she was twenty-six years old. Nate Olsten was thirty-two years her senior; Barb felt that her personal investment would one day pay off in her favor. She was correct. Waiting wasn't that difficult; she even liked the man. When Olsten passed, the inheritance money alone was good enough to pay for the barren land out the wild plains of Oklahoma, a place she could start completely over. The fields had been used as cattle land, crop lands, as well as underground and off-the-books racing, dog fighting, horse and livestock events as well as a good location to brew up hardened illegal moonshine during the years of Prohibition.

Many years had passed since the BSO was legally called the BSO. Barb had sold the place to a single man by the name of Brian Scott in 1991, after the big house had been built; the one she never got the chance to live in. Throughout the many years she ran the place, both above and below board, she maintained what is referred to as the *"small house"*, an 1800 square foot ranch style bungalow on the west side of the shorter end of the property. Though not exactly small by any stretch of the imagination, it did pale in size to the nearly 4000 square foot mini-mansion Barb herself had commissioned before she had contracted an uncommon respiratory ailment associated with many who had spent years in the higher altitudes before safety precautions had been implemented. When Scott took over, the smaller house had become his office of sorts; a meeting place for still more illegal and illicit activities. Barbara Susann Miller Olsten passed in her sleep at the Cotton Ridge Home for the Aged at the age of 88 on January 4, 1992. She died completely alone.

Brian Scott, the son of another rancher in the area, had grown up in the world of drugs and free style living. If he had to make an actual living he probably would have chosen pimping for an organized prostitution ring or gaming; whichever he could get by with putting for the least amount of effort. Because his parents had been as successful as they were, Brian never fully committed himself to any sort of long-lasting program including education; he was a man of very few ambitions, but the ones he had usually cost someone else their time, their money, their own efforts, and usually much more. His mother's son rather than his father's, Brian persuaded his mother Carmine Scott, to buy the ranch for him for his 30th birthday just before Christmas in 1991.

Because Brian Scott had the same initials as Barbara Susann, and changing the names of anything such as logos, business papers would mean putting forth effort on his part, Scott continued to call the ranch by the more recent name of BSO; perhaps claiming the *"O"* for *"Operation"*, *"Organization"* or even *"Owner"*. The man never made anything he did public. Anyone's guess was as good as the next guy's. From the day he purchased the place it became overran with illegal activities including tables being set up in the smaller house for card games, roulette tables, and ferro boards.

You name the game, Scott allowed it to be played, and of course, the "*house*" was favored in every hand.

When his father Jacob "*Jacky*" Scott, himself a bit of a gambler, was asked by a local sheriff's deputy whether or not his son was running an illegal gambling operation, the old man shrugged his shoulders and told the lawman he'd need to drive up to the big house to ask the man himself. Jacky Scott indicated that the smaller house, as far as he knew was being used to store parts, engines, and motors for his son's other hobbies which included motocross racing, stock cars, and classic automobiles being restored and stored in the blue barn; the one most officials felt was the crux of the real action on the premises. It had been rumored that sex-stalls had been equipped in the blue barn, and for a price, a pretty little *filly* would put on a rather inviting peep show, like they had in the bigger cities during the great depression era. The nostalgia was too much to turn away from. Scott's peepshows vending machines were set up to take cash only, and the smallest denomination would have been a ten-dollar bill. Technology was gaining strength in automated machinery; just like a soda pop vending machine, his stalls took currency and never returned change.

Alyse continued to read the various injunctions levied at both Brian and Jacky Scott for their involvement at the ranch; it had in fact been confiscated as a part of the overall investigation into the activities that continued both openly and in secret. It wasn't until 2019, just a few years back, that the property had been legally returned to the Scott family, but with both Jacky and Carmine having passed and Brian serving more than 60 years at the El Reno Federal Prison, the land, barns, houses, and all things resembling fencing were then made available to be sold through a police auction.

Brian's worthless defense attorney Frank Kirlston, hadn't even gone through the case when he was appointed the assignment. It wasn't as if Brian or his parents couldn't afford an expensive lawyer, they could, but believing they couldn't be touched only proved to be one of their mistakes. Burying dead horses on his property without reporting their deaths to their owners and then charging them for months and in some cases years, was another wrong decision, but one the Scotts were apt to repeat as often as they thought they could get away with. The final straw, notwithstanding the illicit sex games and shows, had to be that Brian Scott allowed the manufacturing of methamphetamine on the premises. The small house had been gutted and every inch of it restored as part of the minimal compliances required for its resale.

With Canadian County and Oklahoma County vying for the rights to sell, a state assessor and survey team put the legal land description still within the boundaries of Oklahoma County officially. After a year or two of more paperwork, every realtor this side of the Mississippi River was trying to find a buyer suitable for it who could pay the minimum requested assessment of just over $500,000. It was the rest of the funding that proved to be their downfall. Due to the ownership of the place being in the jurisdiction of law enforcement, the remaining balance on the place could not be extended past three years. Within thirty-six months of its purchase, the $450,000 principal had to be paid in full. This kept just about any real offer off the table.

Since it was not technically owned by anyone in particular, the land, barns and fencing had been placed under the management of a horse trainer who had agreed to board and train horses, taking on a typical lower-end administrative type salary for himself, and giving any overage to the county clerk for recording. One day, it was hoped, the land could be bought, the houses, and barns as well as all the fencing could be repaired and someone could call it their own. Currently, under the meager overwatch as it was, dozens of riders paid various amounts for boarding both useful and unused animals. Ed Holmes being giving the right to collect payments and return any overage to the county, was also allowed to board his five horses for free in exchange of keeping an eye on the place. Something he managed to do with some level of integrity, but not as much as perhaps should have been extended.

"Let's meet up tomorrow at the barns and go over the numbers again. I'll drive out there now and pick Melora up, she's probably had about enough of the complaints and questions she'll have to field from the girls thinking they own the place now. I haven't been there in a few days, but last Saturday when I was

walking about the pastures I was called a name I won't even think to repeat to you, simply because I parked my car in a spot that her highness, one Cathy Craigstone tends to park her truck. God forbid we live our lives as the minions we are with goddesses like Cathy floating around in their shiny buckles and boots.

"If she had half a thought she'd have made an offer on the place. I think most people assume it's owned by the Scott's other son Matthew and his wife, but they weren't even listed in the old man's will from what I was told, Alyse. Who does that?"

asked Jule, *"Who has a favorite kid? Makes you wonder if Matthew was actually a Scott to begin with, or if he figured out how his dad and brother lived, and wanted nothing to do with him."*

Alyse flipped through her papers and found a paragraph worth reading about the other Scott sibling;

"He was in the cattle game for many years, but when his wife's family moved to Galveston and opened up hotels and resorts the two of them washed their hands of anything having to do with the name Scott, and took up with the Standfields. I mean, if you're going to be ridiculed on a daily basis, but you have the opportunity to make bank on the beach, maybe you do it. I would...says here he gave up any rights to it when his brother went to prison. He and his wife didn't want the tax liens and headaches." She answered.

"I'll catch up with you tomorrow at the barns, and I'll bring the contract with me. Did you want to write me out a check for $50,000 now for the down or wait until you've spoken with Melora about what her plans are?" asked Alyse, all but knowing the answer.

"I can wait. I'll bring my checkbook with me of course. I put in my briefcase this morning just because...but I may need to dust it off. We just don't write checks these days. I can't believe the county won't take my Visa!"

With that, the two women put their papers away in their respective cases and parted ways with Alyse making her way back to her Land Rover, a vehicle she felt was perfect to reflect her choice in professions, and with Jules finding the keys to her 1968 Volkswagen Beetle. The difference between the two of them notwithstanding, allowed Jules to think to herself, even if only in a sort of passing manner, that she'd never really been much for showcasing or grandstanding. Maybe she considered herself a bit more like Sam Walton in some ways; if you know you have it, you don't have to show it. If you don't have it, then well maybe you pretend you do by flashing something pretty shiny. As she reached down beside her left leg to grab the crank window's knob, she remembered why she liked the simple life.

3

Melora's strong exposed pasty-white freckled arms pulled at the stubborn wooden gate leading to one of the back pastures knowing that if she wanted to she could have stepped between the fence wires to gain access to the land. Her doggedness got the better of her, and after a few failed attempts at forcing the gate to open she used another more direct approach at completing the task. Cocking back her left leg, she thrust the heel of her rough Ariat boot in the exact spot she knew would bring her the result she had anticipated. Cracking a board in the process, she took a mental note as to which gate she had just destroyed, so she could remember to either fix it once her mother had paid for the property, or pay someone enough to have it repaired should Jule decide against the purchase.

Having already plied her mom with the facts surrounding the better reasons for buying the old ranch, Melora Armstrong felt it was all but sewn up; that her plans for constructing and creating a new

Mustang rescue and training facility would be literally just weeks away. At that point, she told herself, she's already behind the Eight-ball, and would need to scurry to keep up with what all needed to be done to the place to facilitate the number of sale-authority horses she intended to buy on the second Tuesday of the next month; which is when she purchased Mustang horses from the Pauls Valley horse containment for the Bureau of Land Management. Calling the operation the *"BLM"* had been something everyone in the horse world had done for years, but with the uprising in political realms using the three initials for something completely different, it felt odd to associate the two; as sometimes she had been gravely misunderstood when she had mentioned buying anything living from the BLM. It was odd to do, but needed to be done, Melora knowingly and openly, now referred to the government agency as the *"Bureau"*.

Moving from fence line to fence line, Melora measured and documented on her phone's note app, just how long a fence was, whether it had damage to it, whether any or all of it could be salvaged, and she added a sort of graded points system to remind herself about each post which should have been no further than ten feet apart, but were lagging at times, making the fence sag in places that could be potentially dangerous to her incoming herd. Even thinking the word *"herd"* gave Melora the confidence she knew she would need to breathe easy once all of the horses were delivered to her newly constructed and remodeled pens. It would be a few more weeks, but it was probably only a few more weeks. A double-edged sword for sure.

Each animal, and there would be twelve, would need its own space to roam about, but nothing more than a thirty-foot-by-thirty-foot pen, each lined up against one another. There would be six on the east side and six more on the west side. Between the paddocks would be a ten-foot lane, also gated at both ends. Each paddock would have its own open gate, and there would be another gate leading from *Pen "A"* to *Pen "B"* and so forth. Counting the number of gates, posts, panels, and types of materials needed was heaven to Melora; she had finally reached a point in her young life that she could say she believed in every decision she was making.

She was happier at this moment than she had ever been, and somehow this feeling was capable of erasing years of closeted depression and anxiety over being hurt emotionally and physically as a small child during the overly extended custody battle that raged between her parents. No child should have to be subjected to what both sisters were put through, but that was a long time ago, she told herself. Today, at age thirty-one, both single and independent, Melora Ashleigh Armstrong felt stronger, braver, bolder, and healthier. She was about to step into a new self and it felt great to do so.

Back at the blue barn, voices clambered about awkwardly and without so much as an inkling of authority. A nasty taller buttercup of a youth, Bree Morgan had decided a couple of years before that day, that she would be the queen of the barn. Bree gave out orders without taking anyone or anything into consideration if it meant she couldn't do or have whatever it was that she wanted. Her second in command, the daughter of Cathy Craigstone, a girl called Lily, was slightly younger than Bree, not as tall and certainly not as bold. Lily clambered right back to her idol as if to mirror any and everything sputtering out of Bree's clenched lips.

"First, her mom drops her off, and she's clearly over eighteen, I wouldn't be surprised if she's even twenty. Who doesn't have a car at twenty? What a loser. She's out there measuring things, looking at the old pastures as if she's going to bring something out here to stay in one. She'd put out a pretty-penny to fix that shit up before she could put anything in it." Morgan droned.

"...and why would she go out that far anyway? I guess she doesn't have a decent horse; that's my guess. She knows she only has a gross hag and can't afford a stall. That's probably it." She continued.

"If she can't afford a truck she can't afford a stall."

Added Lily, trying her best to make the same facial expressions as her older hero. *"She's definitely a loser. She wears Ariats and they're gross. I mean, she probably has another pair if she shows, but..."*

Before she could finish her thought, Bree interrupted Lily with her signature open-mouthed expression of shock to say,

"Show? What the hell are you going on about, you idiot. She can't show if she can't afford a truck! If she's taking her haggard-assed horse out to the back pastures with all that shit out there to get hurt on, she can't afford to buy gear to use or show clothes. She can't afford the entry fees, stupid.

"What would she show anyway? A broken-down Appaloosa that has a head the size of a walrus! Maybe she and Keegan Tanner use the same horse so they can afford to even be here. God, I wish someone would run over that bitch the next time she steps into the driveway. I can't stand her or her spotted dog!"

Bree's ugly and angry words spewed toward the open air in front herself and certainly in front of Lily since Bree Morgan would never have allowed such an underling to walk in front of her at any time, no matter how much she knew Lily wanted to be just like her. Lily Craigstone thought hard about that last statement concerning an even younger boarder named Keegan Tanner. She knew Tanner had an older Appaloosa horse that some said was part Arab, but she didn't know she had owned a spotted dog as well. Once she was able to pull apart and put her thoughts back together, and it took some time to do so, Lily understood the nuance of her friend's words; the dog comment was said to implement that the horse itself was a dog; an unworthy pest in *"their"* barn.

The Appy was something Bree would not have been seen with, let alone have owned for herself. Lily could however, conceive that Bree and her father David Morgan could own such animals to lease out to others, because it was something Bree had mentioned she wanted to do in the future. Bree had mentioned owning a dozen average horses, renting them or leasing them to riders, and doing what's called a half-lease so that two people paid her each month to ride the same horse. She could use one payment to pay for board and pocket the other half. Only a few people at the barn could have dreamed of having enough money to make the scheme work. Lily was warned twice never to attempt it; she took her sanctioning well enough.

As Melora made her way up to the paved drive of the blue barn in time to see her mother's car pulling up into the same spot she had parked in earlier; the spot Jule Armstrong had decided would be her parking spot on a permanent basis, with signage to boot, if and when she plopped down the money to buy the place. Seeing the white Bug pull into the spot Melora knew her mom well enough to know Jule was making a silent statement. In less than a few minutes time, Lily made her way from Bree's side towards Jule to meet her as she exited her car.

"If you don't mind, that's where my mom parks. We sort of have assigned places here and it's just that..."

her words again were interrupted abruptly by those of the more direct if not condescending voice of the self-proclaimed queen herself.

Bree flipped the tips of her hair back over her shoulders and said,

"You need to move. In fact, since you don't care what you're seen in, or what you drive, there's a spot just outside the big manure pile to the south of the barn."

Rolling her eyes for dramatic effect, which accentuated her overtly drawn eyebrows; looking every bit as if in some sort of off-Broadway pantomime, the wench droned,

"If you know your directions. It's that way."

Then, turning on her heel, she pointed in the exact opposite direction of the southern pole before popping her gum, shifting her weight, and giving Jule that *"try me"* look she thought was so effective on most people.

Closing the door before checking the handle to be sure she had properly locked her car, Jule smiled that smile that basically acknowledges that she has heard the twit, but that she chooses to do what she will do because she can. Turning her face purposely from

Bree's, and addressing the meeker yet not very innocent Lily Craigstone, Jule gave a slight sigh and waited a full two seconds before answering,

"I'll be OK. There's plenty of space in the parking lot, if your mom wants to park her car, there's what...ten, 15 spots on either side of where I parked. It will be OK."

Shaking her head as she passed between the girls, Jule managed to stop Bree's next sentence just in time by turning and facing the mini-wench before giving her the same evil-eye she had given Melora and her siblings growing up; the look that silently dares anyone to say another word on fear of being cut in pieces and sent out to sea for fish bait. Silence fell in the barn immediately, but from the corner of the wash rack another face had tracked what had been taking place. Keegan Tanner hadn't seen Bree Morgan put in her place ever; it was something she couldn't wait to express on TikTok accompanied by the 16-second video Keegan had managed to take.

Two clear voices could be heard denouncing Jule and Melora as being less than mediocre and insignificant trash; words that couldn't be repeated easily. Keegan didn't have to repeat them, she had recorded them.

"What are you looking at, freak?"

Bolstered Morgan, as she casually strolled around the rough edge of the stalls to meet up with the twelve-year-old at the first wash rack.

"You'd better shut your face and keep to yourself, you're not worth talking to let alone listening to. If your mom wasn't drunk all the time she'd see how ugly you are. She'd start drinking if she saw you. I bet that's why she's always drunk. She has you for a kid. I'd kill myself I you came out of me."

Bree's words could only hurt. She hadn't learned the art of being tactful, she had never accomplished the feat of being kind to anyone. Keegan's heart sunk another half inch in her chest before putting her phone away. At least recording the words, she had she could prove to her mom that Bree and several others had been mistreating her at the barn and making them wash their horses if she was expected to be allowed to ride in any of the worked arenas; inside or outside.

Larissa Lowell, Keegan's mom, had in fact been a drinker and one without much care in the way of keeping up with her children. If she picked Keegan up at all it was only because she either ran out of money to buy more liquor at the Cactus Rose where she both worked and hung out, or it may be that she hadn't always been a lush and could muster up the withal it took to at least appear to be somewhat responsible. Lowell had been a rather steady rider when she was younger; perhaps even a qualifier for the top shows in the state, but with her first pregnancy at the young age of fifteen, she had all but ruined her chances of making the circuit.

Year after year Lowell tried to regain her place in the shows, but she simply couldn't stay sober enough or out of the various beds of the various cowboys who came to the State Fair grounds or up at the Lazy E in Guthrie, to prove that they knew how to ride a bull or pull it down long fast enough to bring home a big fat check. When nearly every attempt to gain an inch cost her more than a mile, the woman resorted to anything she could to stay afloat. Unbuttoning her blouse, wearing tighter britches than perhaps she should, Lowell set out to find herself someone, anyone who could stay on the back of a hard-nosed snorting bull long enough to buy whatever she needed them to buy.

Three of her four children, all but Keegan, had been the product of a one-night stand with this or that cowboy; she knew their names, but they would have denied even meeting her if she had stepped up to ask for help of any kind. Both of the men had been married when they had met and slept with Larissa. At some point Lowell made an attempt to let one of the wife's know just exactly how she knew her cheating husband. To her chagrin the wife laughed whole-heartedly in Larissa's direction before shutting the door to their elaborate equine trailer rig, stating that she'd be a number among many. She wished Larissa Lowell luck on getting blood out of a turnip, but she thanked her for giving her more ammunition to do whatever she could when she got around to leaving the man in the future.

Keegan's father had been in love with Lowell; he had wanted to marry her, but with her history with men, and her inability to trust, the best he could do was to at least be a part of Keegan's life until he was killed in a hit-and run accident while crossing the street somewhere in Tulsa. Keegan was seven at the time of his death, and by state law, because she was his heir, an executor was set up for her. Being the sole recipient of his estate, Keegan would someday be able to afford a better life for herself. Though Lowell tried every which way she could think of to get at her daughter's inheritance, the executor had been true to his fiduciary burden. Keegan Anne Tanner would have to wait another six years before becoming one of Oklahoma's youngest millionaires. If only Larissa had known before shutting the man out of her life; it was again, another reason for her drinking.

Making her way to both Jule and Melora who by that time had turned on the back lamps of the barn to illuminate the north side of the barn where the famed manure pile resembled the Muschat's cairn in Edinburgh, Keegan introduced herself.

"*Hi. I know you're trying to buy the barn and land and everything. I heard you on the phone last night when you were in the gold barn. I'm Keegan. I mean, Keegan Tanner, I'm the hand here I guess. I mean, I guess you can say that. I'm not paid or anything, but if I wash their horses they let me ride when they're out of the arenas.*"

Such an introduction seemed both impressive and sad at the same time. Both Melora and Jule fell silent in the presence of such an innocent and devoted face as the one set before them. Keegan, with her long straight brown hair and more freckles than could ever be connected, stated also that she had been at the barn since it opened this last time. Her mother had worked at the Cactus Rose for a long time with the people who had testified against the last owner, and they were the ones who the police had trusted to watch over the barn. Keegan also mentioned that when Eddy (presumably Ed Holmes) had asked her to keep an eye out for anything stupid or scary, that she, the twelve-year-old was doing the work and not only not being paid, but was possibly putting herself in danger on so many levels.

Jule spoke first.

"Keegan, it's really nice to meet you. You seem really smart for a girl your age. I bet you're about what, twelve?" she asked.

When Keegan's smile broadened she knew she had hit the nail on the head. Having been in insurance for as long as she was, Jule could just about age anyone she needed to and come fairly close each time she did.

"Are you saying that you wash the other girls' horses and they let you ride when they are finished riding? Is that what you mean? They pay board, but so do you, right?" asked Jule.

"I do pay board. I mean, my mom pays it, but we pay board for Candy to be in the pasture. She's not in a stall. We can't afford that, but she has a run in, so she's OK. Tina and Freya Davidson have horses in the same pasture as me, but they're just horses that they loan out to people for money. I can't afford one of them. I got Candy at an auction last year for my birthday. She was $200 and both my mom and all my brothers paid $50 each for her. She's the best horse in the world, and one day I'm going to win the NBHA and then go to the Wrangler NFR after that. Candy may be dead by then, she's twenty now, but I'll get another horse and train her too. It can happen."

The girl excitedly explained.

"My name is Jule Armstrong, and this is my daughter Melora. We're thinking about buying the place, yes, and I guess you said you overheard us talking about it. Have you mentioned it to anyone? The girls up front didn't seem to think I was worth talking to, so if they thought I was buying the barns they didn't seem to be too friendly toward me. You seem to understand how important it is to be friends with the owners. That makes you about ten times smarter than any one of them." Jule stated.

"Hi, I'm Melora. I'm going to...well, if we buy it, I'm going train Mustangs on part of the ranch, the back part over to the north and west probably. Have you been out that way to see what all needs to be removed from the pasture? I didn't get a really good *look. It looks like maybe it's overgrown, maybe there's equipment or parts of tractors under the dirt and grass by the big pole. Do you think maybe you could pull yourself away from washing their horses and go explore with me? I could use the help."*

Melora's eyes smiled as she addressed her new young friend.

Keegan's face lit up with such joy at the thought of being included in whatever anyone wanted to include her in.

"Yeah, there's a lot of stuff out in those pastures. The north one is worse. I don't know if you can even see most of it, it's partly covered up with dirt and more stuff. I'll help you though. If you need help, just ask!"

To be asked to help was all she ever hoped for, her willingness to serve simply oozed from within her. Jule's gave the two of them a glance before heading back to the front office area by the lounge to check in with Alyse as to what time she would meet her in the morning.

Upon arriving at the office door, and finding it open, after she had purposely locked it when entering the blue barn, Jule's found not only had the office area been entered, but the door to the private lounge had been jimmied as well. Three teenaged boys roughly between the ages of 16 and 19 were laying on two sofas covered, literally covered with three or four underaged buckle bunnies wearing less than they would at a lingerie showing.

Without even thinking about her standing or position at the barn, Armstrong turned on the overhead light and demanded that the girls immediately remove themselves and put their clothes on without giving them even a second's notice or chance to rebut.

"*Get out!*" she cried to the boys, again without taking into consideration that the barn or the property she was commanding from had not been legally transferred in her name.

"Get the hell out of this lounge, and if I ever see your faces here again I'll have the cops swarm in on you for pedophilia so fast you'll not have a chance to zip it up before they hang you by it! You heard me...Get!"

She seethed, allowing her voice to go as guttural as it could. With such power in her command they moved in all directions, any direction but toward her as she reached for a crop whip that happened to be resting on the side of the desk in her soon-to-be front office.

"*Dare me Mister,*" Armstrong demanded while staring down the face of a bronzed sweaty youth giving her a slight challenge before resorting to calling her a bitch as he exited through the back door of the lounge.

When the girls had dressed and made their ways out of the bathroom which was connected to the office, Jule asked if any of them were boarders, and if the boys had been boarders. When they didn't answer her she shook the crop whip a bit to imply she wasn't above using it on them as well. One girl straightened to say she was not a boarder, but one of the boys had been. He was in rodeo and going to college nearby. He had been training under the old trainer and had the keys to office, but knew how to fix the knob on the lounge to get into it if he didn't have the keys on him. Jules wanted a name, she didn't get one, not from any of them, not even the one who had been brave enough to speak to her.

"Let me just say it, I'm not going to tolerate it here, not now, not ever. I don't know you, but you don't belong here. Every last one of you are under 18 years old and if you gave a damn about those boys at all, you'd stop messing with them. They could spend the next thirty years in prison for what I caught them doing with you tonight. Get a clue ladies, they don't want you for your brains! I know this because you just proved to me and the world that you don't have any brains if you're going to let yourself be fooled by those idiots. You're beautiful, every one of you. You don't deserve to be used or treated like crap, and I know you're too old to spank, but maybe if you'd been taught when you were tiny to love yourself you wouldn't find yourself googling over that rot in the first place."

When she realized that the girls had all but stopped listening and were trying to leave, she wondered how they would get home if none of them had a car.

"Do you need to call your parents? You can use...well, you have cell phones. Just call them and have them come get you. Don't come back. Not if you're not boarding. The locks will be changed tomorrow; maybe tonight. I don't know how late Home Depot stays open."

It was a statement of rhetorical means, but one of the girls piped up to say that Home Depot closed at 9:00 p.m. She knew this because her father worked at the one in Oklahoma City. She also mentioned that Pimble's Hardware in Cashion had locks too, and they were open past 9:00 p.m. on weekdays. Jule shook her head, thanked the young girl for her intel and asked again if she knew the name of the rodeo boy she'd been canoodling with. She didn't know his name, only that he drove the white F250 with the red roll bar. That should be easy enough to figure out; that is, if the boy had the balls to return anytime soon.

When Melora walked into the office using the front door rather than the one Jule had entered from inside the blue barn their eyes met. Jule knew instantly that her daughter had something important to tell her; she had that look. Melora's face was straight, no smile, no twinkle in the eyes, nothing. Keegan came through the door just behind Melora, with virtually the same expression.

"Someone dumped about a ton of shit on your car. It could have been Tucker Banderoff, he's the kind that would do that, and he has a hitch to haul a trailer too. I mean, I didn't see him do it, but his truck was parked out by the pile while Melora and I were scoping the pasture and taking pictures of the stuff you'll need to clear out."

"Keegan, did you get a picture or anything of them doing it? If they dumped it on my car they had to first load it onto that trailer you were talking about." Jule asked.

"The trailer already had shit on it, I mean manure on it. It was already full. It's the one they use in the pastures every day, but they were supposed to put it on the side of the pile. They put it on your car instead....I'm sorry."

She said while shifting her weight uneasily. When Keegan saw the other young girls leaving through the back door of the lounge she shot Jule a look of curiosity.

"I'll explain it in a minute. I have a call to make"

Jule gave Melora a look and a flick of the head before saying she'd need to get a couple of shovels to dig her car out from under the mess.

"But, before you do....listen to this call. I think you'll like it."

Pulling her cell out of her pocket, placing her fingers on the keypad and hitting the recently called numbers, Jule reached her friend and realtor Alyse Bedford at home.

"Alyse, can you come to the barns? I'll have the check written when you get here, and listen, can you bring a couple of beers? It's been that sort of evening friend...do you mind?" she asked, waiting for a response before answering.

"I'll see you in about 15 minutes; and by the way, we're calling the place the Bay Sorrel Ranch. We'll need to change the logos; and the locks."

4.

Brooke Stark was Jule's younger daughter, the one who wasn't into horses. She wasn't into farm life, country living, or anything having to do with being out in the woods unless she and her family decided to hike, fish, or go camping. She was an urban woman, and unlike her sister Melora and her mother Jule, Brooke found it a great deal more comforting to have those needed and convenient conveniences such as running water, toilet paper on demand, and maybe something resembling an electric coffee maker. She wasn't the type to go a few days without taking a shower, shaving her legs, or wearing the same clothes over and over again. Maybe, she imagined, she had been born into the wrong family, but she actually loved being the different one while growing up. It made her feel on-target most of the time, as she was able to give her older sister the goading Brooke felt she needed every time the older one would question why the baby was such, well, a baby.

Being only Fourteen months younger than her older, so much older, sister, Brooke often felt that being the baby had its privileges such as being able to literally point to something she wanted while watching their older brother scurry and trip over himself to make sure the baby was taken care of. Melora had been his *"baby"* before Brooke came along, and it wasn't as if Rogan had stopped giving Melora literally everything she could ever possibly imagine as being needed by a toddler, but the new baby was another story altogether. The new baby was helpless in Rogan's eyes. She couldn't stand up or crawl too far. She couldn't voice her every desire like his older younger sibling could; no, it was Rogan's self-imposed sworn duty to be sure little Brookie was protected and served at all costs. After twenty-nine years, and although she had married, Rogan still had strong feelings about raising his little sister correctly.

Brooke had to laugh a little, as over the years the words *"protect and serve"* would become a staple statement in the Armstrong house; Rogan had signed up for active military duty the week following his high school graduation. Now, at age thirty-four, having been in the United States Army for over eight years, followed by his growing tenure in the Oklahoma National Guard's most elite 45th Infantry, he was a First Sergeant, ready to command up to 600 men and women at his word. The only human he had never been fully capable of demanding or commanding had been his youngest younger sibling, little baby Brookie; the one he had spoiled to the utmost hilt. Brooke's eternal gratitude and respect was certain, but there was just no way in hell she'd do what her brother told her do to; not unless he asked really nicely and promised ice cream. When Brooke behaved in such manner, Rogan retreated to gain the assistance of his second charge; his first baby sister Melora.

It was this very craving for ice cream that Brooke decided to use when she placed a call to her brother while he was on annual drill somewhere in the hills of Arkansas. To hear her explain it to her husband Braydon, you'd have thought Rogan had all but given up his life-long pledge to make her every whim come true within a reasonable and timely manner.

"It's just ice cream, Bro. You owe me. You know you owe me. I don't know exactly why, but I could probably guess it has to do with me not telling Mom what you did with Carli Brightmon on Halloween - - I'll pause for dramatics if you need me to. One...two...three...do you remember now?"

She asked the man holding the other end of the conversation.

"Yeah, uh-huh...that Carli; that night. I didn't tell. Should I? I mean, a half-gallon of chocolate cookie dough doesn't seem like a big payoff to me."

She teased and continued to rib her brother.

"Brooke, as much as I would love to stop what I'm doing, which is training a bunch of idiots how to put-up tents and make fire, I can't just stop and drive three hours to bring you a pint of ice cream. No, that sounds like a husband duty to me, and Braydon is probably a lot closer to Braum's than I am. I'm in the Ouachita mountains. I can't even believe I'm getting reception right now."

Her brother mentioned, only somewhat irritated at the call; but he was actually surprised his phone worked that high up and that far away from civilization. The fact gave him a little peace of mind.

"Do you got a minute?" she asked, *"I'll tell you what happened today when I did this stupid video interview for a very progressive insurance company who will remain nameless."*

She asked as if she already knew he would probably try to decline her offer of enlightening him, but since she hadn't actually given him an actual possible way out of the situation, he more or less surrendered himself to the fact that she would be moaning and complaining to him for the next foreseeable future; something he and she both knew her husband wasn't apt to do if she had attempted to vent in his direction. It wasn't as if Braydon hadn't been used to her off-color comparisons when it came to how she had been treated or subjected to by would-be employers, he just knew the woman was better off finding a job where she could work for herself and not have to deal with actual people, which included bosses.

"No, really, it's good, I'm good, you're good. Go ahead, I'll just give these guys the green light on taking the next hour or so off so they can either kill themselves by falling off the next cliff, or maybe drown themselves in five inches of water. I haven't had a good set of recruits in three years; but no, go ahead sis. Tell me all about the idiots and how they abused you."

He said, as he held the phone between his ear and shoulder, while shaking his head silently at the men he had put in charge of getting his messages across to the others. Silence was his specialty; the man could command anyone by simply staring at them, raising his eye brows, and literally pointing or making another articulate military hand gesture which made probably more sense to the underlings.

When one or the other privates asked a specialist if First Sgt. was on the phone with his wife again, the specialist retorted that First Sgt. Armstrong wasn't married. The woman he was usually on the phone with, and depending on how he responded, would be either his sister Melora if he was able to get a word in edgewise, or his sister Brooke if he could only grunt, nod, agree, and then eventually tell her he was sorry she was going through whatever it is, and he'd do what he could when he saw her next.

The men would typically end up laughing over the matter; most of them had sisters. One quip from a nameless soldier tearing open an MRE, or meal-ready-to-eat, landed quite close to their commander's nerve when the loud mouth mentioned that sisters could be a pain in the ass, but someone else's sister could be useful. Upon hearing the words exit the private's mouth, First Sgt. decided to take a late evening run through the woods, creeks, rock beds and anything else he could think of in order to silently express himself about how he felt about the quip. The next two and half hours were exhausting for everyone, and the fact that his sister's voice could keep him motivated and on track over at least half of the trek made the quest that much more enjoyable for the man; not necessarily for the others.

"I put in my application because I thought maybe I'd like to work from home and do the whole in my pajamas thing. I could be up on the computer at 8:00 a.m. and I could get the kids off to school since I have a wireless headset. They're not going to know I'm driving down the road a few blocks. I could call people, make changes to their policies, and even sell something if I wanted to. It all seemed really cool. It doesn't pay that much really, but if I can stay home and make my own coffee that's a big plus." She started.

"Anyway, they send you their digital application and you have to fill that out. If they like you I guess, they push you through to the next level, which for them is a video interview. Not a Zoom where I can see them and they can see me, but it's a video

thing. I had to find a quiet spot and hold my phone since Braydon's usually behind me on his computer. They didn't have a blur option! Who the hell doesn't have a blur option on interactive process? It's stupid because if I'm at home working I'm not on my camera; but anyway, I had to hold the phone out and my arms aren't as long as yours or Braydon's. I think they could see the boogers in my nose." Brooke joked.

"The first questions are so lame. You have to answer them using the S.T.A.R. method, so if you don't know what that is, it stands for: Situation, Task, Action, and Results. They even made a little video to tell applicants that they expected all of the answers to follow the S.T.A.R. method, and they were like super anal about it. How do you do that when the question is, 'Why do you want to work for us?'

"I mean, can I tell the truth, and say, 'OK, here's the situation, I'm broke. I need to work to pay my bills. The task would be that I think it's best if I apply, fill out your forms and take your assessments, which I guess could fall into the action category as well.' I'm thinking that's the part they want you to do the best on; so, you can explain who you are and how grateful they should be that you decided to apply. The result, I guess I could say 'Yeah, you hire me', but I don't know, the whole thing is stupid." She lamented before taking a second sip of her stale coffee.

"That ice cream would have been really good right now, Bro., just saying. I'm trying to figure out if

my next answers were any better. I didn't tell the truth by the way. No one does. They want you to tell them real events and that's far too personal. I just make up stories and do my best not to sound too sensational when I go on about my superpowers or my innate abilities to read minds and use some sort of Jedi power to force them to pick me.

"One of the questions," she laughed, "...was 'Tell us a time when you had to deal with a critical change in the middle of a situation. What was it, how did you handle it, and what was the outcome?' Damn! I mean, OK, I could have told them about the time I was diving off the cliffs in Mexico and as I'm free falling I realize that the beach is further out than I thought it was, so I had to do some sort of a weird push-thrust move in the middle of the air to make my body go out another five or six feet so I didn't kill myself. Do you think that would have worked?

"I didn't tell them that. I made up something about going to Japan with Mom on tour with her books and I got lost in the airport and couldn't find the terminal I needed to be at so I could fly home. I told them I was Fourteen at the time, and I couldn't speak Japanese; but I was able to use hand signals and draw out things so they could understand me. I said I managed to find my way back just minutes before the plane took off; and they believed me."

When her brother didn't readily answer, Brooke asked him if he was still listening, thinking maybe his phone had ultimately lost signal.

Rogan hadn't stopped listening, but he hadn't really been listening that well to begin with. He had learned quite a few years back to just grunt in an affirmative or negative tone, depending on the circumstance, and to say things that would either end the call or continue it, depending on what he needed at the time. Such was their communication; such was their relationship. Both loving one another, but as the years had firmly found them moving in completely different directions, they found Facetime and phone calls to be easier than driving back and forth from the greater surroundings of Tulsa to the flatter plains of Norman, Oklahoma, where First Sgt. Armstrong's unit was stationed.

"Still here, but I have to let you go. I'm on a run with the boys and I think one of them may have found a kitty to play with."

Rogan's euphonism was understood to mean that either a bobcat or a mountain lion was going to need to be contained or dealt with. The siblings ended their call making those promises they always made; one to call again, and one to accept the call when she did.

"OK, I'll call you back, I guess. Have fun in the woods. Don't forget to check for ticks." She warned.

"I'll take your call if I can, and I thank you for your kindness little sister. Be sure and kiss the kids for me."

Rogan's nephew and niece meant the world to him. The fact that she had named her first born Oliver Wayne after his Rogan Wayne, meant even more. Oliver's little sister Ariel would probably learn from her mother just how to manipulate and take over the life of her older brother at some point, but for now, Ariel Iris Stark would have to be satisfied with beating the boy at chess and other board games, he had the advantage over her when it came to online games.

Rogan knew he couldn't hope to see Oliver off to college at the University of Oklahoma and expect him to beat the living tar out of their biggest rival, their own interstate opponent, the Oklahoma State Cowboys on the gridiron. There would never be another Bedlam game; this thought hurt everyone one of them to the core; the Armstrongs were a divided family with Rogan and Jule being for the Sooners and somehow both girls rooting for the Cowboys. Rogan knew this was the last year the Sooners would play in the Big twelve Conference before heading off to the SEC. If he wanted to see Oliver succeed it may have to be against Florida State, Georgia or maybe Alabama; something he wondered if Ariel may be a part of since times change rather quickly, and girls were taking over more of the punter slots on the rosters.

5

The property with the houses, barns and out buildings as well as its many eclectic pieces of paraphernalia were sold collectively, not independent of each other. When Jule Armstrong signed her name to the dotted line, and offered her earnest check she was putting her claim to the whole of it. Every last barrel that was used to run around, every last hook that held every last bridle that didn't actually belong to a boarder, became her property the second the authorities signed the final papers at closing just thirteen days after her encounter with the boys and their manure antics.

Within minutes of the actual signing the two women, Melora and her mother, took to making a true inventory of the place, having first posted a ten-day notice for all boarders to either make new arrangements for their animals and themselves, or to make full application to remain a client customer of the

Armstrong facility to be renamed "*Bay Sorrel Ranch*". Having no interest in filling out the application to be chosen to remain on premises many of them had been using without paying into the collective kitty, all but 21 horses and eleven names of boarders were found in the box set up to collect the paper applications. When Melora had suggested having the applications both online as well as drawn up on paper, Jule had nixed the idea saying she wanted wet signatures from any and everyone who thought they would be accepted. This way she had proof that they had agreed to all the new rules and regulations which were laid out again, several days before the closing took place at what was to become her personal office just off the lounge in the blue barn. It was the first time Keegan Tanner had ever heard the words "*wet signature*", but it made sense to her.

With the day having approached and the signatures affixed, Jule Armstrong's bank funding was set in place, and within hours of the bank's doors opening, she walked out with the papers needed to post saying she was the new owner of the facility, and that from this day forward, all posted rules and regulations would either be adhered to, or a person could find themselves being asked to leave the barn on a temporary or permanent basis. For the most part, the rules seemed rather boiler plate and ordinary, as Jule had been diligent to find them online through other horse-related venues around the country. Some rules were more apt to be written and obeyed through local laws and restrictions, and still a few were added for her own peace of mind. The one that stuck out in everyone's mind was that the hired hands would not be cleaning the inside stalls over the weekends. On Saturdays and Sundays, all indoor stalls would be managed and maintained by the owners of the animal in that stall, and not by an associate or affiliate. If the owner was incapable of cleaning the stall, arrangements could be made.

Melora walked up behind her mom while the new owner took another gander at the posted rules she expected everyone to follow.

"*Do you think they're fair and unbiased?*" she asked her daughter, but not necessarily willing to change anything if the new manager of the barns thought they may not be up to date with the changing world around the two of them.

"*I mean yeah, for the most part they are. I've got a few more I'm going to add, or run by you so you can add. I need a bit of leniency and even autonomy when it comes to managing the barns. You'll be in the office most of the time, but you probably won't get down here until after 10:00 a.m. and half my day has been burned by then.*" Her daughter angled.

"*You know you have carte blanche with me; you can do whatever you think is best. Just be sure to either have it in writing so they can see it, or best, have them each sign saying they understand it. I'm not going to dicker back and forth with these high-steppin' barn-mammas who think their kids' shit don't stink. The way I see it,"*

Jule gestured with her right index finger pointing over toward the feed storage,

"Anyone who boards here will either feed what we buy or they can bring their own feed and keep it in their cars or trucks. Hector, Celinda, you, or me, we're the only ones actually feeding animals from the feed storage. I don't want their bags of feed here stored in our storage, and have them come up saying that someone's been using their grain, stealing their whatever. I saw where one person wrote her name on the bottom of her salt lick; did you see that?" asked Jule before adding,

"She took a big Sharpee and wrote her name on the bottom of each of her three salt licks, and when one of them ended up in another horse's stall, she had every right to complain about it. Who steals salt? I guess the answer to that is whoever owns that grey mare on the end. Who owns that grey mare on the end, Melora?" asked her mom.

"That would be Bree Morgan; the one who also owns the heavy pregnant Paint right next to the grey mare. She's got more money than we do, but yeah, she'll take whatever isn't nailed down if someone isn't really looking. She probably thought she'd be back here in the morning early enough to move the salt back

to Jodi's stall. Jodi's blood bay is just under 17 hands; damn. I thought Brutus was tall at 16.2HH. That puts Einstein, Paul Abernathy's horse as the tallest horse in the barns at 17.1 HH, with Little Lady over there being the smallest at 11 HH flat."

Added Melora, with a hint of pursing her lips to blow Little Lady an air kiss or two.

"Does Little Lady look like a horse to you, young lady?"

asked Jule, knowing the word *"pony"* wasn't often used around either one of them. Ponies weren't horses, and they both understood the difference.

"I think my mother said it best when she told me growing up that you tell a stallion what to do, you ask a mare, but you pray before you deal with the ponies."

She laughed.

"Speaking of ponies or people with pony mentalities, did you see where Kurt Banderoff called in and left the voice message on my new office phone? I haven't had the number one or two hours when I get a message with his huffing and hot-air blowing about his son being kicked out of the barn. I didn't kick his son out; the boy didn't fill out an application. I'm not in any way obligated to follow the crowds or do what has been done. I almost called him back and let him have it, but I remembered my promise to God that I'd be a little more civil now that I'm not working my

insurance investigations; I'm an author you know, I have to show a bit more restraint. I'm supposed to appear dignified, as they say."

Melora hadn't seen or heard the message, but she had had just about enough of Kurt Banderoff from both the barns and out on the streets of the county roads where he must somehow feel that owning a huge Dodge dually gave him more than the legal limits of how much space on the roads he could take and at what risk and speed. The man sold car insurance too, for Pete's sake; but here he was barreling down the country roads without his headlights at dusk, in a silver painted truck, thinking he was God's gift to the motorways. Why some local LEO hadn't picked him up by now was questioned. Surely, he's not picked up the habit of reckless driving just over the past couple of months. It seemed like nearly every other day Melora and Kurt were on the same roads at the same time, one either needing to pass the other, or one being too stubborn to give way. It was a dangerous game to play; one Jule had mentioned twice to her older daughter to play with extreme caution.

"I know, 'think with your insurance', you've told me that a million times, Mom. I do, too. I think before I speed up, I think before I slam on my brakes, I think before I lean out of my window and flip him off too; but since the dust from his manic driving seems to always cover me head to toe, he never really sees me doing that. Still, it makes me feel better knowing I did."

She laughed before adding,

"We're not letting his son back into the barn, not after what he did to your car, and after he and his friends think that the lounge is their sex club; he can go....well, he can, and he knows he can. He probably already does."

She stated, as she made a face to show she had even offended herself with her last statement. *"He's sixteen or seventeen years old, probably seventeen I guess. I could be his mother! I'm...damn, I'm old, Mom. I don't want to think about it."*

The two women continued to make their rounds through the two main barns, the storage barns and out buildings, making sure they had taken photos of everything so they could do a full inventory of what all had been left at the place and what was or wasn't included in what would be considered theirs to dispose of. Mostly, the two found needless accoutrements and gear such as old tools, a wagon, parts of another wagon, shovels and spades, mostly broken or in need of repair. They did find quite a bit of twine, binding materials, a few ladders, buckets, wheelbarrows, and one of those old-fashioned pitchforks that could be refurbished or what is now called reengineered to become a work of art. Wouldn't that be the end all she thought, as Jule picked up the pitchfork in one hand, hunkered over it somewhat, and pretended to be the old man in the famous painting.

"C'mon Mabel, I need you to pull your hair back, and stand next to me and be my wife."

She giggled, teasing Melora in her best old man voice.

The plans to sell off whatever they could through listings in the papers, online through Marketplace and Craigslist were made; Melora thinking also about adding a page to the new website for the ranch, which would list items for sale, trade, or barter. That may be a way to clean out the barns and outbuildings while at the same time making money to buy fencing and materials she would need to fortify her pet project of bringing in a few Mustangs to train before finding them their forever homes. Melora had all but idolized her mother as she was a young girl growing up, to know that her own mom was one of the state's premier barrel and pole racers.

Jule's horse of choice had always been the wild Mustang, and her means of obtaining them legally seemed to fascinate the young girl as well. A lot of people bragged about how they'd go out to the canyons and literally rip a horse from its herd to bring it home and try and tame it. Stories about her mother's childhood had always been her favorite; whereas her sister Brooke preferred to hear about Disney princesses and the like. Melora liked to pretend she competed with Jule back in the 1980s; sometimes she'd even allow herself to win; but when she did she felt both a little guilty for taking the glory and a little upended knowing that the chances of her abilities going up against those of her mom when she was Melora's age would have been next to impossible.

"How did you ever tame the sorrel gelding you used to win the all-around back in '86? Was it natural horsemanship, or did you come up with something on your own? I don't think Clint Anderson was around then, right? He's more of the turn-of-the-century type; who did you follow, Mom?"

She asked, thinking maybe she had heard beforehand, but wasn't quite putting her finger on it.

"Who did I follow? I guess no one really. I did what I was told by Chuck West and his hands over there at the Chisholm Trail Ranch, the one we think is so quaint now when we pass by it on the way to Wal-Mart. You remember it; it has the huge white barn next to the three silos, and maybe only five acres of paddocks and pasture. Well, it used to be nothing but pasture and fields. I mean to tell you, it was over 160 acres for sure, and maybe closer to 300 acres. It wasn't all fenced off either; we didn't do that back in the day. We had land to roam on. I found the horse in the paper, he'd been picked up in Nevada, literally off the side of the road, and the ol' boy that brought him back to Oklahoma swore he was the Devil himself. He even named him Diablo."

Jule said, lowering her glasses because they were about to fall off her nose anyway.

"I remember that much. You hated that name and when you got him you changed his name to Gabriel, saying he had a message to tell or something. I don't remember all of it. Tell me again."

Melora begged softly, taking a seat on an old half stump of an old oak that somehow survived every winter and every dreaded Oklahoma summer that had ever been thrown at it.

"Before I tell you about Gabriel, I'll have to tell you about my first horse. He was a brute. Daddy picked him up from the Chester Ranch out in Yukon, it may be considered part of Piedmont now. You know the one, it has the statue of the giant Angus bull up on top of the hill. It used to belong to a famous movie star, a western movie star of course, and he bred quarter horses. Daddy worked for them at some point. He did electrical wiring for them; I couldn't say what all he did. I know he let them put a hitch on his trailer and he hauled both cattle and other livestock here and there for extra money.

"One day he and Mom came up to me and told me they had a surprise for me. I wanted a horse too badly, you know, I was about ten years old, so yeah, I was about to be past my prime." She laughed.

"The old guy, the movie star, I can't remember his name now, he brought Daddy to the barn and told him instead of paying him that day he could let him have this horse of his that was a champion himself, out *of champion bloodlines, and he was in about a dozen movies as well. He was a black, jet-black horse. He was taller than short but not really big, maybe 15 HH. He had four white stockings; one was shorter and in the back. His mane was cast to the left and he had a big star on his forehead with a double swirl. The old man told my dad that the horse was about fifteen years old and in great shape.*

"Daddy, not knowing a thing about horses agreed to the trade since he knew he'd make my day, my week, my month, my entire year the second I laid eyes on the thing. He was just too stunning for words. Well, as you may have guessed, I was speechless. I couldn't believe my luck, and I was going to be the best danged rider this side of whatever since I had the best champion horse and we were going to be known world-wide. It's always that way, but let me tell you something you already know. If something seems too good to be true, girl, it probably is.

Within six weeks of me getting that gelding, he was dead. Dropped in his stall at the same ranch because that's where we had to board him at the time. The old man came out to the house himself to tell Daddy so he wouldn't bring me out to see him being buried. It broke my heart into a million pieces, but do you know what really broke my heart sweetie? Seeing a woman riding my horse the next summer at the county fairgrounds, and seeing her taking prize after prize after prize. Daddy never put his name on the papers, and that old Slick-Willie took the opportunity to write to the AQHA, the American Quarter Horse Association, to say he'd lost the papers, and got himself a second set. He sold my horse to the woman I saw, and there wasn't a damn thing any of us could do about it. That was one of the first times I realized that horse people truly sucked.

"But it all worked out. I lost out on 'Sonny Driftwood', but I saved up my money myself the next year and I bought Gabe from the man I told you about who found him and brought him home to train. I wanted to give him a dollar to make it legal. No one was going to sell my horse out from under me again or come get it claiming I'd stolen it from them...people do that."

She paused for a minute, took a long sip of her afternoon tea and told her story.

"Gabe was an angel. He just needed to be shown that he was valued. I bet he was around something like three or four when I got him. The man in Newalla had him just over a year, so he was probably a little over four when he was gelded. Cutting him was the best decision I've ever made with a horse. I haven't ever owned another stallion, and he's the reason why. They're nuts...well, no pun intended...they're crazy if they're left unaltered.

"You'd be a fool to keep them around your place if you weren't breeding and if you didn't have a big enough place to keep them penned up without fear of

them getting out and either hurting you, themselves, or another animal. He was gelded, I let him heal up a few weeks, and then his training started. I let him know I was going to work with him, not force him to do anything, and as we grew to trust one another he and I were one of the tightest partnerships I've ever imagined; God's truth. I'm sayin' the horse was smarter than most people for sure, and he had talent; real talent.

"It could have been all the brush he had to maneuver around out there in the wild, or it could have been that he really just liked going around little round canisters, but whatever it was, if he saw one he put his head up and began to stomp. He was going to hit the ground running before he clipped the edge each time perfectly, and made his turns without so much as a breath between him and that barrel. I had to lift my leg each time. I guess the judges thought I had trained him that way, but I really didn't. He got so low sometimes I could have scraped my knee on the ground before he found his footing and was tearing back to the gate."

Jule recalled.

"I think our best time was a 14.6, but that may be a record I have to prove to myself now. We didn't have all the fancy-schmancy gizmos we have now to time things. We had the digital clock and ol' Bubba over there clicking the clicker! If you pissed off Bubba or any of his family you got a bad time for sure."

Where it may or may not have been fair treatment, it was in fact the way things were during the years Jule Armstrong competed in high school and other competitions. Her own high school didn't have a Rodeo Club, and she was given special permission to ride for a rival school; something that didn't always set well with the folks back in her own community. After Jule's winning years being accredited to another school's name and colors, it didn't take long before the Hoover Highlanders found significant budgeting for equine sports to play a role in the future of their own.

Hero was in fact, her hero, but Gabe was her knight in shining armor. What she learned about horses, the Quarter Horse taught her, what she learned about living, the Mustang would take credit for. Hero was a bona fide gentleman wrapped in horse flesh; the same could never have been said about Gabe. He was a brute force to be reckoned with.

6

Retired Bethany police officer Stephen Mueller made his way through the once open-to-the-public front office door leading into the private offices of Jule and Melora Armstrong. The large opening having just been remodeled a few days beforehand, Mueller brought with him several buckets of lighter grey paint, brushes, tape, and some tarp to stand on while he and Jule found themselves reliving several of their glory years from when the two of them had been a thing back in high school.

Mueller admits to anyone willing to listen to him that giving up Jule for another horsey woman was a mistake. Even though the good officer had been in love with Lisa Billings, he hadn't quite given up all of his feelings for Jule. Stephen and Lisa were married in the summer just after his sophomore year in college; Lisa had graduated from Hoover with a little bit of a baby bump, but nothing she couldn't conceal with her commencement robe. Mueller was a farm boy, raised a bit further north and east, somewhere near Guthrie, Oklahoma.

Since about the time Mueller and Lisa had separated and divorced, a little over five years prior, Jule had become not only one of the more prolific authors to ever come out of the state of Oklahoma, but she had mastered a means of being the most talked about former student at her old school considering not many of its graduates went on to anything other than one or the other state universities. There had been a few boys make the college rosters and one even went pro, but it was basketball and in a football state like Oklahoma, the round orange ball isn't quite as prestigious. Another Hoover grad had made it to the big time in broadcasting, first as a radio host, and then on the local news before taking her talents out of state. It wasn't rare for someone in the smaller communities west of the capital city to make a name for themselves, but it wasn't all that common either.

Equestrian Juliett Armstrong's name was tossed about both in a grand way and in a way to make a few tilt their heads; she had been called every name under the Sun for her riding abilities, but she had also been considered a traitor by many who were old enough to remember her before Hoover High School had its own Equine Club. All of her 16 first and four second place trophies lined the walls of another school which did have a club; the trophies stood proud in the freshly built handmade cabinet her father had constructed to showcase his daughter's winning prizes. Though the schools' respective Boards had met on a number of occasions to try and rehome the old brass keepsakes, they remained at Chesterfield; and probably would remain there. Hoover's loss yes, and sometimes Jule's thorn in the side. Explaining the discrepancy had been rather annoying.

"Stephen Jonathan Mueller, I think you out did yourself here; I only have four walls to paint that color. We can take it back to Home Depot if you want. Melora hasn't decided what color she'll cover her walls with just yet. My office is about twelve by twelve and hers a bit smaller, maybe ten by twelve. Mine has the outer wall with the windows and the door, so we may get away with just one can. I'd hate to see you have to eat the rest of it."

Jule thought out loud, before suggesting that the lounge, restroom, and hallway could use another coat, and as long as the paint was already here, she didn't see a reason not to pay the man for the errand of running up to the hardware store in the first place.

"Nonsense, I have had these cans sitting around for a few years actually; thought I was going to paint the exterior of my house before Lisa got it in the decree. I offered it to her but she decided to sell, and you know the rest. I found that condo close to yours and not to seem ungrateful or anything, but when you left last month I did have to keep your old lawn in shape so you could sell it and call yourself one of the uppities."

He laughed.

"And...you know, I didn't up and sell it. You're the maintenance man for the Conner HOA you know, it's your job, literally your job to keep all the lawns in pristine order. I can't help it if a few wild flower seeds found their way into the freshly cut beds under my windows. Did you trim the avocado trees? There's three you know. Feel free to either keep them or uproot them, but if you do end up taking them out, please also feel free to carry them here so I can replant them just outside the little pole gate over by the white barn, which used to be called the gold barn." She directed.

Once the two of them had taped up and measured out the appropriate amount of paint to finish the interior walls of her office, the door to the office creaked sending a shiver of unexpected shudder through Jule; she hadn't remembered hearing it before. Jule called out rather sharply to whomever it was who thought they could just walk through a door that had a big fat sign on it reading "*Do Not Enter*".

"Hey...hey, who is it? Who's out in front?" she called.

"It's Angie...Angie Banner; I'm here to see someone about buying some of the old equipment that you had listed on Craigslist."

Came the answer, even though the sign on the door had also clearly read to go around to the South entrance.

"Angie? Angie, I'm Jule Armstrong, this is my...um...Stephen Mueller. I'm the owner and the one who listed the machinery, but there is a sign clearly posted for all of our safety. We're remodeling and can't have people just walk into the room like you did. We could fall off a ladder, or drop something on your head by accident. When you leave, you'll need to do so through the back entrance, to the South."

Jule instructed, as she reached behind Angie to be sure the door had been closed securely. Opening the door again, she stuck her head out and around he jamb to see if the note had somehow fallen off, but no, it was still securely taped right where she had left it. Stephen must not have locked the door behind him.

"The machinery, as I mentioned is untested. I haven't tried to start anything. They may or may not work. I listed them all according to their blue-book value, or what would be the equivalent to that. I called them all fair or poor, rather than to say they were in good shape. Before you buy any of them, I'll ask you to sign a waiver stating that I am to be held harmless should any injury occur after you take them off the premises; is that OK?" Armstrong asked, but rather indicated.

"I'd want to start 'em up I guess to see if they work." Banner protested, but so that there was absolutely no mistake made, Jule reiterated that she had not started them, she had no intention of doing so, and if someone wanted them *as-is*, that is how they

were listed, and how they were being sold. They were listed at the lowest possible price, something she may have gotten at the scrap yard for their metal content.

If Angie or anyone else wanted working apparatuses, they were going to have to either search for them, or hope for them, but as far as the Armstrongs and Bay Sorrel Ranch were concerned, all items listed were listed *as-is*, and would not be cranked over on the premises just in case they did have issues that could cause an accident, fire, or any damage. Those were the guidelines, and Jule wasn't a woman to be questioned; especially on her own land regarding her own property.

"I have a piece of land up in Luther, and I run about 60 to 70 head of black angus. I'm hoping the tractor still works, and the three attachments seem to be the right fit for the hitch, so would it be alright if I just tried to turn it over once?"

She asked, however the look in Jule's eyes told her everything she needed to know about whether or not that would be a possibility. No meant no to Jule Armstrong. It was never going to be yes, not after it was determined to be a no.

"Angie, is it?" asked Stephen, walking with the woman, putting a bit of distance between Angie and Jule.

"I've been in the farming business less than most, but I can tell you from the looks of it, that old engine hasn't been cleaned or messed with in any

number of years. Even if you were to try and crank it over, the dirt and gunk would then get into the engine and really mess it up. That old thing will need a full overhaul one way or the other; you'll either have to blow it clean first, and hope nothing seeps into the mechanism, or you'll have to do a total refurbish on it. You'll need to get a good mechanic who knows farming equipment, and you'll have a better chance of it running for you. At least the three attachments can fit another tractor using a similar hitch, so if you want it all, fine, but if you only want the hook-ups, maybe Jule will sell them separately, I can't speak for her." He finished.

Actually, thought Jule, Stephen had done a pretty good job of speaking for her and had said just about what she needed or wanted to say without being too firm, or harsh over the matter. To a woman like Jule, who had always listened and followed the rules, it was incredible how a person could read the ad and clearly see that the words "*...may or may not run, haven't started it, and I won't have it started on my premises*" could then come in and ask if she could start it up once. Then again, the same woman had just marched through a door that had been clearly marked, hadn't she? She had.

Jule wondered if the woman would try and ask her to move the tractor to the street so she could start it up. If she did, Jule had already surmised in her mind, that would be one of those last-straw scenarios where then Angie Banner could then find herself kicked outside the gate with a size nine Justin boot up her butt. Stephen's explanation was far nicer than Jule had been going over in her mind. She thought maybe she could use an even-keeled thought master around more often; and if he's a cute as Mueller was and always had been, well, even better.

As Stephen walked the wayward woman out to the west side of the property to see the old John Deere, he looked over his shoulder to catch a glimpse of his old flame shaking her head in what he had remembered was her look of pity. Jule was standing back there about to laugh inside her throat, but she would end up clenching her teeth before she let it out of her mouth. She kept things like that to herself, it was part of her good ol' Southern charm to be sure. Jule's mother Ruth Ann Bennett had been of the more genteel Bennetts who found their way from Virginia to the hills of Tennessee in the early part of the 19th century before settling in the west where the land was flatter; better for crops.

Jule's grandfather Raymond Bennett had traveled west to Oklahoma to attend the University of Oklahoma, down in Norman, where he had studied Geology; he was in fact, one of the first landmen in the state to drill for oil successfully in the 1920s. He had also been a full back on the rugged football team that made itself known as being one of the tougher units to ever scrimmage against; let alone face off in a real game. Their longtime veteran coach Bennie Owen had been a master at game strategies. The 1920 team took a 6-0-1 record with four of those victories and the only tie game being against conference opponents. Two Sooners that year had been recognized as All-Americans. Juliett's grandfather missing out as the third only by a few yards to Roy "*Soupy*" Smoot.

Being brought up by two of the more Southern vintage families around, both her father's side, and her mother's strong-armed side, had left indelible marks on the soul and demeanor of their first born. Juliett Leigh Armstrong was, if nothing else, a Southern woman with the cordiality and the politeness to prove it, even if she could cuss a sailor under the table when those times specifically called for such diversion of manners. For Mueller, it was enough to know that Jule had stayed in the door to watch as he escorted the buyer to the dusty waylaid prize. Having decided at that moment that he'd definitely spend as much time as he could painting walls, stripping baseboard, whatever it took to spend another few hours with someone he had hoped to get back into his corner of the world.

When Melora made her way through the fields dragging a long pole with barbed wires hanging off of it, her mother hadn't taken a second glance before asking if she needed help. When the answer came that the situation was under control, Jule headed back into her office to make the changes she needed to make on her original plans, to include adding a brick-type veneer to one of shorter walls to make things pop a little, and feel more rustic; the place felt older than what it was to her, and she wanted to keep the vibe going. She thought about the old bookstore in the mall that seemed to cast her into another time warp each time she crossed the threshold of it; she wanted that for her office as well. She wanted something more wholesome than what she knew existed less than a mile from her new front door. The city was closing in on the last remnants of the old countryside. Time had not been a friend to any of the people who wanted the county to remain quaint or quiet. Those days were gone, but Steam Punk was acceptable.

Entering the back door of the two office spaces, Melora peeked inside to see if her own office door had been shut; she couldn't remember.

"I need a new lock I think. I don't want people just walking into the office space like I saw that woman do. She literally stood outside, read the sign, and turned the knob before walking into the place. I think new locks would be a fresh start, but I need one on my office door, when I actually get an office door. I'll have papers and contracts inside my desk, I don't want anyone to steal them and say they didn't sign one."

Melora was thinking out loud, but in a way that made her mother a bit too proud.

"I thought I was keeping all the contracts in my office." She stated.

"No. I'm the manager, Mom. I need to keep them, and deal with the idiots, and you know the others. I know I shouldn't call them that; they're not all bad, but we don't have to accept them just because they filled out the applications, you know that, I hope. I'm going through each one of them, and if they get bad reports from their other barns or from judges or people at the shows, I'm not letting them board here. I want good people with manners. If I wanted a bunch of no-manners I'd just stick with the Mustangs and not have the place turn out so peopley. I know, that's not a word."

Spoke the daughter in a most meaningful mature manner.

"Why Melora Ashleigh, I do declare," teased her mother,

"You sound so much like me; I think I'm looking in the mirror!"

With that, Jule hugged her daughter just a little before saying that there was actually a door that had been purchased some time ago, but had not been used. It was in the inventory, but Jule hadn't listed it on Craigslist or Marketplace, as she thought maybe she would use it either in one of the barns or in one of the two houses on the premises. It was going to open on the wrong side, with the door knob on the right, but she felt her daughter could live with that.

Hector Alvarez, the real hand, had been the barn hand for several years, and he had pointed out the door as well as some useful rope, tools, and plumbing supplies that had not been added to the lists for sale. Alvarez, though in his mid to late sixties, was still very willing to continue as a groundskeeper and stall cleaner; but had asked if he could possibly have weekends off as well as normal holidays.

Without blinking, Jule had agreed to both requests, adding that his salary would be increased soon as well, and if he had need of repairs to his home on the property, all he needed to do was ask. Before they could come up with anything in writing, Jule had sent over a text to Hector's wife Celinda to ask her for a list of whatever she believed needed to be fixed, knowing that the faithful and somewhat introverted Hector would be less than forthcoming about spending her money for his needs.

Celinda's list had been hand delivered the same afternoon Stephen and Angie had shown up, and with the list came an invitation for both Jule and Melora to come for dinner at the Alvarez house; a little two-bedroom manufactured home which the two of them had been sharing since before Barbara Olsten had sold the place to Brian Scott. They had known and did know, every inch of the property, both barns, both houses, and every knot in the fences along the more than 100 acres. Their experience and expertise was genuinely appreciated, and would be rewarded.

7

The Pinterest-inspired hearty egg sandwich she made that early morning lacked more than she was willing to admit. Maybe it was the fact that she hadn't added cheese, or it could be that the toaster hadn't finished toasting both sides of the English muffin, but something was off about it. Jule took a big bite before addressing Stephen's request to fix the one she was trying to wrangle. He was always like that; even in high school. He was the taller of the three boys in the Mueller family; and had a head of hair from the time he was really young. Now, a man in his fifties, he kept his mop-top shorter, but it was still quite thick. The grizzled-grey only made the man more attractive.

Steve Mueller couldn't help himself when it came to Jules, as he called her. He was either under her feet trying to help, or he was under her feet just so he could be closer to her. Either way, he missed the way he felt about her when they were kids. It was a feeling that flooded back to him every time he thought of her.

"Have you ever actually owned a horse?"

Jule asked, while trying to side pass him in the kitchen somewhere between the heavy marble-topped island in the middle of the massive room, and that area between the pantry and the refrigerator that told another story altogether.

"If I had to guess, now that I'm staring face-to-face with this thing, it looks like the space was custom made for a larger unit at one time. There's enough room here for either another trash can or maybe a utility hook where I can store the brooms and mops and stuff."

Her words spoken more or less as a means to throw off the fact that she was waking up in her new huge house with an old boyfriend. How in the name of God's green gardens did that actually happen? The place was far too big, there was no way she could ever want to afford the heating or cooling costs, and these were the thoughts she tried to force in her brain so she didn't have to entertain the fact that she had just woken up next to a man she had always wanted to wake up next to.

"I have never owned a horse. I think the last time I even sat on one was back in maybe 1986 when you graduated and you had that party at the Chisholm Trail; you made all of us ride off into the sunset with

you. I think I fell off. You never knew it, but yeah, I think I fell off." He laughed, trying to remember if he jumped or if he had been dumped.

"The reason I'm asking you isn't because I want you to buy one or anything, God knows I wouldn't wish that on anyone. How we afforded it back then is a mystery to me, but it does make me wanna dig my dad up and give him a big enough hug to put him back into the ground. Can you believe," she continued,

"...that my parents probably worked evenings, weekends, or something so I could stay in horses. I never thought about it then. I don't think I ever really told either one of them thank you. I just went about my business you know, living life, being the cheerleader, being the rider, being the whatever else I could fix my mind to being or doing. God, how did I have that much time on my hands? I get half of my plans completed now and think about cutting my other half into pieces to see if I can sell them off or get rid of them for good. Did we have more time when we were younger?" she asked.

His face said it all. He could tell she was spinning her wheels, that she was a bit nervous about the decisions they had made the evening and the night before. He used the extra space between them to assure her that he wouldn't approach again until or unless she was fully comfortable doing so. *"Maybe I should..."* he started, only to be interrupted. It seemed that after more than three decades she remembered that he would often make an excuse to retreat so she could have more space, more time, more anything he thought she may need or want.

"No...I mean, no, please. Stay. I'm just...well, I'm just me. The same Jule I was in high school, the one who told you no and then lost you to Lisa Billings. I didn't know what I was doing. I didn't know if I was ready, or if I wanted to find out; you were a good guy then and well, you're still the same good guy now."

She spoke in a lowered tone, but one of confidence.

"Maybe if you just...held me for a little while."

She mentioned, catching his eyes and the corner of his mouth as it curled just a bit.

"Well," he added, *"...maybe just a little while."*

When they had settled onto the lounge sofa, both loosely dressed, both nibbling on the half-attempted breakfast, Jule went over the reason she had asked about whether or not Stephen had ever owned a horse.

"Horses, as you may have guessed, are really expensive to maintain. They eat all the time, and that's where God comes in with His grass of course, but they do need more than just grass. They need grain, they need better thicker fiber, that's where the different hays come in; the number of hays would amaze anyone, but there's also grains. Horses tend to eat oats you know, and some folks me included, buy the rolled

oats to feed them, both because it's a better grain and because it's cheaper than some of the manufactured pellets.

"If you don't know what you're doing, and you feed your horse too much Johnsongrass, sorghum or Sudan grass you're all but introducing gas issues to their bellies. Even alfalfa has to be done in small doses."

She rambled, before turning into him to be sure she wasn't boring the man with her latest bit of intel. His wink was good enough, and she continued her conjecture.

"What I'm saying is, you run into a big expense for just one horse, and you do it every single month because it eats every day all day. You have vet bills, boarding bills, farrier bills, the cost of gear you use, tools and tack. You have fall and spring shots that have to be given, worming supplements. If your particular horse needs joint supps or anything like raspberry pellets to calm it down, you're looking at spending anywhere from just under $400 a month at a place that allows you to keep your horse in a pasture to maybe upwards of $700 dollars a month on the average; that's with the standard vet bills, God forbid your horse gets sick or hurt."

When she had finished, she gave a sigh. It was a reservation really, more of a release than anything else. She realized that for all those years she and her family used their uncle's extended yard as a livery for her gelding if she couldn't board at the C.T. Ranch. She hadn't paid for an ounce of grain, a twig of straw for bedding, nor had she ever put out a single dollar when the horse needed medical attention. Had she really been so blinded by youth not to have given the gratitude necessary for even being remotely thankful? These and other thoughts invaded her mind while the two arms of her former now current beau seemed to find their way without much of a struggle. She wasn't eighteen; she wasn't an idiot. She had decisions to make and felt her new life was ready to accept someone into it. This was a completely new feeling; one she hadn't been accustomed to in more than twenty-five years.

"I need to call my mom. I mean, not at this second of course, but I need to call her and thank her for what she and Daddy did for me all those years. I think the only time I really acknowledged that they put out any real effort was when I caught a ride down to Houston for a rodeo, I think I was nineteen, I could have been twenty, I'm not sure. The guy that took me demanded more than gas money, and when I refused he off loaded me and my horse about ten miles from the event barn. Needless to say, I missed the show, but worse than that, my parents had to come save me."

She kept the back of her head planted into his chest while she spoke, more or less reminiscing rather than telling him directly about the times of her life when she was sure he and his new wife Lisa were either about to welcome their first daughter Stephanie into the world, or maybe she just wanted him to know she wasn't always the strong and tough-as-nails woman he believed her to be. She was fallible.

"*The jerk!*" spoke Mueller, half wanting to ask if he knew the guy so he could give him an ear-full so many years later.

"*If you'd have called me, I would...*" he started to say, but realized if she was 19 he would have been twenty and he knew exactly where he was at that age.

"*I guess I wouldn't have done much, huh? I was sort of, you know, married at that time and depending when it was, I was either changing diapers are getting ready to do so.*" He admitted.

"*We haven't really caught up much have we? I took the Cottonwood job, but since I didn't live on the premises I didn't see you much. I bought the new condo, and what, only three months later you moved. It was a part-time thing for me, but I kept it because I did see you from time to time. Over the past five years I've been employed there though you've been either writing, traveling, making everyone at the Hoover reunions jealous with green envy. Oh, it was really bad when you didn't show up because you were in Europe last summer at the tail end of your book tour.*

"*Lisa was there of course, she and her new husband. It was all I could do to avoid them and try not to drink myself into oblivion. I only went because Dub and Rob wanted to go, and since I always did what my cousins wanted, I went to their reunion. I guess I was also hoping you'd be there. Why those things, those reunions are always about who drives what, who owns what, who out drinks the others, and maybe what their best golf game consists of, I will never know, but there she was, Lisa I mean, going on about how you'd gained at least 50 to 60 pounds and she'd seen you rolling down the aisle at Atwoods..."*

he laughed, *"...as if you still owned champion horses when the world knew you'd give them up for the keyboard. I wanted to slap that woman, and you know what, if I had been that jerk that booted you off on the side of the road, maybe I would have slapped her, but I'm...well, me. I can't hit a woman no matter what I guess...but I wanted to."*

He sweetly mentioned as he stroked her short-tufted hair, and traced her left ear with his index finger, the way he knew she liked to be tickled; *"I wanted to."*

Jule Armstrong couldn't stop the snort coming from both her nostrils at the thought of the meek and silent type Stephen Jonathan Mueller, the boy wonderful from all those years before, wanting to raise his hand to the woman Jule had never particularly liked, but found to be a natural nemesis. Slapping her wouldn't have been appropriate of course, but through her giggling and her nose-calling, she purposely allowed herself to pretend she had seen it happen.

"Well sweet pea, and man of yesterdays, we'll need to get going if we're going to get all the things on my list at Home Depot, Lowes, Costco, and wherever else I need to go before...wait, she thought I gained 50 to 60 pounds? I mean no...I was a stick in high school, but I got over that clearly enough. After having my three kids I may have put on 30 pounds, let me think about it..."

As she thought about what the scales may say about her weight at age fifty-four she remembered that age eighteen at graduation would have been somewhere in the range of a hungry skeleton versus that of a full-figured woman with actual rounded breasts; something she could only have dreamed of having in high school.

"OK, so what's 152 minus 115? Is that 50? No, wait, it's...dang it, I don't do Math. Math is a four-letter word and I refused to use it."

She said as she raised herself from Stephen's chest, took his face into the palms of her hands to get a better look at him before kissing him, and then she added.

"I know this much, she lost and I won! That's so much better than a slap."

8

Melora strong armed her way into her mother's new office a few weeks after the closing of the property; her face pale, flushed with a strange tinge of what appeared to be anxiety, a condition her middle child had suffered with for years when she became scared or upset. As her daughter lifted her cell phone into the air she began speaking so quickly and without making much sense. It was all Jule could do to try and calm her daughter long enough to at least try and piece together the parts of her message that stood out the most.

"Whoa! Honey, slow it down, don't mash all the sentences together like you do. I can't pull out the good parts. What are you trying to say? Slow it down, Melora." She tried.

"Mom, Jodi William's mom reported her missing and there's an all-points bulletin to be on the lookout for her. She was here last night after closing hours; I saw her around 11:00 o'clock."

Her daughter explained. *"Her truck is still parked out by the north fence."*

Jule thought about which one Jodi Williams was. She couldn't put a face to the name. Was she the one with the 17 HH bay? Maybe, that rang a bell. Cocking her head to the side, Jule asked if Jodi's horse was the blood bay with the thicker snip. It was weird how she could remember the horse, but not the rider most of the time.

"Jodi and Lily were helping Keegan pick up a puzzle in the lounge that Bree Morgan tumped over. You left what, around 8:00 or 8:30? I stayed in my office, and apparently something happened in the lounge just after 10:30. Bree left, but Lily told Keegan she needed to clean up the puzzle mess and to stop being so lame. I wasn't there, Keegan told me later what was said. When Keegan stood up for herself she all but scared Lily to death, who then left the lounge panicked but went the other way, not out the door, but out to the barn. A few minutes later, Keegan was washing her hoodie and jeans when Jodi came in with Lily from the barn and told Keegan they would help her clean up while they waited to see if Larissa was going to come by and pick Keegan up or leave her overnight again."

As she said that last part, Melora realized she had let yet another cat out of the bag that should have been, or could have been sensitive information. Melora sat down beside her mom on the overstuffed sofa in the main office to explain.

"*Mom, when Larissa doesn't pick Keegan up she stays here...well, over in the lounge, and I drug out the puzzle earlier to have something to do with her while we got to know each other better. Bree came in and started her usual rant about Keeg being a misfit and a loser so you know I stopped her. I told her I didn't care how much money she had or what her family's name meant in these parts, I wasn't going to let her be at the barn if she couldn't stop being a bully to the younger girls. I told her, and I'm telling you now, I guess, I don't see her fussin' at the older ones.*

"*I see her rally around the older boarders, especially Paul, who she may be sleeping with, if I'm honest, but anyway; I left to get the contract to show her where she and her mother had signed saying they agreed to be cordial and welcoming to all boarders and visitors, but when I came back the puzzle was all over the floor and Keegan was at the sink washing off her sweatshirt where the Coke she was drinking had spilled all over it. Bree was gone, Lily was too. I guess that's when Lily went to get Jodi.*"

Melora would have stayed to help, she explained, but Keegan said she had it under control. The young barn manager continued to express her disbelief at the way Bree had openly and wantonly knocked over the puzzle, spilled the Coke, and insulted Keegan after Melora went to the office. Melora had made up her mind before that particular incident in fact, that the fifteen boarders she had agreed to allow at the barn was about to be fourteen; and she was actually looking forward to making the call to David Morgan to let him know his brat daughter was both unwelcome and in fact would be banned from the place.

"I haven't called him yet, Mom. I hadn't told him yet. I mentioned to Keegan that I only wanted fourteen boarders, but I hadn't told Morgan yet. I was thinking about it, and maybe Keegan said something and it set Bree off, I don't know. Here's what I do know, at least it's what Keegan says, and I have to go by it, because it lines up with what I know I did. She said.

"Last night, when I was closing up, I realized Keegan was still in the lounge. She was putting the puzzle together, you know, the edges of it. I told her I would come in tomorrow, which is today, and help her put the other pieces in place. Bree came in and was rude, I left to get the contract. I left, and I didn't see Bree, but I did see Lily, Emily, and Jodi Williams in the barn. Emily was with a man I assume is her dad, they were getting into a truck and leaving, he didn't even wait for her to close the door before he drove off.

"I got in my truck, and drove home to the small house, and I don't know why, but I looked at my clock. It wasn't flashing or anything, but it said '11:01' so I know when I left. Apparently, while I was in my office, Lily had joined Bree in the lounge and Bree became indignant and tossed the puzzle, at the same time

spilling the Coke all over Keegan. Bree left at that point, and Keegan went to wash off her hoodie and jeans. Lily left the lounge and went the other way, back into the barn. I came in right at a minute or so before 11:00 o'clock, because I got home and the clock said, 11:01."

"Keegan just told me that Jodi and Lily came into the lounge, Lily apologized, and went outside to ask her mom if she could stay. She had called her, but since Cathy was already pulling into the drive, Lily just went outside to talk to Cathy. Keeg looked out the window and saw Lily standing outside talking to her mom. Keegan heard Lily ask to stay another 15 minutes or so, so she could help with putting the puzzle together, but she was really helping Keegan pick it up. She wanted her mom to think she was in the lounge with the cool kids.

"She admitted Mom; Lily admitted to Cathy later that she and Bree had been responsible for it making the mess in the first place. When she and Jodi were outside talking to Cathy and Cathy was being mean to Jodi. Keegan said when both girls went outside around 11:20 or so, that Lily's mom got out of the car wanting to know what was taking so long, and why Jodi Williams was with her daughter. I guess Cathy and Jodi didn't get along that well.

"Keegan heard Cathy Craigstone say that if she knew Lily was inside with her, with Jodi or Keegan, that she wouldn't have let her stay. She pulled Lily by

her arm and forced her into the car before spinning out; there are still tire marks you can see them. They're in your spot." Melora continued.

"Mom, Now Jodi has been reported missing, and it's all over Tik Tok!" Melora complained.

"It's on Tik Tok?" asked Jule, *"...not the news? It's on social media, but that could be a lie, sweetheart. It could even be something Bree Morgan put out there to make it look like Jodi is missing. Are you sure it's real? You get too excited sometimes."* She warned.

"Mom, it's real. Let me show you."

Melora spoke as she reviewed the small cell screen and moved her fingers across a few buttons to que the minute-long video featuring the Chief of Police in Kingfisher where the Williams live. Jason Miller of the Kingfisher police stood stoically straight-faced while he reported that the *"minor child, aged 17"* named Jodi Elizabeth Williams was considered missing and in danger; apparently she took a prescription medication twice a day and when she hadn't returned home the night before, she missed her nightly dosage and again the morning dosage. The medication, Chief Miller instructed, was critical and without it Jodi's blood pressure could spike instantaneously. She could die of heart failure if she is not found and given treatment.

"I had no idea she was on medication like that." Jule whispered.

"It never dawned on me to ask if any of our boarders needed special accommodations for any disabilities, I mean other than the ones you can see. We have the ramps and all, but if this young girl needs this serious of help, we need to try and retrace her movements if we can."

Suggested Jule, without thinking about her morning duties, including her 10 o'clock Zoom meeting with her manager Mike Maguire to go over the next big thing on his mind as it pertained to the branding of her brand, whatever that could mean in terms of an author being a brand. Jule had tunnel vision at that point. She and Melora both began searching every inch of the two big barns before recruiting Hector and Celinda Alvarez to assist.

"Can you help us look along the fence lines, maybe in the sheds? I'll take the white barn, Melora's got the blue barn. I think I see Keegan in the feed stall..."

She told Hector, *"I'll get her to go around the pastures to see what she can see. This being Sunday, we'll not have as much traffic other than those coming in to clean and ride. They can help too. No one rides, no one does anything until we've searched the entire premises. I want that understood."*

Jule instructed, as all ears listened and followed her words to the letter. Because they were so focused on finding their fellow barn boarder, no one noticed the slim figure of a man slip past the blue barn open doors and head for the lounge. If they saw him, they probably assumed he was there to help find Jodi.

When the next hour had passed without anyone arriving at the barn, or anyone who had already been there, making any progress in finding Jodi Williams, Jule called them together to go over where they had looked. Jodi's truck, an older model Ford F150 XLT was a bright royal blue with a cute horsey vanity plate with pink horseshoes surrounding the frame. The tag itself read simply *"Cowgirl"*. The rear tag, the legal tag in the state, had not only been bent from where she had obviously backed into something, you could hardly read the lower half of it. Jule wondered if the girl hadn't been stopped a few times, but let the "*mom*" in herself go for now, there would be time enough to straighten out the tag and the kid another time.

With the blue truck still on the gravel outside the north pastures, Jule thought perhaps the driver had lost her keys in the tall grass somehow, and had taken to walking home, but she also knew that Kingfisher was a good eighteen to twenty miles from the barn. She could have called someone; she could have caught a ride, but there were no new tracks that Jule could see leading up from the muddy entrance to the back or even to the front of the office area where it would be most likely where she would be picked up.

Questioning Keegan seemed to be the most logical next step.

"Keegan, what time did you, Lily, and Jodi finish picking up the puzzle or finish trying." Jule asked the near-teen.

"I started after Bree knocked it over, but I stopped and washed off my clothes first, and the floor...and the walls. It was just when her dad picked her up, so just before 11:00 o'clock or so, and then Lily talked to her mom and got permission to stay another a few minutes. Lily called her on the phone, but her mom was already in the parking lot. That was also around 11:00 o'clock I guess. Since it was Saturday night, you know, they can stay until 11:00 so they do most the time.

"Then when Lily left Jodi walked out with her to the parking spot where Cathy always...where you park now, and I heard Cathy say something like 'I didn't know she was helping you. I wouldn't have let her stay.' Which I thought was really rude. Jodi never came back in. I thought she would so she could at least say goodnight or goodbye, but she didn't. I waited a few minutes and turned out the lights. I just drug a blanket out of the cabinet and went to sleep. That's the last time I saw her, so about 11:20 maybe, but I'm not sure, it could have been before that."

Jule thought it out again, from a logical standpoint. If Melora's clock in her cab had registered 11:01 when she literally lived maybe one minute from the barn, it had to be no later than 11:30 p.m. when Lily was picked up because Melora said the gate locked at

11:30 on the nose; there was a timer. It wasn't logical, nor was it even probable that Jodi would have gotten into the Craigstone's dually if she wasn't well liked by Cathy; Cathy didn't drive her over to her truck. It was more likely that Jodi had simply walked either through the blue barn to cut off a bit of space and time to get to her truck, or since the weather was good, she may have walked all the way around the barn to get to the north side of it toward the north pastures, it's a good three- or four-minute walk from the lounge. Either way, there are flood lights illuminating that side of the property. The only chance of her losing her keys and needing to call someone would be right out there by the truck where she had parked. That's the only thing that made any sense. She didn't leave the property; the gates were locked. She would have had to call the emergency number to get someone to let her out.

She must have walked through the barn, or around it, and maybe when she reached for her keys she dropped them. Jule laughed at herself, remembering the year wasn't 1985 and the kids these days, everyone these days, has a flashlight on their cell phones. Even if she had dropped her keys she could have just used her cell to light up the ground! How odd, she thought, that when her mind went into "*mother mode*" she resorted to the years when she first became a mom, not the later years she's been more successful as one.

Jules asked Melora after the search had been concluded, if she had called the Chief of police in Kingfisher to let him know that Jodi was last seen on the property sometime around 11:00 to 11:20 p.m. The answer she received was that she had not been in contact with the Chief, but that it made sense to do it. Jule decided because she was the owner she would make the call, however, just as she was about to place the call her phone alerted her to the reminder she and Maguire were to meet in less than five minutes for their Zoom to discuss branding. As callous as it seemed to her at that point, bringing law enforcement onto the property to search for a missing minor in desperate need of medication, seemed to scream trouble for her from a book manager's point of view.

Instantly, Jule realized the second she placed the call, Mike would try to talk her through the next most probable motions; telling her it wasn't good for business, and since the girl wasn't on the property, it needed to be handled with kid gloves. She felt that if she mentioned all the facts to Mike he would want to handle it from his point of view; but if she didn't tell him he would wonder why she had not contacted him the second she was made aware of it so that he could handle it as professionally as possible. It just seemed too impulsive of her perhaps to assume she and or the property were in fact connected.

Since Jodi had not been found, it wasn't as if she had suffered a heart attack on the premises and was lying around somewhere between the blue barn and her truck. That point was obvious.

"*Mac!*" she smiled while addressing her friend and manager, keeping him so very far in the dark for good reason,

"*I can't talk just yet, we have something going on, but I'll get back to you in a few minutes, I promise. I hope that's OK.*"

She managed to fake her way through a moment of necessity. When he agreed to the new call, Jule placed the more important one; she called Chief Miller in Kingfisher, to inform him of what she felt was imperative.

"*Chief Miller, my name is Jule Armstrong, I'm the new owner of what used to be called the BSO ranch just south of Cashion.*"

Waiting for his response before continuing, Jule explained to the lawman everything she had been told, and the actions that had been taken that morning, before realizing that what she did could possibly have destroyed any true or real evidence in the case.

"*I know you did what you think was important, but ma'am by walking all over the property, opening doors, moving things, and literally walking through what could have been foot tracks, tire tracks, or even a body being dragged through the mud into the pastures somewhere, you may have compromised something. I don't mean to, and I don't want to say you did something wrong, but I do think you should have called me before you went off looking for the girl."* He scoffed.

Though his chiding wasn't meant to be too harsh, his words made sense, and they burned through Armstrong as if she had purposely taken a rake and covered all of the clues that could have been discovered.

"Ma'am, what I need you to do is hang up the phone and call 9-1-1 in your county to report what you just told me. I am in Kingfisher County. Your barn, I believe is still in Oklahoma County, they'll need to take the first report from you, but you can tell them you called me and we'll take it from here. Thank you for your help, it really does make a difference."

Though he tried his best to sound as if he meant what he said, the tone in his voice struck deep into Jule's mind, her heart, and her soul. She wouldn't forgive herself if the girl's disappearance couldn't be solved because she had ruined any chance of finding the needed evidence.

9

Fourteen applications had been chosen by Melora Armstrong as the names who would be selected to board at the new Bay Sorrel Ranch. When asked why the facility had been given such as simplified name as to describe two shades of horse flesh, Melora's answer was simple as well. The two colors of Mustangs most overlooked and mostly forgotten by their would-be owners or trainers are the bay horses and the sorrel horses. Of all the thousands of animals out in the wilds of the American frontier just waiting to be gathered, sorted, auctioned, and trained, it seemed that more than eighty percent of them were either a normal average brown or a normal average red coated animal. Only the really bright and shiny ones received the most attention. Melora and Jule wanted to give something back to the underdog; or in their case, the underhorse.

Most Mustangs roamed their entire lives out in the western states of Colorado, New Mexico, Nevada, Arizona, and even some in California, Utah, or Idaho, but generally speaking, they were collected from federal properties around the four corners and further southwest. Melora had applied at least three times to work for the Bureau of Land Management in the past, but because she hadn't finished her formal college years in a timely manner, things didn't work out for her the way she wanted it to. In her dreams she would become the best Bureau coordinator, or someone whose job it was to protect the animals at all costs.

Having grown up around conservative-minded people, Melora never thought twice about the means or methods being used to gather the herds. Once she became an adult, did a bit more research into the matter, and realized that there were both good and bad methods being utilized, she had thanked God and her lucky stars that each time she had been turned down for the positions she had applied for; as she couldn't imagine being a part of any program that wantonly abandoned and slaughtered horses for the sake of making quotas, or fulfilling a metric of some sort. In some ways they were saving the animals, and she held onto those thoughts for her inner comfort.

Her involvement from about her twenty-fourth year had been to buy a horse or two, train them, find good homes for them, and repeat the process. Once, when she was just over twenty-seven years old, a few years in the past, she had entered the Mustang Makeover, to see if she could challenge herself and a random animal to meet all criteria needed and required for a 100-day challenge which culminated into a climax with the top ten contenders competing for a grand prize of $40,000 cash and other prizes such as saddles, tack, year-round hay supply, and of course the obligatory media cover, which Melora wasn't necessarily interested in. In fact, just as she had entered the competition her mom had entered her own competition of writing; her second and third Highland romance novels had hit the shelves of Barnes and Noble, and while she rarely saw her mother during that year, it was oddly strange that the day of the big competition for herself would wind up being the exact same day her mom's live interview with the BBC-TV was taking place at roughly the same time of day. She would miss watching her mom take that next leap, but then again, her mom would miss her possibly winning the grand prize.

As it turned out, Melora had placed 4th out of ten, kicking her just shy of any monetary prizes, but she did take home a buckle, a new tote bag full of things that she could use in the future for whatever horses she wanted to train, and of course, the obligatory media coverage that alerted everyone to know that she hadn't made the cut, but that she was to be congratulated for having been at the dance in the first place. That sort of coverage, she believed, never really needed to be shared. In some ways, it only lent itself to creating more emotional distress than she had already felt about having pushed herself to the limits she did; no animal in her opinion, should be forced to do this or that and to do it within such a short amount of time simply to be shown off. She knew in her heart that every horse in the final arenas would end up losing their training within a week following the challenge.

Training wasn't about making the horse dance, prance, bow, or twirl on command. A Mustang wasn't a puppet. It took diving into the deep end and nearly drowning in her own mistakes to realize that her devotion to the training of these great creatures would mean a great lack of media attention and a lot more one-on-one and face-to-furry-face communication to build the bonds needed to proceed one step at a time. Mustangs, she knew were not like other horses; not by any stretch of the imagination.

An average horse, say a quarter horse, for instance, has been bred in captivity for going on countless generations. Their DNA has been altered so often to meet new or desired features to bring about a certain muscle structure, or perhaps to bring out their speed capabilities, whereas the Mustang is a mongrel, a mutt. They have been inbred in smaller herds most of the time; they have been cast away, forced to forge on less than what was needed for daily nutritional need.

Mustangs aren't to be governed; they are to be communicated with. When one faces off with an ordinary farm animal, again, something like a quarter horse, a paint, or even a thoroughbred horse, it's taken for granted that the human is in control. With a Mustang the roles are absolutely reversed; and both the human and the beast know this to be true. Before a Mustang can be controlled it must be willing to be so. They can be herded, gathered, forced into pens, and pushed around, but when they are met one-on-one, and given the opportunity to share their mind and their infinite spirit, they will return to their natural force; it is a thing of grace and such beauty. The word *"majestic"* has no truer meaning than when describing the American Mustang.

For Melora, the Mustang was the only breed of horse she had ever wanted to work with in that she remembered the tales her mom told her about her own experiences. While growing up as a girl she had seen the movie *"Hildago"*, a western portrayal of the American Mustang in all its glory. Though the story itself was, of course, embellished for Hollywood purposes, the love of the breed was seared into the girl; she would do all she could to help them. The story of the famed spotted horse in the movie is based on a grey stallion owned in the 1800s by a man who traveled with and performed for a wild west show. In the movie, the horse is taken overseas and wins an important race that only the top breeders of Arabian horses and the like could ever hope to win.

She knew the movie wasn't true, but the spirit of the animal was very real and she knew that to be very true. Her first horse had been an older black Mustang mare somewhere in her mid-twenties that her mom had picked up for a few hundred dollars. As a kid Melora climbed all over that horse, believing her to be the tallest, fastest, most amazing horse to ever live. Again, reality was a completely different story altogether. She was asked at least a dozen times over the years how many Mustangs she has owned, and her answer was always the same, *"No one actually owns a Mustang, but you can befriend one if it has a mind to do so."*

As she measured the pastures for the new fences which were expected to be brought in over the next couple of weeks, Melora wondered if when she approached the beaten old ruins of the abandoned junk laying around the back half of the pasture which included an old truck bed, a camper, part of a tractor, and other scrap pieces her mom was planning to have hauled away, if she would come across the body of their new boarder Jodi Williams. In the three days since her disappearance no one had found the slightest clue or come across even a lead that would shed a bit of light on the ongoing investigation. Jule's worries about how she had orchestrated the search in the first place and how it could have been the reason all leads had remained unfound, seemed to multiply in her daughter's mind three sometimes four-fold. Melora had six senses, not five. She knew things, and her mind was working overtime on this one point.

Once again, refusing to approach the piles of junk embedded in the ground, she questioned herself if she had the courage to train a wild animal with the dedicated and hard-headed gumption it took to bring about the needed responses from the animal, why was it that she couldn't force herself to walk up to an old truck bed and look up underneath it to see if she could find a shoe, a jacket, something that could lead to the finding of a young girl who very obviously meant more to the universe, and of course to God, than any horse ever could.

She knew her limits by this time in her life; at thirty-one she felt that she had lived the lives of three women her age. She had been through not only the divorce and an embattled custody case at a very young age, she had rescued her little sister from a pack of dogs a few years afterward. She had managed to sing and record several songs with popular music artists, mostly because her mom's connections in the writing world, but she was pretty good too. She knew she could have chosen music as a full-time profession, but a 16-week concert tour with an unlikely metal band had convinced her that life on the road meant far more than just traveling, setting up, singing, and getting paid.

The compromises, the long hours, lack of sleep, and too many addicts and freaks in charge of the entire affair led her to remain firmly planted on the terra cotta right beneath her boots at all times. No more world-tours for Melora Armstrong, not unless it involved taking her lasso to Australia to pick out a few brumby horses to bring back to the States. When she put her mind to it, Melora was exactly like her stubborn and over-the-top over-thinking mother. She could be annoying obstinate when she needed to be; which usually happened when she was trying to protect herself or someone she loved.

Keegan's bright smile was all it took for Melora to return to her senses after staring at the rusted clutter and debris in the tall grasses of the back fields.

"You don't think she's under there do you?"

Asked the twelve-year-old with enough surprise in her voice to send Melora right back to her first anxious thoughts about the chances of the girl being found beneath the rubble.

"I mean, we can look."

Stated Keegan, before grabbing a thick long stick from the ground to use as a poking device. The confidence level of the kid surprised the new barn manager to the point of taking lead in the matter, exchanging her crop whip for the handy branch, as she moved forward and toward the edge of what could only be the tattered shabby remnants of an old flatbed trailer; or part of one anyway. It had been demolished at some point, by some trauma, but also weathered over several decades of being left right where it sat. It took a few minutes before she realized what she was seeing, but when her eyes fixed on what she knew could only be the legs of a human, Melora's soul quickened within her. Immediately, her voice gave alert involuntarily; she choked a little, coughed and almost dropped to her knees.

Leaning herself against the stick, she straightened herself. She turned from the edge of the flatbed, the corner of it lifted just enough to conceal what she knew would prove to be the body of the missing girl. A swarm of flies had mingled and gathered up underneath and inside the camper shell resting near the flatbed. The camper was half buried, half leaning awkwardly as if someone had purposely managed to pull it up out of the ground before moving it to cover the upper half of Jodi's remains. There hadn't been the pungent smell that people talk about; not when they were approaching the ruins, but when her eyes fell to the scene, and her ears heard the buzzing of the insects, she knew the truth. The only thing Melora could think of in that moment was to shield any of what she was viewing from the eyes of her young charge; she couldn't let Keegan come closer. She couldn't let her have that image in her mind.

"Keegan, listen to me. Do not come closer. I want you to do exactly what I say, do you understand me?."

Melora asked, before instructing the girl to run as quickly as she could to the barn and to tell Jule where she was.

"Don't come back out here, do you understand me. Do you hear me?" She demanded, *"...just go tell my mom where I am. Tell her I'm calling 9-1-1."*

Warned Melora, as she cautiously removed her phone from her pocket when she realized that a swam of flies had begun to move out from under their shielded hide to investigate the intruder. When the dispatch operator answered her call, Melora took a breath before reporting what she had found.

"Hello, this is Melora Armstrong of the Bay Sorrel Ranch out on County Road just south of Cashion. I think I've found the body of Jodi Williams. I can see something but I don't want to get any closer. My...my..."

and then, before she could say another word, Melora realized the full impact of what she was doing. She had found the remains of a girl she had last seen being not only so helpful and understanding, but from all of the brief conversations she had with Jodi in the days leading up to her last, Melora was struck by the genuine care the teenager showed to her two grade horses; ones others at the barn would have purposely shunned, or even found a way to harm. Jodi Williams was one of the good souls, maybe that's why God had sent Melora to find her; how He had stopped Keegan from investigating without her.

Gathering herself into what she would have referred to in horse training as being collected, she spoke again, this time with more controlled confidence.

"She's dead, yes, she has to be, there are hundreds of flies and I'm smelling it now. I guess I hadn't before. If you want me to I'll stay here until you..."

As she tried bravely to finish her sentence, Melora's face flushed; she realized she was just about to collapse. In agreement with the directions of the dispatcher, Melora let the operator know, *"I'm going back to the barn. I can't stay here. When they get here I can tell them where she is. I'm sorry, I can't stay."*

10

When Keegan hadn't turned up for her normal day's start for riding, cleaning, and pushing herself onto and into everything Melora hoped to accomplish for the day, her heart ached the same as it did just weeks before when she realized that the last time she had whimsically passed the lounge that late spring evening and saw the Williams girl for the last time, that perhaps she may someday never look up to see that face that reminded her of the soft underbelly of a catfish; so freckled and pale, almost pink. Keegan Tanner had a way of bringing the woman back to her senses, especially when she did the Math and realized at thirty-one she could easily be the girl's mother.

Why Larissa Lowell at somewhere between clueless and stupid couldn't figure out the best thing she ever did in her life was to create such an amazing kid, was far beyond the imagination of the manager turned friend. If she did nothing else with her life,

Melora told herself, she would not only help the kid be all she could be, she may even try to find a way to adopt Keegan if the opportunity ever truly arose. Before making another sweep of the blue barn's vast riding arena to see if it had been watered and worked so the riders could have fresh footing, Melora walked the exterior of the place to see if her mom's car was in its place. She needed to go over a few of the new ground rules before posting them for the boarders to either absorb and adhere to, or if she was going to have to go through yet another come-to-Jesus moment with a few of them; a method she had not only learned from her mom, but one she was getting pretty good at considering how often she had to go into the matters with the kids who thought they knew more than anyone breathing around them.

"Mom, was I a total poophead when I was a teenager? I mean, I know Brooke was and for the most part still is, but I can't remember really ever talking to you the way I heard Bree Morgan spew off at her mom here at the barn, before she and David Morgan finally came to grips with him taking full custody. I'd have waved my hand in that girl's face and blew her a lasting good bye kiss for sure, but you either put up with me or I wasn't that bad. Which is it?" came the question, but her mother cut her off before she could go too far into it.

"Keegan didn't show up at class today and her mother just called me to ask if she was here at the barn

yet. Seems a couple of girls at school yesterday said she was crying in the bathroom and again at the counselor's office. I haven't spoken ten words to Larissa Lowell but all the sudden it's my responsibility to keep up with her kid and I'm supposed to know why she didn't show up to school and where she might be now."*

Spoke Jule, allowing her words to taper off before turning to her daughter to answer her regarding her past behavior.

"I don't remember you ever spewing off at me, I would have put you on the ground if you had. I may have forgotten it, but I'm sure you wouldn't have. No, you were pretty chill I guess. There was the time that, like Keegan's doing now, you decided not to show up for classes but it was during the custody case and you were staying with Gramma so God only knows where you were, she couldn't be bothered to keep an eye on you and all the cattle on the ranch at the same time. The woman got up at five in the morning and had finished her chores before the Sun came up. If you got up and dressed yourself and caught the bus to school that was on you. When you didn't show up and your sister told on you, that's when we knew you were missing. You're too quiet. I don't think a single teacher even counted you absent; they just assumed you were hiding in your hoodie. I don't see that happening with Keegan, do you?"

asked her mom knowing the answer before asking.

"Mom, she's really gone. If I find her out where the rubble was or hanging in a barn somewhere I'm going to lose it. I can't do that again. I've reached my limit on body finding; just so you know, and if you can't tell me you're going to help me find her then don't tell me she's gone. I just couldn't take it. I think I really am growing fond of that kid. She either reminds me of myself, or maybe who I wished I was at her age. Keegan Tanner knows more about horses than I ever did; she's taught me things now that I didn't know. I'm thirty-one Mom, I was Thursday of last week old when I found out that a gelding needed his sheath cleaned to get pebbles out of it so it doesn't get infected. Why in the hell did I not know that? Why in the hell is a twelve-year-old telling me these things?"

She asked a face that seemed more than interested to help her find another young boarder who may have decided to use the property as a means of playing hooky.

Though the lounge showed signs of evidence that Keegan had at least been sleeping there, it wasn't necessarily recent. It could have been a day or two since either of the Armstrong women had traipsed through the blue barn to find the lounge doors open by means of the spare key only they and Keegan were aware of. The key was still missing, not on its peg behind a painting of an old cowboy tipping his hat to whoever viewed him doing so. The painting was called *"Manners"* and for the life of her, Jule couldn't see herself removing it from the wall of the hallway leading from the lounge to the bigger barn. It just felt as if it lived there, and had lived there too many years to be taken down or thrown out. No one in their right minds would have wanted it; it was serving a greater purpose now. It protected the whereabouts of the spare key.

"She has to know she has friends, doesn't she?"

said Jule, but she looked a little uncomfortable at having mentioned it in such an inquisitive manner.

"I mean, she's too friendly to be friendless, why would she feel the need to go into the counselor's office to cry, if her mother was the one calling me to ask where she could be? Maybe it has something to do with her mom actually; now that I say it out loud. The Cactus Rose seems to be her haunt most of the time, God only knows if her other kids, her sons, are in school or out on the streets. I don't know. Did Keegan say how old they were, if they lived at the house or whatever?" asked Jule

"The only thing she's ever really said is that she has three brothers, and that none of them has the same father. Larissa was a bit of a buckle bunny and a rodeo groupie in her day. Of course, Keegan didn't tell me this, but I think Larissa had sex with just about anything that straddled a bull to either keep up with

her friends doing the same thing, or maybe she thought one or the other of them would settle down with her and earn enough on the circuits to bring home a steady check, I don't know.

"Keegan's dad was a good one, but Larissa didn't think he could hold a candle to the bull riders. He was a banker or finance guy, I don't think he'd ever even groomed a horse, but his kid sure knows everything there is to know about them from the inside to the outside, from the tip of their ears to the frogs in their hooves. I can't tell you mom if I've ever met anyone so genuinely interested and infatuated with horses. If she could be one she'd no doubt be a unicorn; she's that special...that different."

When they had made another pass from the south to the north and from the west to the eastern gates of the ranch, luck had its way at last. Melora's eye caught a glimpse of what looked like a red raincoat, just like the one she had seen Keegan wearing a few days before. The girl was hunched or kneeling in the run-in where her small Appaloosa cross was newly pastured. Moving Candy from the north pasture made sense because the vet had mentioned the horse had a tendency to founder on richer grass. The mid pastures, the ones next to where Melora's Mustangs had recently been delivered, were sparsely patched with grass, the sandy soil on that part of the property made a better paddocked home for the animal.

"*Keegan!*" cried Melora, as she ducked under the top wire of the four-strand fencing that ran the length of the pasture.

"*Where have you been? Did you not go to school today?*" she asked.

"*I woke up late and decided to stay home, well, here. I decided to stay here.*"

She answered with a bit of shyness having admitted out loud how she felt about the barn.

"*You didn't tell your mom. She called my mom saying a couple of girls saw you crying in the bathroom yesterday and at the counselor's so we thought you were upset and maybe that you ran away somewhere.*"

Melora's face bending down a few inches to see if she could detect any emotion or expression to give her a clue as to what might really be swimming around in the head of the girl.

"*Well, yeah, I mean, I was crying yesterday and I was in the bathroom when I broke down too. Mom said she was going to sell Candy and make me stop coming here if they haven't found out who killed Jodi. She said it was a dangerous place. She said it always has been, and that before Jodi died another girl was murdered here about 30 years ago and no one ever found her killer either. Mom isn't sure I should be around you or Jule. She said that you're the one who *told me that Bree wasn't going to be picked for the roster and that when I told her, well, I told Lily, she told her mom, and then I heard Jodi and Cathy outside, I thought maybe Cathy and Lily killed her and drug her out to the pasture to be eaten by coyotes or something."*

The story was an amazing one to be sure, but how many actual leads could be pulled from that sort of speculation? The question bothered Melora somewhat, but not as much as the need to comfort her favorite boarder at a time when she felt that comfort was needed.

"So, is your mom thinking she's going to sell Candy so she doesn't have to pay board, or does she really not want you here with us?" Melora asked, again, trying to make eye contact. When Keegan rolled her lips inside her mouth, her friend realized the truth. There was something more wrong with the horse, not with Larissa Lowell.

A thousand black birds swooped through the skies overhead while a hundred more or so pecked at the grass seeds of the spring grasses as they tried their best to take hold. A few low hanging grey clouds threatened to burst open on top of the two friends before they could make their way back to the main barn to discuss a few accommodations which may fit into the budget of Larissa Lowell; allowing her to unburden herself of her youngest long enough for Melora to ask questions about potentially making the arrangement more permanent if she could. Using a kid the way Lowell did was unacceptable; it was cruel and it reminded her of how she felt every time a counselor or court-appointed psychologist would ask her questions about her parents; about who she wanted to live with.

Melora thought she loved her father, she really did, but what could a little girl know about such things? Daddies and moms are supposed to be married. They're supposed to stay married. They're supposed to love each other, to love their kids. They're supposed to take long car rides on weekends, go to parks, play in the sand at the beach together. They're not supposed to fight and say ugly things. In Keegan's situation it could only be worse; her father wasn't around to defend himself even if there was a fight. He was gone. He had been the good guy. He had loved her. He had said nice things. If her heart was true to itself, Melora was about to break into a dozen pieces, but she knew she had to be stronger than she had been; it was her turn to be the adult now.

Though the people in the area still called the ranch the BSO even though it had been years since Barbara Susann Olsten had owned it. Convincing people to call the place by its new name, which was *"Bay Sorrel Ranch"* may take some time, but in some ways making it happen would take on a life of its own.

"I need you to help me Keegan." Started Melora, standing to her feet, and inviting the red-coated school ditcher to do the same.

"We need to get people to start calling the ranch by its real name. It's Bay Sorrel Ranch, and we're not saying the word 'The' in front of Bay Sorrel Ranch. It's just Bay Sorrel Ranch. In order to get people to know that, we need to make videos, post them on YouTube, Tik Tok, and maybe start some threads on Reddit to ask questions about it. You know, make it more than just the place where bad things happen; which I know is really bad timing considering what happened to Jodi. Can you help me do that? Can you make a few really cool videos and post them?"

The delight in her eyes told the whole tale. Keegan couldn't have been happier if she had been gifted three Appaloosa Arab mix horses that looked and performed exactly as she knew her best pet Candy had when she was a much much younger horse.

"Let me start by cleaning the area where the sign is, that way I can say I work here, and I am one of the reasons the ranch is so great; can I?"

She questioned, only to be told it was the most perfect idea ever. Before too long the two of them had managed to not only let both of their respective mothers know of Keegan's whereabouts, but they also managed to get the two moms talking, to make arrangements for Keegan to have a better living arrangement; one that would free Lowell up from her not-so-motherly routine, and allow Keegan to not only catch the bus on time to make it to school, but those bully girls who sent her off to the bathroom crying because she had on the same clothes as she had worn a day or two before, and there wouldn't be any more trips to the counselor at the request of her protective teachers who felt something needed to happen. Before the girl could be taken from her by the courts, Lowell saw the writing on the wall. She could maintain actual custody, and give what she could give to the child; which was freedom from living a life of embarrassment.

Because the big house was in fact too big for any of the Armstrongs to consider calling it home, the house would be put up for sale, and the smaller more reasonable house would become home to them all. The four-bedroom, three-bathroom estate seemed like a mansion to Keegan, who had been sharing a one-bedroom apartment with her mother for the past several years. The new arrangements put her in a double-walled protective state of being held accountable both by Melora, who she so aptly called *"Lora"* and Jule, who in some ways became the grandmother Keegan had never known as Larissa's own mother had remained in Idaho where Larissa Lowell had been born and raised. Having never met her actual grandparents, Keegan found herself and her new circumstances not only something to be proud of, but something to maybe even brag about after her Lora took her to Kohl's to buy a few new outfits to be seen in; to be new in.

11

Though they had not been instructed to do so, Jule had the entire north and western pastures stripped of literally every bit of debris, rubble, or stubble that could be used or investigated by the various legal authorities to garner any would-be evidence in the Jodi Williams case. Once an autopsy had been performed, portions of it had been shared with the property owner in order to better question her and Melora about anyone or anything they could come up with regarding who could have not only detained Jodi, as it seemed she had been, but who or what could have forced her into the north pasture where it was determined she was murdered. Once given the go head, Jule cleared it all out, hoping to help clear the ranch of its haunted reputation. Murder is blunt, not mysterious and ghostly, rumors needed to stop.

Blunt force trauma to her head had been the method of injury, the manner of death being of course, homicide. Line 21a of the Oklahoma Certificate of

Death had been marked with a circle surrounding the word "*homicide*" rather than "*accident*" or "*injury*". When an individual died of natural causes, the police officer explained to Jule, there is box in the middle of the certificate for any medical notes or comments. Had Jodi succumbed to her blood pressure ailment rather than having her skull crashed in, the words "*pulmonary hypertension*" would have been present.

According to Officer Mansfield of the Oklahoma City Police force, pulmonary hypertension would result due to the effects on the arteries and sometimes in the lungs and heart when the blood pressure builds to a point where the muscle can't control it. Symptoms would have been fast or faster racing heart, shortness of breath, or even appearing to be tired, really tired. Nothing like that had been present in Jodi Williams before being lured to the pasture or taken there. Keegan had just seen the girl, there was nothing wrong with her breathing. When the autopsy came back, her blood work indicated that she still had sufficient medication in her system to take care of any spike that could have taken place.

That's not to say however, that when she was approached, or detained, that she didn't become scared and possibly scared enough to begin exhibiting these types of symptoms. Maybe the person who lured her or took her became scared themselves and rather than try and deal with her conditions, they panicked and struck the girl. She would have either been in front of them, with her face toward them, as she was struck on the right side of her head, the blows appeared to have come from a left-handed person, or someone using their left hand.

There wasn't as much blood as one would have suspected; this led detectives to think she died from the first blow. The blood on the boards of the bed of the old trailer indicated that she had been struck, was bleeding while standing, and then once she fell to the ground she may have been covered up, or pushed up under the loosely held together apparatus consisting of the side of the flatbed and the edge of the overhead camper. Since it hadn't rained after the event, but before it happened, there was the possibility that the blood that was found pooling under her head had gathered only after she was in a prone position. The blood covering her clothes indicated she had in fact been standing when the fatal blow was struck. According to the coroner only one hard blow had been delivered; and maybe a second after she had fallen. The fatal blow was sent to the right side of her skull, up and over her right eye.

"I'm not 100% sure about it Sgt. Mansfield, but I do think Cathy Craigstone is right-handed. She thought she and her daughter Lily were going to be chosen for the final boarder roster, and I remember seeing a pen in her right hand the evening she left Lily to help with the mess she and her friend Bree had created." Stated Jule.

"*Bree Morgan? Would that be Breanna Diane Morgan who you're referring to? Because she's the next person on my list to go see and ask questions of. She and her father swear they weren't at the barn that day; both of them put their whereabouts at the Lazy E Arena up in Guthrie from about 4 o'clock to midnight.*" Mentioned the officer.

"*That's not true. Bree was at the barn from right after school, so yeah, around 4:00 o'clock, but she left right at or after 10:00 p.m. according to both my daughter Melora and our barn hand Keegan Tanner, the one Bree and Lily harassed that night. It was Bree and Lily who created the mess that prompted Jodi to stay longer and help. She usually parked her truck out there on the north side..*"

Jule stated, pointing with her index finger up toward the first horse barn where Melora kept the family horses now.

"*You're left-handed Jule.*" Stated Mansfield.

"*You didn't tell me that when I mentioned the killer could be a lefty.*" He questioned with his eyes, allowing her the chance to answer.

"*I'm not left-handed, but I did use my left hand just now. I'm actually ambidextrous, but my mom tells me I was born using my left, and over time she conditioned me to use it less often, so I wouldn't be left out like she was when she was growing up. I take it not many folks in the early '40s liked having to make *accommodations for lefties. I use both hands; but no, in case you're wondering, I don't kill people in real life, only in my books, and only then when they deserve it."* She explained.

Mansfield had mentioned Morgan for a couple of reasons. He wanted to verify what David Morgan had said about not being on the property that day, and he wanted to verify if Bree Morgan had been on the property. When she thought about it, Jule let him know that she had been on and off Zooms all day and all evening with her manager Mike Maguire, and a couple of reporters from both the United States and the United Kingdom, as her book *"Tartaned Soul"* had been given another nod that afternoon in the UK for one of the best sellers of the Highland Romance genre; it had surpassed a few more notable books, and they were requesting a Zoom meeting for purposes of telecasting a book review an reading for the following day.

"I came down to the barn a couple of times to my office to get something or other, and went back to the house. I did see Bree twice; once after she arrived, after school, and once when I closed my office and walked back to the house. She was in the blue barn arena with her Paint and the baby foal. We allowed them to stay at the barn until the mare was delivered; we didn't want to upset her any more than was necessary. She gave birth a few months back, and my daughter was about to let David Morgan know he needed to find a new barn; she was going to give him a 10-day notice. That was the night Jodi was killed.

Melora got busy, and hadn't made the call to her father yet, so he wasn't here, but Bree was. When she was picked up, I don't know who saw the driver, but Keegan said she left in a black Dodge Ram. David Morgan drives one, so it's probably his." Jule explained.

With only the word of her daughter and Keegan to go by, she told Mansfield, that he was free to question Melora, but one or the other of them would need to be present if he decided to question Keegan. Jule felt that trying to find a way to ask Larissa to be present would be tantamount to nothing being done in the first place. Larissa was as apt to assist the police as she was to leave the bar at a decent hour. Some things just weren't going to happen in their lifetime. When the investigating officer mentioned to Melora that her seeing Bree on the premises at any time after 4:00 p.m. and before midnight would be paramount to his investigation, Melora acknowledged the gravity of the situation, following up that she could take a lie-detector test if needed. Of course, that sort of thing was never really used in most cases, but it was comforting to the officer to hear she was willing.

"Can I ask you something Sgt. Mansfield?" asked Melora, wondering why they hadn't used sniffing dogs or cadaver dogs to find or locate the body, his answer was that they didn't know they had a body until she found it. Jodi was considered a missing person who was in danger of dying from lack of medication, in

which case her body would be obviously displayed somewhere; either in her truck if she had driven off, or she would have most likely have been seen in the open if she had passed out on the premises. Until Melora came across it in the field, no one would have imagined she could have or would have gone out to that particular area given that it was so full of debris anyone could be hurt especially at that late hour without any overhead lights.

"You did us all a favor. Dogs are used when we know we need them. It's really expensive to pull out the K9 units if we don't need to. Our trainers are top notch and they are compensated because of it. There is however, in case you ever need it again, a group of rescue and search dogs up at the Bridge Creek Stables in Crescent. They have a team or pack of Bloodhounds and a couple of Bassetts that will pull double duty until they find their targets. They've won awards and everything. I guess you can look them up online, but I've given you their name. The thing is, if you get a hold of Rodney and tell him Jimmy Mansfield told you, he may let the dogs come out and do a dry run to see if we can find another scent to follow."

As Mansfield was explaining his thoughts he took a second to pull out a notebook and scratch a few words, then decided to act upon his thoughts. It had been several weeks since the murder, and maybe there wouldn't still be anything to go on, but if the killer left his scent near the scene or at it, maybe the dogs could find something. If they could, it would give the case another chance to bring the ranch into the media again, for less than desired reasons. Jule could just about see Mike Maguire's eyes popping out of his head when she got around to explaining it; as she knew she would need to do so.

The Oklahoma City, Bethany, and Mustang K9 units were called and the whole of northwest Oklahoma County as well as the Northeast of Canadian County and maybe even some of the more southern reaches of every farmers in and around Cashion watched with seething curiosity and misplaced excitement at what may happen once the dogs were released. Precautions were given both verbally and by written notification posted on nearly every post leading from the entrance of Bay Sorrel Ranch to the back barns lining the north pasture that Monday morning. Big five-foot square cardboard signs with large black block lettering reading in essence that no one was to attempt to distract the dogs from doing their job. Anyone interfering with police business would be subject to arrest and would be charged with obstruction of law.

The BSO had been a most unpopular tract of land in those parts for years, and it had not really gained much in the way of being trusted just because the new owner was a well-known, even famous author. Word around those parts was that she may have murdered the girl herself just for the publicity, but most people who had any sense to them at all discounted the rumors as soon as they had been shared. Since most of the nonsensible rumors had seemed to crop up either over Sunday coffee at various local churches or over cornbread hash and potlucks at the same churches, Jule decided to try her luck at visiting a few of the local places of worship to at least let her face be seen; this way, she figured, she could prove that the good Lord wouldn't strike her dead in their midst, nor would He allow the roofs to cave in if she walked through their doors.

Over her five decades of living, Jule Armstrong had been a staunch Baptist. She was a believer in Christ, a follower of His teachings, and it didn't matter to her what the good souls at these places said or thought about her, she knew her walk with her God was solid as it could be. She had even prayed a number of times to have the killer or killers revealed to her somehow so she could assist in the investigation instead of just being the center of everyone's attention for having had the gull to buy the joint days before the girl was murdered.

It wasn't the murder that created the stir so much as it was the fact that the killer or killers were at large. Most in the area, because it was a few miles from Kingfisher where Jodi had lived, didn't know the girl. They had no idea that she had taken so many ribbons and accolades for her riding abilities because most of her riding was done up in another part of the state. Why Jodi Williams had decided to board at the BSO when it was being called the BSO was unknown. It seemed that only Lily Craigstone and maybe a few others even knew who Jodi was; why she had chosen a barn so far from her home could mean that she either thought about moving once she graduated, or maybe she worked in the area somewhere and it was closer to go to the barn and get a ride in before heading home.

When she was younger, that's exactly what Jule herself had done. Jule's home in Bethany, Oklahoma was about six or seven miles from the Chisholm Trail Ranch; but she had worked at the little grocery store just a half a mile west of it. Driving past the ranch before going home after she pulled a 4:00 p.m. to 8:00 p.m. shift three times a week to meet criteria for her D.E.C.A. class at Hoover High meant that she could have a bit more sunlight to ride in before pulling into the crowded driveway where her siblings and parents vied for better parking spots each day. If it had been left to her, like Keegan did, Jule would have camped out in a barn or something to be closer to her horses. Maybe she remembered these things when she thought of Keegan. She wondered what she could remember when she thought about Jodi Williams.

12

Nobody wasted their time or energy trying to distract the hounds as they made their nosey way through the fifteen-acre paddock called the north pasture. Taping off areas they had traipsed through, two of the K9 unit officers took visual-aid digital recordings of the latitude and longitudes of the exact locations, while a third officer wrote descriptions of what he saw in his pocket notebook for future reference. Seven dogs had been brought to the location from various departments nearby, and were given samples of Jodi's scent through articles of clothing her mother and father had not washed or disposed of since her demise.

Not knowing who the other person or persons could be, the dogs collectively hit on something and began tearing off in unison toward the blue barn, ending up by the area where the previous managers had piled the manure from the various pastures before loading it onto flatbeds to be distributed evenly throughout the grounds. It was the same area where Tucker Banderoff had parked his truck many times; the one with the hitch that fit the trailers that pulled the manure flatbeds. The dogs couldn't stop barking once they approached the flat top pavement where the pile had been removed.

"Looks like they found something, maybe someone."

Crooned one of the K9 officers before using his camera-type devise to record the exact spot on the Earth where the dogs had hit.

"What do you know about this spot Ma'am, and by this spot, I mean exactly this five-foot-by-five-foot square approximately. The dogs seem to really like it." He added.

"I can't say with certainty, because the last time I knew of someone being parked there or standing there besides myself, was a boy by the name of Tucker Banderoff. He drives a..."

She began to explain before being shut down by Officer Ted Jablonski, the third K9 commander who not only knew the name, but absolutely knew the truck he drove.

"You don't have to tell me who that kid is Ms. Armstrong, he's been a pain in our ass for about as long as he's been driving. Thinks he's God's holy gift to the road, and he'd be the only one to think that if he old

man wasn't as quick to agree with him as long as he can share the title. Those boys have been on our radar any number of years and for any number of reasons. Are you telling me, that he parked his truck here recently? Do you know if he was here that night? Did anyone see him here?" he asked.

Jule could only repeat to Jablonski what she had told Mansfield, she hadn't been down to the barn or the ranch pastures much during the day that entire day because of her other line of business. She could ask Keegan or the other boarders if they had seen Tucker Banderoff, but with his popularity being so vastly animated when it came to the younger boarders, she wasn't sure she could get a straight answer out of any of them except Keegan. That day had been all but quiet to begin with, unusually quiet in fact, for a Saturday.

After speaking with Melora about who had come in to and who had left the barn, there was only a handful of boarders, a farrier who had been commissioned by Craigstone and Morgan, and maybe the attorney, the one who rode the big Dressage beast in the first stall. The horse's name was Einstein, a 17.1 HH Hanoverian purebred used not only for his flash and high-headed posture, but his coloring was outstanding. Einstein's blood-bay coat gave an amazing sheen encompassing several shades when clipped each year. His rider, was a high-maintenance man by the name of Paul Abernathy.

Paul had made the cut for the roster not only because he was willing to pay the new board fees without questioning, but he was a noted rider who was known by many to have a good personality and reputation at the Red Feather Tack and Feed Store off Broadway in Edmond. Not many people do their due diligence and leave solid references, but Abernathy had. If he was questioned, Melora advised, the person doing the questioning would need to know the man is a criminal or defense lawyer, a Pitbull-type from one of the larger firms downtown. Her warning was taken in genuine by detectives and officers on the scene.

When Paul Abernathy answered his phone his first question wasn't the identification of the caller, but how the caller had his number in the first place.

"I'm Sgt. James Mansfield. I'm calling as a courtesy before giving your number to a detective who will be following up on a murder case we're working here in the far northwest quadrant of Oklahoma County where you board your horse. Your name came up as being one of the few people who had been at the barn the day or evening of April 8, and we need to do our own due diligence to ask you a few questions." The good sergeant informed the man.

"Before we get started, I'm told you're an attorney, so that's good news for me, because it means you'll answer my questions without hesitation and without any funny business because you and I both know if you don't answer me I'll bring your name up

to the ABA and we'll make more of it than needs to be, are you ready for my questions or do we need to speak at another time?"

asked Mansfield, all but sure he would be conducting his interview forthwith.

Upon determining that not only Abernathy had been present at the barns between the hours of 4:00 p.m. and 10:00 p.m. it was also recorded that he had left the barn somewhere between six that evening or just a few minutes thereafter. He did let the officer know that Leah Cotman, a forty-something year old nail salon owner had been at the barn. After she rode a while, she gave Dean Stovich a ride home. Dean had been training under Abernathy for just under a year. Stovich and Cotman left about the same time as Paul had, as Paul remembered needing to wait before pulling out of his spot to back up and drive away from the barns.

No one had been at the barns after the hour of 11:20 p.m. that either Melora, Keegan, or Lily could remember. Her mother Cathy Craigstone had refused to answer any questions put to her unless she was served a warrant; something she felt wouldn't happen any time soon, but she did allow her daughter to answer as long as she didn't say anything that she hadn't been told to say. According to Mansfield, Lily Craigstone only repeated what Keegan had mentioned regarding the Williams girl, and that was to say that her mother and Jodi had quarreled about a minute over Jodi being accepted and Lily not being accepted for the roster position; something Craigstone blamed Jule for, saying the parking spot was not a reason to thump a kid's dreams, and causing her to not be chosen as one of the boarders. The parking spot had no bearing on a decision to cut the Craigstones; personalities to the side, Cathy had been banned at a number of barns in the past, and neither Jule nor Melora wanted more barn drama.

What neither Cathy or Lily had told the police, but Melora was quick to do, was that the Craigstones were not chosen due to Cathy's reputation at literally every other open barn in every surrounding county. She had either left owing a lot of back board, or they were being sued by Cathy for minor infractions including but not limited to, harassment, tampering with the health of their livestock, or something similar and again, from every last barn in the area. The BSO only accepted them because they had cash to pay and couldn't pin anyone to the wall for any wrong doing. If no one was really in charge, there was no one to hold responsible. Even after she had been asked to leave, Cathy Craigstone often lurked around each barn to be seen or cause a bit of trouble if she could.

Mansfield asked for a list of the people who both made the cut and those who didn't make it, so he would have a few leads to follow up in case someone was jealous of Williams for getting the green light. Keegan's name appeared first on the keep-list but a digital number value of zero was placed beside her name where the outside pasture boarding fee should have been.

"You're not charging Keegan Tanner anything to board her horse, but you're charging Shaina Cleveland $700. I know Shaina. She and her family go to the AME church that my wife and I attend. You're not charging Shaina because her family has money and this Keegan kid doesn't are you? Because that could look funny to some if you did." questioned Mansfield with a bit of added attitude.

"Sgt. are you asking me if I'm racist? But maybe you're doing it in a nicer way than just coming out and saying it?" asked Jule.

"Well, I mean Shaina is paying $700 a month, and looks like almost all the other boarders including this Paul Abernathy is paying less than she is. She's the only black girl on the roster, I think she's the only one anyway."

"Sgt. are you going by the girl's name? I mean, you said you know her, she goes to church with you. Are you going down the list looking for names that look ethnic? Helene Jackson is black too, Sgt. She only pays $600 a month and she has two horses. One of her horses is a big pure white grade mare and the other is a solid black grade gelding. Maybe I should charge her more for the gelding is that how you think I run my barn? She has both of her horses outside and under the stars without so much as a blanket to cover them, but

you know what, maybe I should let her keep them both in the stalls because she's a beautiful lady of color, and I don't want to be seen or thought of as being a racist."

Chided Armstrong before going on to say that the reason that Shaina Cleveland's horse was marked as a $700 pay was because she, the mare, receives insulin shots given every week by the barn manager, and there's a cost associated with that.

Staring the man in the eyes and trying to remain as calm as she could be under the circumstances, Jule reminded the good man before her that neither her family or anyone in her lineage had been raised to be prejudice toward any man, woman, or child because of race, religion, creed, political stand, or sexual orientation. She was fair and as balanced as anyone she could remember, and one of the reasons she needed be was because she herself wasn't perfect. She knew she had come from a background of being the ones who were called *"white trash"* and *"hillbilly"* most of her adolescent life. It took becoming a well-respected rider as a kid, and a well-known author later in life to be given the well-deserved respect she thought she deserved in the first place.

"If my own mom thought I was charging someone more because of the color of their skin, I wouldn't have any skin left on my ass to sit on, do you understand me, sir?" she asked.

"I do understand you Ms. Armstrong, and I'll be the first to say I'm sorry if I offended you. It was just something that caught my eye, and I thought I would ask you about it, that's all."

With that, the man motioned to tip his hat by the corner of the extended brim before smiling, and walking to his car.

As Mansfield and all the others made their exits, Stephen Mueller made an entrance through the east gates to ask his new girlfriend what the fuss was all about, if she was OK; she seemed a bit steamed. He wanted to ask if the property was OK, he had grown a bit concerned since he hadn't heard much from Jule over the past few days. He of course, knew about Jodi's body being found, but without any true reference or understanding about why a young girl would be murdered there and under such strange circumstances, he had purposely not made his way up to the house to visit Jule considering she wasn't living alone anymore, and even though he was retired, he was often asked to lend a thought or two officially from other departments. Since he was involved with Jule at this point, he would have needed to recuse himself; what better way to do that than to not be present if the police were hanging around?

"I'm thinking I'll either rent myself an apartment or have a place built here on the property. I don't know. I don't want the big house, it's too big. I haven't taken you all the way through it, have I?"

Jule asked Stephen. *"I've not taken you on a tour of it, not all of it. We're cleaning it up and getting it ready for Alyse to list. She thinks she may already have a buyer! She's pretty sure she can sell it within a few weeks actually. Alyse is really happy that I'm pricing it at a give-away price; she says, it'll be off the market soon. I just don't want some snobby old rich guy living there who wants me to tend his garden or something."* She quipped.

"Maybe you shouldn't sell him the tract closest to the smaller house, and then you could build a privacy fence so he would have to stand on the north side out one of those two windows there, to even see you." Matched Mueller.

"Well, like I said. I may get an apartment nearby so I can come up to use the office, but I really don't see myself living with Melora and Keegan for the rest of my life. I'm a cave dog. I don't need much."

As she said it she realized it had been a minute since he had been caught up on all of the barn drama. He hadn't been told about Melora's new acquisition and how she had suddenly become a grandmother to a kid she had only known a few weeks. Turning to face the man, Jule leaned into him, putting a little weight on him while lifting her left leg, bending her knee, and pointing her toes. While he held her in place, Stephen took a little step to the side of his new lover, twirling her in one of those little ballerina spins that people do when they flirt a little more than most.

13

What they did was wrong and the girls knew it. Most of the ones involved in the hazing were more than sure that their actions would never have been considered decent, or even moral. For one or the other of them not to run to the barn owners to let them know what Bree Morgan had bullied them into doing seemed just as mindless, just as thoughtless. It took the confessions of three girls who all pointed the finger at Morgan, for Trisha Bellows to do something about it. The problem was, for Bellows anyway, that if she decided to go with her good judgement and kick Bree and her two horses out of her barn permanently, she'd lose $1100 a month in income. Bree's dad David Morgan would be apt to force a legal side to it, and insist that Bellows also expel the others; that would mean more than $1650 additionally being lost and with the way things were going, it was just not going to be feasible to do it.

"Tell me what she made you do, and why the hell you did it."

Scorned the owner of the High Five in Bethany, several miles south from Bay Sorrel. When Trisha spoke, she did so in a general manner, not pointing to or singling out any of the girls specifically. She hoped at least one would chirp up and tell her what exactly happened overnight in her barn.

Elle hadn't been all that keen on Bree to begin with, so it wasn't as difficult for her to speak; that, and she wanted to remain in the better graces of the barn owner so she could keep her place in the stalls. Her mare hadn't been happier in years. Coming to the High Five, even if it didn't have an indoor arena to use, was a better option than most. She spoke clearly, but not very loudly, needing to be coaxed a few times before her entire story had emerged.

"Bree called us, well, I mean, she texted us and told us all to show up last night after closing hours. I couldn't get my mom to take me so Bree and her dad came by my house around 9:45 I guess. We got here and the others were already here, Bree claimed that picking me up cost her time and we had to hurry." Elle started.

"You mean her dad knew about this?" asked Bellows in a tone less than surprised, but on the side of disbelief.

Looking more like a lost sheep than a young lady, Elle Thompson continued.

"Yeah, he said it was going to be the best prank ever and we could either do it or never expect another favor from any of them again. Since he paid my board last month and let my dad pay him back later, I didn't think I had much of a choice. They do that. Morgans I mean. Bree will be really nice to you maybe three or four times, bringing in your tack, or washing your horse, maybe mucking the stall, but you know that she wants something for it. She won't do anything if it's not going to bring her something in return. He told me to just do what she said and not to tell anyone because if I did...well, you know what will happen, and I guess if I'm late again now you'll kick me out anyway, so I may as well tell you what we did since I'm not going to be here."

As her words began to disappear, and she began kicking at the dust beneath her feet, Bellows encouraged Elle to say what she had started, all the while stepping back a bit to wrangle another boarder who was quietly trying to make an exit.

"You're not going anywhere Jera. You're in on this too. I caught you! Your fingerprints are all over these scissors and I'll have your mother's last paycheck if you try to walk away from me now, young lady."

Trisha had been kind enough to allow Jera's Simmon's mom to do a little bookkeeping for her in lieu of half the month's board for her daughter who hadn't turned 16, and wasn't eligible for most places around the area to hire her at least ten to twelve hours a week.

"Go on Elle, who gave you the scissors? How many of you cut the tails and manes off the horses of the girls Bree thinks need to learn a lesson, and how many of you decided to trim up your own horses to get out of being blamed?" At her last question, the Thompson girl stepped forward and spoke up with clear intention of being heard.

"We all did it. Every last one of us. Jera, me, Tawny, and Chase. She had four pairs of scissors and gave them to each of us. She told us which horses to do, and like you said she thought we needed to do our own horses too so we wouldn't be blamed. I did it, I cut of Elsa's mane some, but when I got to her tail I just couldn't do it. I did cut off King's tail, and I'll tell Cecily Bridges that it was me. We went to school together and I didn't want Chase cutting it too close to the bone; he did that to Marla's gelding and he may have cut his skin. I think he did."

Elle looked around at her friends before her head began to sag and tears filled her eyes at the realization of her own actions. She knew better, and she hated herself in that moment. It wasn't a prank. She knew that now. It was harsh, it was mean.

More than a dozen horses including those of Trish Bellows had been cropped and with the number of shows and competitions coming up it was no wonder that the girls were misled by the one truly vicious-minded fiend in the barn. Having seen the hair on the ground outside her gelding's stall, Trish was apt to begin searching for the culprit. As it had happened the night before, it would be impossible to lay blame on anyone. No cameras in the barn meant she hadn't any proof, no evidence, but she knew enough about the younger boarders to know the deed wasn't done by an adult. No one at the High Five was in such a competitive spirit to molest a horse which could prove as an opponent, no one but maybe Bree Morgan.

This sort of thing wasn't done; not in civil circles it wasn't. The last time something like that had happened to her, Trisha was a junior in high school where she presented her most important event with not only a near-tailless horse, but one she had to scrub for over an hour to remove pink and gold spray paint from its fur. This sort of thing was wrong, it was immoral, and the more she thought about it, the money didn't matter as much as doing the right thing did. She might lose more than she could income wise, but she just couldn't see herself being caught up in barn gossip statewide again, not again. She had to put a stop to it. Bree Morgan was persona non-grata from that point forward. The others may be on probation; that may be the best choice; she would decide at another time. For now, she just needed to get to the bottom of it.

When Trisha thought about it and how the whole thing took place, it made an impact on her to the point of not only reporting the incident to the police and listing David and Bree Morgan as the suspects behind it all, she was able to talk every parent of the actual perpetrators into a meeting to discuss the actions of their children; her boarders. Seeing how Chase Finley was involved the whole thing began to gel. Bree had Chase wrapped so tightly around her little finger he could be talked into doing anything. Trisha knew from rumor and reputation around the barn that Bree had any number of suitors or boys who found her fascinating. She had been further rumored to be one of those types of girls who didn't mind flirting openly with other young girls her age either for the shock value of it, or perhaps she was actually and genuinely interested in pursuing that sort of lifestyle. Trisha herself didn't care either way, but it made sense to keep a mind like Bree's away from causing any more havoc than she already had.

Chase Finley, a boy of somewhat gloomy habits had dealt with Bree's hot and cold mindset for years where he was concerned. He had hoped to make her his girlfriend when she asked him and the others to help her with her little prank, as she called it; he could help her and she might help him. Hair grows back, she assured them, it's not like they were doing any real harm, and besides, she would be apt to mention to Chase, *"If you do this for me, I'll love you forever"* Trisha Bellows could all but hear the twisted lips of the barn bully spewing out coos and whimsical entreaties while thrusting the long shears into his hands and pointing out which horses he could start with. It wasn't hard for the woman to sign the police report naming them all as suspects; even if it meant starting over trying to find new boarders.

For this and other reasons like it, Melora Armstrong had not chosen to accept Bree Morgan into the barn's roster when the boarders were asked to fill out applications for the opportunity to remain in the barn. Her antics at the BSO, as well as at Dreyfuss Stables in Yukon, had led Melora to make her decision. It just seemed that no matter where David or Bree Morgan went they left a wave of trouble in their wake. If it wasn't horse tampering, it was something else. Bree, at her young age, would have been subjected to having been raised in a household of shenanigans; she couldn't have come up with such malice thoughts on her own without first being aware of it from early on. What else could the Morgans be up to, thought the new barn manager of the Bay Sorrel. It wasn't beyond her to dig into the court records of every county surrounding the barn to see what she could find. Court records were, like everything else, found online.

"Lora, did you see where our videos have more than 5,000 views today?"

asked Keegan, her eyes bulging with excitement. It had taken the girl a few hours to film and edit her prizes before uploading them both on her personal Tik Tok account and on the new one set up for the barn.

"I didn't know a barn could have a Tik Tok, but it makes sense to do it, I mean, we're going to be here all day working and playing so why not let the people see us and then they'll want to come out and do this too."

Agreed Keegan before asking if she could do a walk around tour; excluding the offices of course. When Melora agreed, telling her it was an excellent idea, you would have thought the skies had opened and poured out confetti; Keegan's smile could be seen a few counties over if anyone had a mind to look up and see it.

"Oh my gosh, yes!" she exclaimed,

"I'm going to start at the gate, and work my way all the way to the barn, but I'll probably make it like really hazy and walk slowly like a Hallmark movie. Then I'll enter the barns, and walk past each stall showing the horses as they pop their heads out. Maybe I can get someone to wave a bunch of hay behind me and that way they'll all put their heads out, but I can't do it until after dark when everyone else is gone. Then, I'll need to mute the sound because the person will be calling their names and the hay will make noise too, but it's going to be great Lora! It's going to look like we have the most trained horses and they can't wait to greet anyone who comes to the barn...and..."

She couldn't contain herself; the girl was giddy with excitement. Taking notes in her head and making sure everything was just right, Keegan spun around while she danced through the rustic beamed barn, looking for props to use, before deciding she may need to clean the place a little more for best optics; and the music. She had to find the right royalty-free music to play for each video.

Melora was really happy with the names she had chosen for the roster. It was going to be something of a privilege, she believed, for someone to be able to say they board at Bay Sorrel Ranch. When people asked them if there was any trouble at the barn, the answer would be no, drama is not allowed at Bay Sorrel. This was of course, a pipe-dream considering all that had just taken place; but it was a goal that everyone who knew the Armstrongs felt they could achieve. Jule, with her take-it-to-the-limit seriousness about anything she put her mind to, and Melora's accommodating way with people, and especially with wild Mustangs; the new barn was a new beginning for more than just the owner and her daughter. It was something the community could be proud of; at least it would be soon enough.

14

Steve Mueller hadn't been away too many days when his grizzly bearded face popped its way in through the front door of the office space which for all means and purposes had been off limited to just about anyone whose name wasn't associated with Jule Armstrong. Mueller and Tanner were the only ones with the front door keys besides the Armstrongs. Keeping her keys behind the old cowboy's painting had morphed into Keegan becoming that much more mature about it; she had a new unicorn keyring that she sported about, given to her by Melora. Though he could see Jule, and see that she was on a call, Mueller slipped in quietly before sitting in his favorite overstuffed leather chair he had managed to talk Jule into installing for this exact purpose.

She was quiet basically, nodding her head and making agreeable sounds into the phone, and he could tell she had been discussing the latest details from whatever they were calling the discovery of Jodi Williams' body a few weeks prior; the unconscious thoughts of not knowing the full truth hung in the air like floating quicksand. Neighbors and people in the community hastened to conclusions as they always had when the haphazard ranch was involved in anything less than above board; it seemed to always have a cloud hanging low enough over its pastures to cause trouble and certain doubt in the melancholiest of ways. Today's intel which Jule would share soon enough was no exception. Holding her hand over the phone a bit, she leaned over her desk to whisper.

"They found more during the autopsy Steve. Seems Jodi was eight to ten weeks pregnant when she died. That gives police and of course her parents, an entirely different outlook on what may have happened." Jule began, and then closing the call she hung up the phone.

"That was Mansfield, you said you worked with him in Bethany before you retired. I let him know it was you that he saw when he was last here. He was just leaving when you were pulling into the drive but he said he thought it was you. He says to tell you hello, and I'm supposed to mention that he won and you know it. I assume you know it, because I don't know it...you can let me know what he's talking about."

She laughed a little under her breath hoping that maybe something Mansfield had given her was lighter in nature than the rest of their conversation.

"He's OK with us moving the rest of the debris and rubble saying he had all he needed and it was all checked at the lab. The only thing he has a problem with is me destroying evidence to begin with, but dammit, I didn't realize even for a second that I could be doing that Steve. I knew you were a policeman; I should have figured that out before I even asked everyone to help us try and find the girl."

As she beat herself up over the matter, her left hand inadvertently picked up a little laminated folded map of the general area of the greater Oklahoma City area. She felt it was insignificant to mention, but mentioned it anyway,

"Did you know a former Navy Seal and local man, a rancher himself named Dave White invented these things? True story. He owns the little place up on Edmond Road that I took you to last week; where Robin keeps her horses. He owns that place, and a few Nascar type cars, an airplane because he can, and because he has a runway in his backyard. I thought about putting one in the back forty, but decided against it, what do you think?"

She asked, as she maneuvered her way into his open lap, draping her legs to one side, and wrapping his shoulders into her giving arms. Her heart heavy thinking about the poor and helpless young victim, and now thinking twice as hard about her as she had not been alone in the situation. She wondered if Jodi even knew; if that could have been the reason she was murdered, or if the baby was simply collateral damage.

Jule felt that life wasn't that fair to anyone, but especially to a young and vibrant girl like Jodi Williams, who had many roads diverging on her at once. She was a senior in high school; the year everything is supposed to be exciting and preparing her for the rest of her life. She was competing in both English and Western events at the highest levels possible for anyone not yet a professional. For her sake, more than enough good events taking place in and around her life seemed to be stacking up; she was on top of the world. She had many admirers, one of which seemed to be a bit of a poet according to Mansfield. Trinity Williams, Jodi's young mother, had found a slip of pink romantic parchment, the type you would have to go out and buy to actually have in your possession. On the note was a brief and pointed poem of sorts telling Jodi she was the one he had wanted to share the rest of his life with, but for the life of her Trinity hadn't heard the name Chase Finley before in any of the more recent conversations she and Jodi had. Who could he be the mother wondered. Who indeed, wondered Chief Mansfield as well.

Chase had known Jodi since childhood apparently, but he was one of those quiet types that never seem to leave the safety of the woodwork to be unblended. He wasn't seen, he wasn't even known to most. At school he had been an enigma; on every club list there was including Chess, AV, Library Club, the Four-H Club, and even Student Council. He had run for a junior office his sophomore year, but when he was defeated it took the steam right out of him politically, and though he remained involved in the various school social associations, he managed to do all the work but not take much in the way of credit. He had graduated the year before, leaving his mark in the yearbook, but not many knew who the boy was. At least through the magic of photography they knew what he looked like. This was a good thing at least.

"The name Chase Finley in some ways rings a bell,"

mentioned Steve, as he remembered the incident up at the High Five ranch where the horses had recently been molested. It was a bit of a story for days in the Bethany Tribune; he had already retired, but one of his cop friends had called him to ask if he or Lisa had been friends with the Finleys since the paper mentioned Chase had attended the same church where the two had attended when they were married.

"I haven't walked into the First Baptist of Bethany in about as long as I can remember. I stopped going about a year or two before my divorce. The rumors were bad and the conversations worse. I think if I had to think about it, Christians treat other Christians with so much less respect than we should. I have to include myself in on that one honey,"

he said, as he shifted her weight, he pulled her into himself a bit tighter.

"I have to admit here before you and God that I wasn't very friendly to some of those who were trying to be more than friendly to me so they didn't show their true colors within the church walls. I don't know what it is about the place, but people think you can say what you want to say outside the church, but inside it you have to be shut-mouthed and stupid to not see what was going on both in my situation, and now I guess this Finley kid.

"If my memory serves me, he did some of the horse tail cutting and may have even stabbed a horse or hurt it somehow, all because a girl asked him to do it. If he's going off writing poems to Jodi, I don't know why he thinks she's the last one to love. He has it all hanging out for Bree Morgan just a few months after the love of his life is gone...kids. That's why he did what he did at the High Five. That boy's a mess I guess. Maybe he had one of those Jekyll and Hyde minds that can't keep himself straight. He was in love with the angel and the devil at the same time." Mueller said.

With her arms secured around him, and her mind drifting somewhere above the clouds in high thought, Jule wondered out loud if Chase and Bree had come up with a plan to do away with Jodi. If somehow Finley couldn't satisfy one, but maybe believed he had an in with Morgan if he'd get rid of the pregnant one. Could that have been the motive she wondered? Before settling the matter as being possibly too far-fetched for reality, she wanted to at least scratch a few notes about what she was thinking so she could add the circumstances in her next novel. She couldn't or wouldn't add that the murder had taken place at a local author's barn, that would be too close for comfort, but she could change the names to something Scots Gaelic, put the setting somewhere north of the cliffs in Ayrshire, and crank the year back a few hundred turns to a mid-15th or 16th era where men were apt to club anyone over the head for virtually any good reason at all, but cutting a horse's tail could get you burned at the stake in any village. Jule let her mind wander while ears were being tickled.

Months passed, when Chase Finley's name appeared again, this time on the front page of the local papers online and in print; it was heard during the nightly news as well. The young man had been accepted into the prestigious halls of Stanford University at the end of his senior year at Chesterfield. He had not returned to the college following the fall break, and the university authorities were reaching out to officials in Oklahoma to ask for assistance in locating the young man. Jule had turned the news on just before preparing her evening meal with Steve at the new apartment she had chosen to rent; her boxes still needing to be unpacked, had found a new use, doubling as table tops for her world-famous Mississippi chicken over rice.

"So, Chase Finley is missing now. He probably murdered Jodi and thinks he'll be caught. They'll do a DNA test on the baby soon, and maybe come up with him as being the father. He's probably taken one of his dad's rifles and offed himself in one of those old rickety deer stands in Kingfisher county between the city and Okarche. If I were writing this out, and trying to make it as pathetic as I possibly could, that's exactly where I'd put the boy.

"No, wait, I'd have him writing a long note to his mama first, so she doesn't have to find him. He'll tell her where he is so she can get someone from the church or maybe her brother Phil to go find him swinging from a tree. Forget I said he would take his dad's shotgun or rifle. If he wasn't going to do that to himself he may have tried to do that to Jodi as well. No, he's hung himself. He's up there in the woods and maybe used an extension cord...."

She tangled within her own mind.

"He's unplugged his mother's sewing machine, taken the cord with him, and purposely drove himself to the woods where he'll be found. He left the note on the desk by the machine, because she'll sit down to hem something later in the day, find the note, and send out her brother Phil...I'm assuming she has a brother, and I'm assuming his name is Phil. It'll be too late to see anything without a good lantern, so he'll take his truck, point the headlights into the open gated area after he drives as far as he can into it without getting

stuck in; but there he'll think he sees something hanging low enough that it could be a body.

"Phil won't know that the dead weight of the boy will bring both of them crashing to the ground, but he cuts him down best he can, he uses a step ladder that he had in the back of the truck. When he does manage to climb out from under the weight, he realizes that there isn't so much as a drop of blood. He'll wonder about that for a minute, thinking the noose must have quickly broken the boys neck, and that will remind him of when he used to watch shows like Bonanza and Gunsmoke, where there wasn't ever any blood even when people got shot. He'll think about Perry Mason and how he and Paul Drake found dead bodies without blood, but he'll remember that Perry Mason isn't a western, and he'll go back to his love for Gunsmoke. For a minute the man won't know if he's eight or forty-eight and he'll want to run home to his own mother's house to be held and comforted.

"Choosing to end his own life rather than face what he did was both cowardly and youthful; how could Phil hate Chase for it? He carries the body to the back of his truck and calls the local police because he doesn't want to get into trouble for molesting a corpse or wrongfully disposing of one, he saw that on Perry Mason, not Gunsmoke, and he knew he didn't want to have to face a jury of his own peers. He places another call to his little sister to let her know her baby boy has been found, and that Jesus has him now...."

She looked into Steve's face as he finished the last bite of his food, only to realize she hadn't even started on her plate.

"Got more cornbread?"

the man asked, not even addressing the fact that the new story in Jule's mind was far more modern than what her first thoughts had been about something happening high up in the boggy moors of a faraway land; this was a modern tale. He wondered if any of it could actually ring true.

15

Mike Maguire called her for the sixth time trying to reach her, but Jule had left her phone on her desk while she took her first trail ride on her new property. Both her daughter and Keegan had their phones, and since her larger than most iPhone seemed to always come out of her back pocket when she rode, she felt it was much safer at home or at least locked up on the office anyway. Melora had a side pouch on her saddle; it might be a good thing to find at Atwoods next time she took a trip to Norman or Kingfisher.

When she returned, and her legs were able to hold her up again, Jule complained openly about the fact that she couldn't remember horses being that thick in the past. Reaching for the edge of her desk to grab the vibrating cell, she realized also, that she had taken the ringer down to silent. She hadn't returned it to normal since the night before. Steve had stayed over;

which in and of itself was reason enough to keep the world at bay.

Maguire had arranged not only for the new launch to be handled within a week of the release of her newest new book, he had managed to find a sponsor to bring her and himself to Scotland to give the book an authentic release in the Highlands themselves. Archibald Books had raffled off three of the books, all signed, and with each book the winners would spend an evening with the author over dinner, again paid for by the book distributor, and they would have near implicit access to her through a two-hour question and answer session with the ability to record themselves and take selfies. Jule had even promised to spend a few minutes of their time together reading from the book if they took a fancy to that. Erin Morrison, head clerk of the book distributor felt that Armstrong's agreement to do so would bring about a flood of interested rafflers; and she was right.

"Mike, thank you. I can't say it enough. I don't think having the launch at the barn would have been the thing to do. It's wonderful, but to be honest, with all the events that have surrounded it, and we haven't really had the time to clean it with all the new boarders being vetted and the twelve Mustangs Melora brought on, we're just not there yet. I can't think of a better place; no better place. Ayrshire is perfect." She told him.

The days passed and when the time finally arrived to make her fifth trip to the best place in the world, Jule had all but decided she would not be going alone. Yes, she had her manager Mike following her from Las Vegas, they were to catch up in Chicago before making the trip to Glasgow; but what she really wanted was to see how sexy her new boyfriend would look wearing her family tartan in the form of an authentic hunting kilt, complete with sporran, hose, boots and jumper. Not being one for pomp or finery, the black boots would always outshine any dress shoe purchased for the purpose. Jule had a thing about big bearded men wearing kilts, and even though Steven Mueller couldn't boast of having a rounder belly, the way Armstrong preferred, he would be dashing in the pleaded garment of her ancestors...and maybe he'd be just as dashing while stepping out of it as well. She imagined the latter thought over and over again in various scenarios to the point of making herself blush.

The Highlands surrounding Ayrshire, Scotland, an area situated several miles west of the grand city of Glasgow, couldn't have been more on top of their game than they were that fine Saturday morning in early June. Some words to describe the area could be fresh, clean, crisp, or even brilliant. Others, those who used the impending weather as a more suitable guide to more realistic claims could refer to the bogs, the crags, the majestic cliffs that hung dramatically over the clapping waves of the sea; but whatever it was, Jule was there again, atop the hills and moors of the world she loved so deeply and wished in her heart that a visitor's visa wasn't what separated her from feeling permanently a part of this world.

Most Americans, she told herself, wouldn't know what a real kirk was, or a cairn, or even a glen. These words had become names in the States, their ancient meanings long forgotten by the average person who used the words to cling to the life given to them by history and so much more. Growing up in Oklahoma City's enormous metropolitan expanse had all but thwarted any desire for Jule as a younger soul to seek out her roots and find out more about her past, her hearty ancestry which had been singularly Scottish with a tiny exception of one or two percentages thrown about from places like Italy, France, and Spain. According to the DNA test she and her siblings had taken in 2010, and again more recently after it was discovered that the newer tests can tell you more, Jule found that she was over 64% Scottish; giving her a better understanding of herself. Never again would she allow anyone to call her stubborn without letting them know it was a noted family characteristic; not a flaw.

Jule walked the lengths of the hills, the mossy rocky moors, that seemed both irregular and wholly perfect at the same time. Their many qualities, neatness and rustic glory bequeathed a gentility she could never find within the borders of her own state. Oklahoma as a state, was just over a hundred years old, where as she had stepped into a world whose last thoughts of being anything resembling civil had been several centuries in the past. On top of the grass-carpeted hills, she sat alone in her thoughts, but not in person, as Steve had not been the least resistant to join her on the next book launch and tour. Her eighth book in the series titled *"Tartaned Spirit"* had been poised for release within a few days of the murder; her manager Mike Maguire had taken painstaking measures to keep that and other tidbits of information out of the press where Jule's name was concerned.

"I see what you mean about this place feeling both welcoming and foreboding," mentioned Steve, before approaching her cautiously from her left side.

"You're a might too close to that edge sweetheart, if you don't mind..."

He spoke quietly, while moving her gently, taking her elbow into his hands, and directing her a few feet inward.

"You're scaring me with your curiosity. That's a five-hundred-foot drop and it's all rocks from there. Even if you did survive the fall, you'd crush yourself on those boulders. We don't need that today. I don't want that ever." He smiled.

Their trip to the Highlands would prove agreeable in so many ways, ways that an American tourist would claim to be lifechanging, while a more local Scot would say was just another day in the air. How wonderful to think that every day of their lives they could walk among the giant mounds before them. That they could see the green covered lands and have all the many thousands of years of history right before them; yet she knew that most Scots weren't hardly even aware of the older more insignificant battles that raged right under their homes and streets. Most of the battles they were aware of, the ones taught in schools, had been given less and less study over the waning decades and had reached a point that when discussing the matters with those she believed should be capable of carrying on a conversation about it, Jule Armstrong found that not one of her conversationalists had even heard of Clan Armstrong, nor did they really even care to learn about it. For most, it was something that happened, but wasn't happening now. It made her wonder if she had become as cold about her own nation's history.

"When was the last time you dug into something that was rumored to have happened in America, but you only had the teacher's word on it, Steve?" she asked.

The situation somehow seemed a bit romantic to the man, and there was certain intrigue to the question. He looked about and realized the scenery about him held endless opportunity for him to draw upon, but he wasn't quite understanding how it would be that he came up with anything resembling an answer. Staring at her, he brushed his hand down the back of her head, feeling the close-cropped cut she had paid for the day before they traveled. The length in front made her look rather pixie-like, and it reminded him of the dancing elves he had read about in books when he was a kid.

"I don't know what you mean about things that happened in America. I guess I took the word of the teacher, like you said, because I didn't think for a second that they may want to lie to me about such things. I did find out recently that George Washington never had wooden teeth; that was sort of a kick in the head for me. We're told he did, but turns out they were made from the teeth of slaves and some were made out of bones of animals. There's that place in Arlington that has a dental museum, and they mentioned it saying the books for the future should be changed. Is that what you mean, sweetheart?"

He asked her while dipping his head just over her shoulder, going in for a good solid hug.

She loved him. She knew she did. It wasn't a new love, nothing like you'd expect if you found someone and got to know them, thinking they had a million things in common with yourself. She loved him from what she remembered him to be, the person he never changed from, the man she believed was good then, and she should have fought like hell to keep. She wouldn't let him go now, and bringing up insignificant things as she did from time to time only served to remind her of the grip she lost every time she understood her heart to clench at the thought of the man; she had so carelessly nearly handed him to Lisa Billings all those years ago. It was a mistake she could never recover from, but one she could set aside knowing that in the very instant, he was holding her and they were in a world she had tucked so firmly into her heart that didn't only seem magical, it was truly a pure vision within her soul.

The hour of the day was closing in on them. In Scotland, the sun set rather quickly and at an hour much sooner than in the Sooner State. The evening at length was beginning to slowly and densely thicken around them; one by one the people she could barely see in the first place, began to make their decent down the hillside. Many fearful tales of dreadful events taking place upon the tops of lonely moors had flooded her brain when she allowed herself to create and conjure what would take place in her newest and latest novel; but it was nothing to the hopes she had carefully packed with her when she had asked Steve Mueller to accompany her to the United Kingdom to launch the tour of her new novel; lucky number seven had been amazing. Would eight be great, she wondered. Her hopes extended through dinner as the two made their way to the cobbled streets of the quaint village at the base of the craggy cliffs.

Making their way through the drizzling skies wasn't hard for Jule, as she had easily recalled nearly every spring evening in Scotland being either wet or threatening to become so. She hadn't decided if owning a really good umbrella was the way to go, or if everyone she knew carried disposal types, not worrying whether or not it became all but ruined after a few sturdy gusts. Gusts of course in Scotland, had nothing on the wayward and often unpredictable winds of Oklahoma; but just as when she found herself unaware of their upheaval back home, she had nearly taken a flight by one before Steve caught her saving her from falling, this time into the watery pools that lined the curbs of the old streets.

"Woman, you're determined to leave me! I won't have it. No one and nothing is going to grab you, or take you out of my arms; I hope you understand that. I'm simply not willing to go through the hurt and misery again."

His words, whispered, seared through her soul. Though she couldn't exactly express her feelings without saying something silly or inappropriate; she had managed to nod her head and press herself closer into him, sharing the heat between them, or as much as their wool coats would allow them to do. They stood breathlessly close and enjoyed the heat.

"I don't say it enough Steve, you're the reason I don't date anyone else. When I lost you I lost everything. I wasn't able to fight for myself anymore. I think that's why I ended up with Lance, the girl's father. I won't go into it, it's way too much and too painful to talk about but I'm so happy to be with you right now. I'm never going to leave you if you think I'm the one you want. I want you to want me. I really do...and just as I said that the song just...yeah, sort of....popped into my head." She laughed.

Together they both began singing under their breath and between laughter.

"I want you to want me. I need you need me. I'd love you to love me, I'm beggin' you to beg me."

The old Cheap Trick lyrics seemed to flow from them both, oozing into the air around them, leaking into their hearts and forcing them to become a silhouette against a waxing mooned sky somewhere east of the north sea.

16

Meanwhile, back at the ranch, the names of the Fourteen applicants had long been posted and they were all but accepted by everyone who had made the cut. Most of the English riders had not quite made their introductions to those who rode the Western style, and vice versa. Melora took note of each of the people, writing comments beside their names so she didn't forget to remind herself who owned which horse or horses, what if any connection they had with other boarders, and which horses were inside the stalls at night versus which ones were outside in the three pastures.

Of the pastured horses, she noted which had both run ins as well as automatic watering holes allowing the animals to be as comfortable as they could be, and which drank from troughs. Not wanting to continue using the plastic or even metal deep 100-gallon galvanized stock tanks sold at both Atwoods and

Tractor Supply. The barn owners before them had used such means of watering, but when Jule decided to make the barn her own, some of the more convenient methods of convenience fell into place. Cleaning out the troughs became difficult for Hector to say the least. In the winter time, a basketball was placed in each water trough to keep the ice broken. Horses enjoyed the game of pushing it back and forth as well.

Along with the auto-watering holes, Jule had approved the install of heaters, fans, lights, and better doors in every barn. The stall door hinges had all been replaced, as were nearly all the wooden slats in the indoor stalls as well. The white barn, formerly known as the English barn, also formerly known as the gold barn, because it had once been painted such a color at one point, was being fitted with new rubber mat flooring, new stall frames, doors, hinges, and gates and the feed for hers and Melora's horses was being stored in a small silo rather than in large fifty-pound sacks on top of wooden pallets. A second and even a third silo was planned for the blue barn sometime in the near future, making Alvarez's job that much easier. The costs were extreme, but if the barn was to have the garnered reputation that Jule needed for her authorship notoriety, it was necessary.

"I'm about to read you the names of all of the boarders Keegan; both indoor and outdoor. I want you to tell me little known facts about them, things I may not know because you've known them longer, are you ready?" asked Melora to her all-too-helpful help.

"Yeah, I'm ready, but if I don't know anything about them can I just say that?"

she asked. Keegan's mother had once told her that if she couldn't say something nice about someone to just say nothing at all. Melora wondered in her own head if this was what the girl meant; knowing she would be all too happy to write something if she felt it needed to be disclosed.

"Keeg, if you don't feel comfortable telling me something I still may need to know it. So, if you can't say something just let me know why, and we can talk about it, how's that?" she encouraged the girl, with a smile and a nod.

"OK, starting with your buddy Deb Robbins. What do you know?" asked Melora.

"Deb is seventeen years old. She seems to be on everyone's good side. She's neutral in the whole Bree Morgan thing, and she dated both Chase Finley and Tucker Banderoff at the same time but she was also dating Mason Freeland and Charlie Bollinger so I can't tell you if she likes blonds more than brunettes."

Said Keegan, giving her first name a good shot at what she thought would be something Melora would have no idea about.

"Yeah, well, that's really interesting, and a bit scary, but really, what I wanted to know is what horses does she ride, how does she ride, does she show,

and can she get herself to the shows because I'm going to start charging boarders if I have to drive them."

Answered the barn manager to a rather oops-faced kid before her.

"Oh, my bad. OK, so Deb is seventeen. She rides Freida the Haflinger and no, she doesn't show because she doesn't have the money, her parents don't own a truck and I think she actually leases Frieda from Tina and Freya Davidson. I don't think she owns her. I could be wrong." Keegan smiled before adding that recently Freya and Tina Davidson had bought at least four of Darrell Hodges horses for that very reason.

"Darrell Hodges" stated Melora, *"He's next; whatcha got on him?"* she asked.

"Darrell is something like sixty or something, he's older than my grandma. He has about ten horses in the back, I'd have to count them. He put one down last month but I just found out about it. He didn't say anything because it was the day after Jodi was found and he didn't want anyone thinking he had something to do with it. Not that we would think that, he's been the nicest man on the planet to me since my dad died. He goes to the Cactus Rose too, and I've spent the night at his house when his wife was alive a million times. He doesn't train his horses so if they get ridden it's because I do it. Deb has the Haflinger and I broke it for him when I was ten, the one Tina bought to lease to Deb." She rattled.

"Ten? You were breaking horses at ten? You know kid, you don't surprise me much anymore. You've been twelve years old for a long time now. This face, it's a mask. I think you were here when Theodore Roosevelt signed Oklahoma into a state, and I think you broke the mule he rode in on as well."

She added before offering Keegan Tanner half of her Sonic fries that she noticed the kid had been eyeballing.

"OK, we're up to number three, and that's Crystal Harroz, Brandi Harroz, and Crissy Harroz, I'm counting them as one since they are a family, and they are all using the same large pen next to the paddock where you stay. I will eventually move them into your paddock, so we'll get a second run in for them. Do you get along with them? Do their horses get along with Candy?" questioned the manager.

To her surprise Keegan had a flat-faced stare at hearing that anyone of the Harroz family members were going to share the three-acre paddock with her horse because that would put four horses on three acres. Something Keegan didn't really think needed to be done, but she also knew people did that and worst at other barns.

"I'd rather just have one horse sharing the paddock with Candy if you can, but if you have to do it I understand. The horses may get along since they are next to each other now and don't really seem to be

bothered by one another. I mean, I think they may be selling the bay anyway, his name is Bullet. Brandi is only three and a half and Crissy is either five or six. They need a pony not a 15 HH paint; but Crissy rides Little Lady from time to time, she's Tina's too. Crystal has a grade Palamino. She may keep them both, but if you can make a deal with her to take the Palomino from her and let me train it I can make it into a better barrel horse for the girls when they get older. They're not going to be able to really compete until they're nine or ten anyway. That would give me a better chance at the races next year since Candy's coming up lame all the time." She confessed.

After a few more words regarding the Harroz family needs, Melora questioned her friend about her smallish older Appaloosa Arab cross. When she finally got around to spilling the beans on her mare, it was apparent that the reason Larissa was more concerned about keeping Candy had less to do with financing the board for the animal, and more to do with what she believed would be future bills at the vet. Candy had nearly collicked twice in the past month, neither time being brought to Melora's attention.

"You don't have to keep it quiet kid. I'll help you if you need me to. I didn't want you leaving the house last week after ten, but I guess now I know where you were going and why. I thought maybe you were just used to sleeping in the lounge and felt better there. I didn't realize your horse isn't well. Do you need me to take a look at her?"

Melora asked, feeling as if she may end up giving the kid news she didn't want to give her.

It was decided that the list could wait, and more attention could be shown to Candy, who had rallied to a degree, but it was apparent to anyone looking at her that she had been aged incorrectly when sold a year before to an uneducated woman trying to make her kid happy for her twelfth birthday. Every little girl wants and deserves a horse, but they don't always get one. Keegan was one of the lucky ones it seems, but because she couldn't dip into the little girl's trust account, Larissa Lowell had managed to do the best she could, asking her sons to chip in to buy what she was told was a twenty-year-old grade mare; believed to be mostly Appaloosa, and with her narrow chest and the high-flying tail on the beast, it was also apparent that there was a bit of Arab blood in her as well.

Keegan wanted to register the horse as a Half-Arab, but without the means and paperwork needed to do it, she simply forged her own fake certificate, one she never claimed to be real in the first place. She listed the horse's official name as being *"Fancy Candy Can Do"*, giving the horse her own birthday of December 2nd, but of course putting the year of her birth eight years before her own.

"Keegan, you know I know you know horses. I also know you know how to age them using the Galvayne's groove on the tooth just behind the front teeth, that upper incisor. You helped me with the

Mustangs after I sedated them to give them their full check eval. Surely, you've looked in Candy's mouth, haven't you?"

She questioned, maybe already guessing the answer.

Keegan's head hung lower than usual, and before she lifted it to look into Melora's eyes she coughed a little. She couldn't seem to say it without the words catching in her throat, but Melora knew. She could see it her friend's emotionless stare, and the way her bright brown eyes lost all of their glow; she knew.

"Candy's about thirty Lora. She's not twenty. She's nowhere near twenty. The groove has not only come down, it's gone away. When we had her floated after she was brought to the barn the farrier asked me why I bought a horse who wouldn't live another five years if I thought I wanted to go into barrel racing. I don't know. I was just too happy to have a horse. I was just too excited to actually own my own horse, and not have to ride on Darrell's horses when he told me I could. I broke the Haflinger and he sold her, but they brought her back. He wouldn't sell her to my mom saying she was more expensive now that I broke her. I broke her! I was the one who did that, and he wanted to charge my mom a lot more for her."

She spoke, allowing her tears to flow, allowing her heart to break.

"Deb leases her because she can't buy her. Tina and Freya's dad bought her for them to lease to Deb. Deb acts like the horse is a mess, but I know she's not. I broke her. Darrell wants me to break them all, but not after that I won't. I told him I would break one and keep it, or buy one now and break it, but he won't let me do that. He said they're all over their late teens and I should get one that's younger so I can grow up with it. I don't want a broken-down horse; I don't want a monster either. Lora, I just want my own horse, a good horse, the right horse for me to train and love."

Cried the Tanner girl, once again finding herself at a true loss for either emotional connection or words to express her inner soul.

When the two left Candy to walk to the blue barn, Melora calmly steered the girl to the left to bring her face to face with twelve unbroke, untamed, unhandled young horses, all of which were unremarkable in every way. They had no pedigree. They had no standing in the greater horse world, what they had was eternal attitude, gumption, fortitude, and a way about them that spoke to the spirits of every celestial being around them.

"You pick one. You break it. I'll give it to you, and you'll not only have the horse of your choosing, but he or she will have the best damn trainer this side of the Pecos. If I was a horse, and someone gave me the opportunity to be chosen by some old man who would never work with me, or to be chosen by a young girl

with fire in her heart whose only desire was to be the best at every sport that involved riding me, I'd be sure as hell marching myself up to the gate to pick her before she could pick me." Melora spoke.

"You pick. There are twelve right here. You don't have to let me know now, but when you do choose, you can put your name right on that title the moment you ride and stay put for more than a full minute....is that a deal?"

She asked looking at Keegan, whose stare had become so much wider, so much brighter, but so very much more intense, Melora knew she had a deal...she knew.

17

The English riders of the barn had gathered off site a few times in order to openly discuss their concerns regarding the new management, the new ownership, as well as the future of the new barn. To say they had varied and articulated opinions would be an understatement as men and women alike, to a person, carried within their hearts and minds completely different reasons for why they wanted to remain at the Bay Sorrel as opposed to moving to another barn; the first consideration, one everyone could and would agree upon, was that the Armstrongs were fair in pricing their boarding facility; which was something that could not be said about other barns within a reasonable distance of it. Where Bay Sorrel sat just at the far western and northern boundaries of Oklahoma County, the nearest full-service facility with a sizable indoor arena was literally a dozen or so miles from that particular corner, and though it was somewhat closer for several patrons, it was nearly twice as expensive.

The Genesis Farms boasted both an indoor and outdoor riding arenas, as did Bay Sorrel, and their maintenance and care for such riding spaces were in fact superior to that of the Armstrong's property. Still, paying over a $1000 a month to have a horse boarded, fed, and supported with a staffed vet only two miles from the barn seemed too much for most. Though the monthly fees included several 30-min lessons each month, none of the riders had no need of such instruction. This and other considerations were discussed among several members when they agreed to meet in Oklahoma City at the Full Circle Bookstore off Northwest Expressway and Pennsylvania Avenue, on the lower level of the famed 50-Penn Place building, a towering structure that had stood for decades representing some of the finer stores in the capital city for shopping, spa-days, and more.

Robert "*Hunt*" Hunter Wainscott, perhaps one of the top riders in the barn for years, had all but decided to withdraw his application for stay in favor of purchasing his own place near Lake Arcadia. He hadn't been in competition riding for several years, but had devoted most of his spare time to training those at the barn who were serious undertakers of their craft; those whose life goals matched his in essence and style. His ideas were warranted of course, listened to, and respected, but most knew and all would know soon enough, that his plans were temporal at best. As Hunt moved about the bookstore, picking and poking at various titles, his fingers edged a book with more or less the most general binding possible. Such a bland cover, he thought, and such an ordinary if boring title for a book that held so much and so rich history of the state of Oklahoma. He read the title twice before setting the book down, then picking it back up again to give it another chance. Titled simply *"Odd Stories of the Greater Oklahoma and Indian Territories"*, Wainscott told himself he may actually learn something that afternoon. The very spot he was standing in to credit the book held mounds of intel about the very real topic of what it was truly like to live in the wild western states at the turn of the 19th century.

Before he had managed to completely walk away from the others to mull over the book, Hunt Wainscott reminded his riding friends not to forget that though they were all chosen as part of the acceptable clients for the Armstrongs, only seven would remain inside the barn with stall usage. This, and this alone for Hunt, was the deciding factor, giving him the nudge he needed to move to the next chapter of his horse-world life.

"Just because you have the money to pay it won't mean a thing to Armstrong, she's not about the money. Everyone inside will pay $600 and everyone outside with the run-ins will pay $400. She's already ordered the construction of four more run-ins for the other two pasture, and another two for the ones that have units already in them. She doesn't care if you're a

banker, a pancake maker, or a teacher, she has set prices. The age and condition of the horse mean more to her than your bank account. Keep that in mind." He suggested.

Mia Nguyen, a rather tall, slender young Asian-American whose parents and grandparents had migrated to the states before she was born irritated the fact that Jule Armstrong wasn't about anything like most other barn owners were about. Having discussed a few concerns with the owner, Nguyen soon discovered that the author turned owner of a barn was much more interested in the experiences of the riders than any other owner she had been associated with. Mia was impressed from the day she met both Jule and Melora, to find out that they had been riders; not just people buying barns and charging fees.

"She asked me if the barn was warm enough to ride or if she needed to crank it up a little. That never happened at Dale Venner's place, and it certainly wouldn't happen at Heavenly Acres. Their idea of an indoor is a rickety old shed without heat or air, and the clods are as hard as rocks under hoof. I paid a full month's rent on the first and was gone by the seventh of the month; no refund, no apologies for the way they overfed my horse. I didn't so much as get a thank you for giving them 23 days of board for nothing. Not only that..."

she continued in the same irritated vein,

"...Carmine Scott had the nerve to say something like she had no respect for English riders. She said we all had daddy-issues.

she stated boldly before adding,

"She asked me at least three times if I was dating anyone, and if I was planning on getting married and having kids. What the heck, I thought. I paid her to board my horse, but she and that bigoted husband of hers would watch me constantly, tell me not to go into their feed barn, and made sure I knew not to flush the toilet paper down their toilet. Apparently, they had a bad system. It was gross. Really gross."

Her words fell hard on the others who had either met and understood her rant, having been acquainted with Brian Scott's parents. Heavenly Acres had been bought by the cattleman next door to the horse farm less than two weeks after Jacky had died and Carmine went to live with her sister in Texas. If someone were lucky to never have come in contact with any of Scotts, they would be lucky indeed. Jacky and Carmine had a way of making themselves seen, heard, and known in the boarding world; they charged a bit less so they could lure in a client only to claim the owners hadn't paid on time, giving them the right to confiscate and sell off any livestock in their custody with an outstanding balance. Usually a barn owner would work with a soul, hoping to remedy the situation; that wasn't the case with either of the Scotts.

After hearing themselves talk about so many other barns where they had all had poor experiences, to a person, they had decided to try and make it work at Bay Sorrel, even giving so much as to compromise the install boarding arrangements. Mia, who rode, but wasn't a competitor at the time, had volunteered to keep her gelding out in the pastures. With Hunt leaving, and opening up two slots, Amber Pickett and Paul Abernathy put in their bid for install care; both were rewarded with such by at least the other members. When it came time to go over the assignments the following day, all would give their personal recommendations, feeling that Jule or Melora Armstrong would readily agree to their arrangement.

"Why is it though, that we can't keep our horses in the white barn since there are eleven stalls and the Armstrongs only have four horses? That doesn't make a lot of sense to me."

Asked Amber, who hadn't really considered herself lucky, but more deserving of an indoor stall in the first place.

"I mean, if they only need four, and we have as many horses as we have, it only makes sense. They could make about $3500 more a month if they let us tack up and stall over there. It's not that far from the other barn, we can walk that far; I would. I don't know about the rest of you." She finished.

Hunt's words were reiterated for a third time by Leslie Merriweather, another aged Dressage trainer and rider, who, like Hunt, had considered buying her own property when she heard about the takeover. She had been through the Olsten-Scott fiasco, knew far too much about Jacky and Carmine to say a word without a full load of blasphemous language coming out of her mouth. She had taught Sunday School for too long, she told herself, to be known or heard repeating what she knew to be true about that family; only the one boy that "*got away*", Matthew Scott, was worth a plug nickel, and she wasn't all that sure about him either. Leslie leaned into the conversation, holding her white round mug of coffee tightly before repeating nearly verbatim what Hunt Wainscott had mentioned about the Armstrongs not needing money.

"Jule Armstrong, I'm told comes from a little money, not like the Morgans have, or even the Craigstones, or yes, Paul, your family. She doesn't have that kind of money, but she does have it, and it's not only from the sales of her books. She was a prized barrel racer in the late '80s and into the '90s. She never made it to the big dance, but she kept herself in the national average for sure. I heard she invested well, and when she set up her children's trust; she has two daughters and a son, I'm told she dropped a cool million in each for their future. That's not the type of money you sneeze at. I think she believes she'll be OK with or without barn boarders.

"I am convinced she's doing the barn thing for Melora's Mustang dream. There's really no other way

to think about it. The white barn, their barn, what used to be our barn in fact, is going to be used almost exclusively as a Mustang training facility. She's said she's going to put in a large round pen on the top side, the west side, then she'll block off the back half of the easterly end for tack, supplies, and what all the girls need for when they break the animals."

Leah Cotman, the only horse owner who couldn't care less about being indoors or outdoors as long as she was able to use both the indoor and the outdoor arena when she wanted to was fast to pick up on what Merriweather had started.

"Melora, or Lora, as I've heard Keegan Tanner call her, told me that she is employing Keegan to help with the horses. They either adopted her, or they have some sort of a thing going where she's allowed to live there now in the small house. At twelve years old I was still playing with dolls. I think my uncle had me try out for Miss Cherokee Oklahoma about the time I was Fourteen, but that was the first time I had ever sat on a horse; during that parade downtown. God only knows I was scared to death the thing was going to throw me.

"Here's Keegan Tanner, the little freckled sprite; daring each animal to give her grief. She's one tough little girl, that one. I couldn't imagine having the gull and the nerve she has. I'm 40! I couldn't stand up to a horse that was snorting at me, kicking, running around throwing its head in the air and whipping

itself into a frenzy. She doesn't even flinch!" Leah's words ended with a bit of an admiring thought; *"Jule has my mother's first name; did you guys know that? I saw it on her invitations; she and the former police officer are engaged now. Juliett Leigh Armstrong and Stephen Jonathan Mueller."*

As soon as she had stated the fact, Leah questioned herself silently if maybe only she had received an invitation to the reception to take place the following weekend. Hunt returned to his book and began reading after relieving his friend Leah from her near embarrassing moment to let her know they had in fact all been invited to the soiree to take place in nine days; two days in fact, following Jule and Steve's return from Scotland.

18

Hunt Wainscott's choice of books didn't disappoint. He flipped through the pages searching for a story he felt had to be included in the annuals of time where Oklahoma's oddities and unusual events and stories that could not only describe and defend the unique history that belonged to the state, but it could also somehow explain it in a way that passersby, strangers, or newcomers could understand it; before settling in and determining for themselves to call themselves true Okies.

His favorite story took place only thirty miles north in a city called Guthrie. Known for its rough and rowdy beginnings, Guthrie had once been the capital of the state until an underhanded group of ruffian politicians literally stole the state seal taking it with them on a train bound for Oklahoma City where they set up a new government proclaiming the city as the new capital. This being a time of recovery from the antics of other interstate conflicts, no one made too much of it, and the thing stuck. His favorite tale about the area remained steadfast with the retelling of the story behind a simple bank robber by the name of Elmer McCurty.

Hunt Wainscott, being of British decent himself, always loved the tale of the son of an Irish immigrant who came to a terrible end of his life, only to embark on a nearly sixty-six-year adventure which saw his body being over embalmed, unclaimed, then used as a means to stave off any would-be criminals in Logan County, by having the sheriff literally prop the body of the dead man up in the corner of any recently occupied cell where a minor offender would be held overnight. The sheriff, to his way of thinking, believed if anyone managed to live through the night sleeping next to Elmer, they'd be either too scared to commit another crime, or maybe they'd just end their own life right then and there, giving Elmer a roommate if the sheriff could talk the undertaker's grandson into repeating his mistakes during his botched first attempt at embalming a body.

McCurty, according to the book and the legend of course, was soon discovered by a couple of roustabouts who dressed up in fine clothing and claimed his body for themselves; Elmer was given a name no one recognized, but he wasn't being claimed by anyone local. The took men took Elmer, their *"uncle"*, to various side shows, circuses where they rented him out as a side feature. He even starred as "*a famous bank robber"* in those side of the road peep shows; the type a person could run across in the early '30s and 40s.

McCurty, who had lost his life in 1911, wasn't actually recovered and buried until 1977, when he had been placed in a movie set warehouse for storage for any number of years. He had been painted several times throughout his afterlife, no one realizing the body wasn't a fake or a leathered dummy. He ended up being used in a stunt for a television action show, only to be run over by a large vehicle, which exposed an actual human bone in his arm. Through science and forensic research, the body of Elmer McCurty was identified, and eventually returned to the Sooner State, where through much fanfare and delight of the city of Guthrie, he was buried alongside another famous or infamous outlaw, Bill Doolin.

Hunt Wainscott and his new bride at the time, had been living in Wellston, Oklahoma. Upon reading about the celebration in the old capital city, the pair decided to dress up in period attire, much like his new wife's family had every April 22, for Founders Day or for the Oklahoma Land Run day. They made their way just in time to be a part of the nearly half-mile long walking precession leading up to Boot Hill in Guthrie's main cemetery to send off a man who had no friends in life; but millions of admirers sixty-six years after being shot dead for his poor choices.

The story epitomized for Hunt what it meant to be an Oklahoman. For him, the story rang clear of the things that can change a man's life without a second's notice. Hunt's father had migrated to the plains, first living in Kansas as an electronic technician for Western Electric, before moving his family; a wife, daughter and young son, to Oklahoma. Hunt had been too young to fight in any war, but had joined the Oklahoma National Guard a few years after high school. It was during his second week of training that he first mounted a horse, having been brought up in the country but had been mostly a farming man, the son of another farming family back in England, one that never had a need to ride a horse. He remember using mules as a boy to plough the tough soil outside Edmond, Oklahoma, but that was when he was incredibly young. Before he turned twelve he drove his father's John Deere, and could clear a forty-acre tract in one afternoon to make ready for the upcoming wheat season. Horses were things to look at, admire, and think about, but until he was a soldier, he hadn't actually been on top of one.

Now edging just under seventy years of age, the man couldn't imagine a day without one. Though riding the English style was mostly a natural next step from soldiering, he also owned a few western saddles, bridles, and other tack, lending itself and him to ride more comfortably on trail rides and around the grounds at Bay Sorrel. Like others, he had been at the same facility for many years, and had been closely acquainted with the antics of Brian Scott, even before that, he had been associated with Barbara Olsten, though he had to admit she wasn't as hands on or approachable as Jule or Melora Armstrong were. With Olsten you hoped to be given an audience. With either of the Armstrongs a text, call, or simple lifting of the head could bring about a meeting in minutes. Times were changing for Wainscott.

After his wife had passed from breast cancer in 2011, Hunt had allowed himself to pour whatever energy he had left in himself to stop competing, and to teach others the best traits he considered to be his own. Casandra's absence had left a hole far too deep and far too wide to fill, but somehow being around the barn and assisting others helped with the pain of the void; at least during the day. Nights were another story for the man, one he rarely discussed, but knew he would need to either deal with soon on his own, or perhaps find a partner to settle in with and perhaps start the next phase of life with.

As the light from outside literally poured through the oversized arched windows of the bookstore, through the stacked aisles, and finding rest upon the various patrons who held their hands to their eyes shading themselves, Hunt thanked his Creator for the thought, the memory, and the light that he knew at this time of day would always remind him of her last smile before she left him. Glancing at his watch, he already knew it would be somewhere between three and four o'clock; that was the right time, the brightest time.

The quietude of his study and reading was quickly interrupted when a smiling plump face wearing bright purple glasses peered through the tall bookcase just to his left.

"*Oh hello,*" she said,

"*I'm looking for one of the associates. I can't seem to find one. This is my first time in the bookstore, and I can't seem to locate anything. It doesn't really seem as organized as the library, is it?*" the spirited liberal-minded woman questioned, the tips of her white hair appeared to be dipped in vibrant pools of glittering royal blue.

Hunt wasn't quite sure what to do at that moment. The woman he thought, could be around or about his age. She was pretty enough, forward and brave enough, and in some ways she reminded him of his sister Trudy; maybe it was the purple shade of her eyewear. Trudy was the one who stood out from her first year of life. Trudy was the one who had convinced Hunt to take a chance and ask that girl by the kitchen at the church to take a walk with him; he had listened to Trudy and it panned out rather well for him. Maybe this was his big sister's way of saying it's time to move on brother boy, it's time to put all those tears behind you, away and outside of reach. "*Go ahead Hunt,*" Trudy would whisper in his ear, "*Talk to her; you'll be fine.*"

"Well, I'm not an associate, per se, but I am familiar with the lay out of the place. I've shopped here for decades. If there's something I can help you find, it would be my pleasure to do so."

He added, thinking maybe he would ask her if she had had her afternoon tea. If she hadn't, he surmised, he wouldn't be too shy to suggest the Earl Grey with a sprinkle of loose blueberry for a different experience.

Leah and Helene had remained in the store long after the younger set had left. Bookstores weren't the first choice for hanging out for anyone under the age of forty it seemed. Leah, being right at the age of maturity, she believed, was about to settle in with a bit of discovery in the fiction and fantasy section when she noticed Helene making her way to the children's section, of all places. Leah's thoughts were mixed, but after a few minutes she realized that at her age, she could very well be a grandmother; so why wouldn't Helene already have grandchildren of her own. No one at the barn had really taken the time to discuss their extended family.

The small and quiet voice inside her head suddenly recalled that she had not known much if anything about either Helene or Mia before these impromptu meetings of theirs. No one at the barn had really been close; they were more formal at times. They respected each other's space, much like one would expect their own horse to do, but these were people too, she told herself. They are colleagues, friends, or at least they could be if either of them wouldn't object to the thoughts of becoming so. With the sauntering of a shy beast in the field, Leah approached her older acquaintance in hopes of returning to their previous conversation. She believed the communication could become a sturdy bridge the two of them could cling to, walk across and find themselves both familiar and comfortable. Her hopes were not dashed.

"I'm so glad you followed me over to the children's place." Stated Helene, whose soft brown eyes had a way of making anyone feel at ease.

"You delight me Leah. I hadn't known your name before today. I thought your name was Leigh, meaning 'meadow'. I called you that in my head for over six years now; please forgive me." She said.

"Helene, if I know one thing, it's that no one ever gets my name straight. My last name is Cotman, but before that it was Blinker, and you'd think I had flames for eyeballs the way I looked at people who couldn't say 'Blinker' without saying it wrong. They'd say 'Blank', 'Binky', even 'Blocker' but I had to say 'No, it's Blinker, just like the little things on your car that tell folks you're making a turn.' It's a miracle only a few of them thought my last name was 'Indicator'." She laughed.

"And my name is Helene not Helen. I can't tell you how many times I've had to say it wasn't. Aren't people just crazy at times?" she asked.

The two women spent the next few moments going over the new barn rules, of which none of them were going to be a problem for either of them, mainly because they dealt with issues that took place much later in the evening or over the weekends. Neither Helene nor Leah boarded their horses indoors, so cleaning stalls themselves on any given weekend wasn't going to be an issue. About the only rule that made either of them think twice about remaining at Bay Sorrel Ranch was the one about not approaching the white barn. The white barn had been such a lovely place to gather for all seasons. The smaller lounge sat four or five comfortably, and was just enough room for them to stretch out and enjoy a cup of coffee or hot cocoa before riding or preparing to do so.

"I'll miss not going to the white barn, but then again, I'm still getting used to calling it the white barn." Joked Helene, telling herself she would possibly ask Jule if they could continue to go to the smaller lounge if possible.

"For years it was the English barn, and we weren't allowed anywhere near the blue barn since all the western riders had it covered. Now, we're expected to share, and I'm alright with that too, but there are more people now, and with the little Harroz girls taking their time so often, it's hard to canter or get into

any real movement with my two mounts. I may end up selling the black gelding to them actually, and I'd be smart to do it. He's about 18 years old, and under Fourteen-hands so he'd be a good pony sized ride for them. It's just that he's so cantankerous at times. I wouldn't want to be responsible for anything if it happened after I made the sale. Does that make sense?" she asked, to a head nodding endlessly in her direction.

"Oh don't do it. Don't sell the horse to anyone at the barn you board at, and don't sell it to anyone at a barn you just came from. You won't hear the end of it. You'll be talked about, threatened, and God only knows what. I've seen it too many times. I did it myself. I bought one of Darrell Hodges horses from him, and within a day or two I wanted my money back. I did end up selling it to someone else at another barn, but I was quick to say I didn't have the horse for more than a week. That thing about killed me. He was not the same horse I was told he was, and I never openly accused Hodges but he must have drugged the thing before showing him to me. When he didn't ride him first, but asked Keegan Tanner to ride him for me, to show me what he could do, I remember her saying he was off a bit, that he wasn't himself. I should not have bought that beast. Keegan wouldn't talk to me for months after I sold him. She hated me. I know she did." Mentioned Leah with a bit of truth to the matter.

"Bree Morgan found me a buyer for it over at the High Five. She said the girl had been in classes with her for years and she was a confident rider. I sold the horse and never looked back, but then Keegan, as you know Keegan will, came up to me a few weeks later and said the horse had dumped the girl; I think her name was Georgina. The horse was called Jerry and he was both starting Cushing's disease, and he needed to be floated. Ol' Hodges told me he had been treated and that wasn't true; then he told me he knew nothing about the horse being maimed with Cushing's.

" Georgina's father called me about six months ago asking me if I felt responsible for the whole thing; apparently the girl couldn't ride well or the horse didn't like her. I think the girl may have been heavier than I am, and I'm not that light Helene. I weigh just over 160 pounds and if the horse is 900 pounds sopping wet I'd be surprised. It was about that time I learned never to trust that Bree Morgan again as far as I could throw her skinny rich ass."

She added before mentioning that a horse, unless it's a Mustang, according to Keegan Tanner, the know-it-all at the barn, could only take about 20 to 22 percent of its body weight comfortably.

"Well, I don't know if that's true," mentioned Jackson. *"I'm at least 160 and maybe closer to 175 and my horse is somewhere between 1000 and 1100 pounds, so that's what...."* She quietly thought through the math in her head, *"...well, OK, it may be, that's less*

than twenty percent, but I've seen rodeos where those big big men ride those shorter horses to steer cattle with and even rope them and tie them up. Haven't you seen that too? They can't be under 160 pounds; they'll likely be closer to 200 or more." Jackson said.

"I suppose, if we wanted to know we could look it up on the internet, but like I said Helene, if I want to know anything whatsoever about a horse, all I have to do, all you have to do, is ask little Keegan Tanner. She's not even capable of lying, and she's so smart when it comes to horses. I bet she becomes either a professional rodeo woman or maybe she'll make her way up to Stillwater and become a veterinarian. They only take the best up that way."

Added Leah, with a bit of pride in her voice. Leah had graduated Cum Laude from Oklahoma State University quite a few years back, and she had used her Educational degree for more than a decade before choosing to instruct instructors rather than trying to continue wrangling her misbehaved students.

"I didn't graduate from college Leah, but I did go to high school all the way through." Mentioned Helene.

"My daughter Traci turns 37 this year. I was about two or three months pregnant with her when I walked the stage. My daddy never knew I was going to have a baby, but I think my mother knew. I was married to Traci's father the day after I graduated;

the day after we graduated. He was the talk of the town with his basketball playing. A baby out of wedlock would have ruined his chances for that scholarship. We married and we made the best of it for as long as we could. By the time she was a sophomore in high school her dad and I separated. We didn't..."

before going into the story any further, Helene checked to be sure her telling of her tales were going to be acceptable to her new old acquaintance or if she was making Leah feel a bit uncomfortable.

"Oh, no, no, no, please. I'm thoroughly enjoying every word. You stand around places like the barn or even grocery stores where you see the same faces for years and you know they have to have a life! No, please, you telling your stories means I'll get mine off my chest soon enough too, if you don't mind." She added,

"Hey Helene, before you go on, tell me, do you like tea? Do you think this bookstore could serve up a good cup? I'll stay if you stay. I'm about to learn, learn, learn, and girl, nothing makes me smile more than cramming more stuff inside this head of mine."

19

As a vivid more alluring vibrant haze of golden sharp rays began to penetrate the coral morning clouds above an apathetic and long-suffering Auld Reekie, Jule peered out the fifth story window of the illustriously stoic stone edifice locally known as *"The Hotel"*. Anyone local emphasizing the word *'The'* did so because of the centuries old reputation the Balmoral Hotel had in the city of Edinburgh. With more than four hundred hotels in the general area to choose from, Jule quietly checked off one of her more intimate goals of making love in the old public house. Nothing on this or any other morning could ruin or even attempt to ruin the mood the author found herself in now that she had been fully appreciated by the one man she often fantasized about even when she was dutifully married to Lance Beall.

Steve Mueller edged his way to his side of the double bed in the small but airy room before allowing his feet to touch what he knew would be a cold marble floor beneath him. He wasn't as young as he used to be, and some of the more energetic moves he and his lover had engaged themselves in a few moments before had left the man wondering if perhaps a hot shower wouldn't help draw some of the kink out of his lower back, knees, and neck. Something he had laughed about as a kid when he overheard his own father lamenting about the indecencies of growing old and making love at the same time. As he stood, stretched, and recoiled from one of the more inflicting spasms just above his right hip, the man quickly sat himself back down onto the disturbed linens, laughing at himself again; at the stage of life he had mastered, even conquered with pride.

"Oh, I'm old woman. I can't feel my toes but my hip is screaming that we are both very very much alive. I don't know about you, but that was one hell of a time for me, and if you don't mind..." he suggested, while patting the corner of their bed,

"...I'll take a slow maybe more lenient approach if you give me half a chance to do so."

She approached him from the open window, allowing the natural curves of her body to ease out from under her peachy colored satin robes. She held his gaze, but purposely chose to stare directly into his non-dominant eye for as long as she could. This she knew would intrigue him. She believed this method to work its magic in ways she could only write about in the past, but knew to be true. To do so, she understood, would build a connection and help both of them overcome any anxiety or stress that may try and interfere with their intimacy; their goals.

Straddling the corner of the bed where he had proposed she retreat, her knees formed a perfect V-shape with her lower half being exposed to him, as she allowed him to do the same, straddling her, their bodies met. She closed her eyes as a surge of excitement began to muster its way through her spirit. Shivering with anticipation, she willed herself to remain calm, to be the heroine she longed to be, the very essence of the women she wrote about in her novels. A slight tightness had forged its way into and about her thighs, the pressure of her position giving her more leverage for what she had intended. She clenched herself from within, not wanting to allow him to penetrate her just yet. Her legs would be his guide, he patiently awaited his que to begin.

Stephen laughed but closed his lips to contain his thrill. Turning her to his side, relieving her of her stance, he kissed her fully. His mouth lining hers and his tongue slowly tracing the seal of their mouths before finding the sides of her own thickened muscle, both rolling, releasing, touching, and retrieving in motions that seemed rehearsed. He dropped his head to her shoulder indicating his desire to move forward; she could feel his smile as he suckled the nape of her neck, barely being able to contain his passion. The scruff of his three-day beard lingered upon her skin, both itching and scratching at the same time. God, how she loved the two sensations; like the smells of lilac and lavender in the same room. She pressed herself closer, rising through her back and hips, lingering as long as she could with each of his deepened thrusts. She wanted more of him.

She lifted her head and cried from what felt gloriously rooted and infinitely pure in pleasure. Tiny tears began to form within her eyes, but she wouldn't allow him to know. He might stop his motion if he understood what he was doing to her, she knew him to be too kind. Denying herself the comforts of age. Biting her lower lip she persisted, she insisted, and he obliged. Rolling her nipple hard between his thumb and fingers he whispered; asking if he could lightly bite, and she couldn't contain her desires. For several minutes she agonized, but with a pleasure so raw and content, her mind all but trailed into a hue-filled mist of satisfaction.

    Moaning, mewling, he deeply kissed her, opening his mouth before sliding his lips over hers again and again. Breathing her breath, giving her his own. Choosing to suck his tongue rather than releasing it, she toyed with the man to the point of causing him to break whatever thoughts he had of restraint. Withdrawing himself from her, he held her close to his body, allowing her to move against him, to rub him in ways he needed and wanted to feel. Slowly she opened her eyes to see his; two grey blue orbs of constant stare before her. Several bright yellow pricks burst through like rays of the country sun shining down on her, she had always been so fascinated with the patterns taking shape in his eyes. She hadn't known anyone else who could claim to truly have kaleidoscope eyes; Steve Mueller would always be that man.

    Before retiring themselves, before what they knew would be their last day in the old country, they allowed themselves one more restless day of play. They would explore each other rather than to try and climb the heights of the stagnant volcanic rocks meditating silently only a half mile from where they lay naked, thoroughly happy, thoroughly alone, and thoroughly together after so many years apart. Promises were made between them that if either former spouse or if any other former lover needed to be mentioned in conversation for any reason, they would first give a signal to the other, allowing them the opportunity to either leave the room, change the subject, or allow the mentioning of the name. No one would come between the two; not ever. This was their vow; one they intended to keep for their remaining years on Earth.

An early afternoon stroll found the two lovers edging their way through neighborhoods rather than walking the bustling crowds of Princes Street or New Town. Johnny Walkers Experience would simply have to wait until they had all but seen every stone, nook, and cranny of the homes of neighborhoods such as Bruntsfield to the north, and the Grange a bit further east. Some or most of the buildings boasting years even centuries of years older than anything the two had encountered while living in the United States. About the oldest building Stephen could remember was the old church in Santa Fe, New Mexico where he and his dad had met to honor Mueller's grandfather; the man loved the Southwest so much. Waldon Stephen Mueller had lived to be a full one hundred years of age; surviving three wives and six of his eleven children. The small brown adobe stucco structure had inside its front entry hall a plaque stating that it had been built before the fall of the Alamo down in San Antonio, Texas. That year was 1718. The church, once a Catholic chapel, could have been built as early as 1690, but even with that more recent year compared to the many hundreds of years that had passed since the construction of the homes before them, Mueller admired each one differently.

"This one has a weird sort of feel to it."

He mentioned, noting that several of the windows had been purposely filled in with mortar or bricks. He didn't understand why each floor would have at least three separate windows covered. Jule explained to him that there was, strangely enough, a time when buildings were taxed liberally by the government by how many windows they had. The more windows a person had, the more luxurious his place would have been considered. The poorer folks who couldn't afford to continue making such extenuated payments simply for the pleasures of looking out the window, began covering them with whatever means they could to satisfy the would-be collectors of tax. It seemed arrogantly silly to her, but it was something she had to understand wasn't a part of her life, but was to be respected for the sake of history.

"OK then, Missy, if you fancy yourself to be such a historian of all things Scottish, tell me why this neighborhood is called Morningside, and why do you suppose the wealthy folks of the City Centre area decided to move out from the big towns to forge their means and ways out this way...way...way." He laughed, twisting his mouth up like he used to when he wanted to see her bite her lip a little. He couldn't for the life of himself figure out what that gesture of his mouth meant to the woman, but if he got the results he wanted to get, he'd do it as often as he could remember to do it.

Before thinking much longer than a few seconds, Jule recalled a story she had heard on YouTube, as a matter of fact, by a would-be historian who had addressed those and other facts not only about Morningside, but about several of the outskirt towns that laced the edges of the old hub of what was being called City Centre now. The kid was in his 30's she thought, a red-headed chap calling himself the '*Ginger Man*'. He walked about Scotland with his GoPro camera in tow; explaining and expressing his opinions on things he saw or came across. Morningside, it seemed, had been mentioned in years past in a plan for the city to have the various classes separated somewhat, but not too far from the city's majority since all of the hired domestic service help would need to most likely walk to their employment.

She further explained that the district was developed as a residential suburb, with as he had mentioned, attracted the wealthier of the citizenry, but also their animals. The fact that over a dozen livery stables could be found in the areas plans was exciting to Jule; someone had to own those stables, someone had to run them, and collect the fares from those who kept their livestock guarded from both weather and foolery.

"Say, that reminds me," Stephen joked, *"There's a barn-themed bar just up the road in a city called Kinghorn; maybe we can hit it up before we leave tomorrow. You can go over the old photos they have on the walls and see if they compare or how they compare to your ranch. I don't think they had riding arenas though, if I'm honest. Makes me wonder now when riding arenas became a thing."*

His inquiry being dropped the second they ran face-to-face with several fans of Jule who had followed the pair from the steps of the Balmoral, waiting for her to return before accosting her to seek her autograph as well as taking selfies with her to show their friends. It was a thing apparently, for groups of people to stand or wait outside the front area of the hotel in hopes of meeting someone who they considered to be famous. Jule smiled, and shrugged, not wanting to appear rude in any way, while Stephen stepped aside and allowed her light to shine around her fans.

Their last day and evening would be cozy, drawing them into a small concert venue off of Clerk Street where a Christian music artist played both piano and guitar at a small open to the public venue. He sang somewhere between twelve and fifteen songs, during his sets; a few instrumentally, and finished with his own rendition of *Amazing Grace*. It was one Jule hadn't heard before, but felt she would never forget. Though she hadn't heard of the man of course, she wondered if he had been popular in the United Kingdom. To her surprise, and also to her liking, she found that he had recorded seven albums, full albums, and a few shorter albums being called EPs, something she hadn't encountered before. He had mastered the skills of managing an audience through telling jokes, short stories about his life, and encouraging them to consider following Christ as a means to find the peace they sought for any and all mental illnesses they may be facing.

The man wasn't an enigma, not really, others were doing the same things he was doing, but his stories of personal fortitude and survival seemed both ominous and redeeming. He had fallen several times; he admitted that. He had gone through rehab, stints in the hospital for both overdosing and stress related feats. He was homeless for over a year at one point before finding his faith and allowing God to control both his will and his actions. When he made up his mind to be a better man, he didn't do it alone; he gave credit where credit was due.

There was something about the man that caused Jule to think about him long after he had closed his final song and she and Steve had returned to Oklahoma.

"I think I'm going to download a few of that guy's songs and even the one album he talked about. His voice was so commanding. It reminded me of you in some ways. His name is John you know, which is your middle name, sort of. You used to belt out the National Anthem each week

for the games; do you still sing? I mean, I know you can, I've heard you a little, but can you do that for me Stephen?" she asked, but rather pleaded in a way.

"Will you drag out one of my guitars and teach me to play it; you said you would in high school. That's why I bought the first one. You owe me you know."

She giggled before turning to him and sweetly asking again. With a face so sweet and as sincere as he knew his new almost bride to be; he refused to refuse, agreeing to give her literally anything she ever wanted.

20

The hands on the big clock out in the barn registered as being just after 11:00 o'clock but no one knew if the thing had stopped in the morning or after the barn had closed. When it was finally addressed, Hector Alvarez moved his long ladder to the wall the clock hung on and asked his wife to stand beneath him so he could hand the clock to her. It would either need to be thrown in the bin out back, or repaired if that was even possible. Since the day he had arrived at the BSO so many years before anyone else now calling the barn their haven or hideaway, Hector had seen the clock but had paid little to no attention to it. It was the old plug in the wall type of clock, and the cord, though grimy from years of wear and dust from the barn, was still intact.

Hector, as many men his age were inclined to do, wore a silver watch on his left wrist. If he needed to know the time he'd simply glance down to see; besides, the clock was in the barn and he wasn't always going to be indoors when he needed to check the time of day. Hector rose with the sun or just before it, he ate breakfast when his wife cooked it, and he went to bed when his eyes felt heavy; who pays attention to clocks, he wondered.

When the very peppy, happy-go-lucky Dr. Lacey Hoel walked into the barn that morning and saw the man leaning over the side of the ladder to get a better grip on the time piece, she instinctively stopped her movement to set down her tackle box to assist Celinda Alvarez with holding the bottom half of the long ladder.

"It's been a million years since we've seen you here, dear. Where have you been keeping yourself?"

asked Celinda, realizing that she hadn't been in contact or seen the equine chiropractor in at least the last two or three years anyway.

"Your face never changes. You could be sixty-five by now and look the same. I can only imagine how blissful that would be for me to look so young, so beautiful...oh, and your smile. I have missed your smile."

Celinda mused as she leaned herself into her good friend; one she knew was good for all the news, stories, tales, and gossip to be had because Dr. Lacey, as she was called by her patients and clients, had the privilege of being hired by someone at nearly every barn in the state of Oklahoma and quite a few in surrounding states as well. Because of her clientele list growing as it was, Hoel had incorporated the use of her sweet husband who she had met on just such an event. Aaron Christenson had been hauling for the Dowd Horse Auction down in Corral City, Texas, when one of the horses he was about to carry off hadn't had its work done. He was held up and the extra forty-five minutes he had to wait to allow Dr. Lacey to toss back her long brunette tresses to work her magic gave him an idea.

"When you're finished with the mule you can crack my back too. I wouldn't mind a bit. In fact, I'll even enjoy it if I can take you to coffee when I get back from this run tomorrow."

Such a line. No other man in her life had been so bold as to ask not only for a date, but to have her manipulate them at the same time. He's a keeper, she thought. It didn't take long before the two of them were seen together on both sides of the Red River hauling and cracking; the two went hand in hand.

"Oh, Celinda," Lacey began,

"I have been so busy! With Aaron's new hauling business taking off, and both of us thinking we might want a baby soon, we've just been working our tails off closer to Texas where his family is. I've all but given up my Kansas and New Mexico clients. I didn't really want to, but now that we're married and living in Ardmore, it's impossible to get up that way. This is the farthest I can come and feel good about not charging someone a helluva lot of money for the barn fee.

229

Anymore I have to have at least four horses or people to work to make it worthwhile."

Her dissertation made sense, and as they both reached to assist Hector with the broken time piece, they smiled thinking to themselves it couldn't possibly be fixed, but Celinda knew her husband would have fun trying. No one really needed the clock anymore because everyone had cell phones to pull out or even their smartwatch, which because it was in fact a watch would tell time. Perhaps Hector believed he could salvage the old thing for the sake of selling it at the Dowd Horse Auction when he caught up with Aaron to see what chances he had to get a few dollars out of it if he could interest someone in buying the thing for memory sake; some people loved and lived for nostalgia.

"I'll see if Jule will let me keep it. If I can fix it and sell it to your husband for say, $30, I can at least feel good about chancing my bones being broken to get it down from the wall!" Hector joked.

Celinda took Dr. Lacey by the hand, retrieving her tackle box before asking her to tell her everything; not to leave out a single rumor. She wanted to hear it all. Dr. Lacey was to scrape her mind from side to side, the older woman told her. She was to think long and hard, dusting off every cobweb to let her know who was sleeping with whom, who had sold what, when, where and why, and she wanted to know if anyone had been smart enough to chase down any real property that others thought had too many issues. If the woman had any intel on what was being prepared at a county bake-off, Celinda wanted to know.

If Celinda had one vice at all, it was thinking she could turn a ruined piece of property into a gold mine. It never happened, but this was her way of living vicariously through her mind's creative passageways; she could dream and she loved hearing about the haunted farms and ranches that Dr. Lacey had been lucky enough to venture onto. Perhaps it was her upbringing near the Mexican border just south of El Paso. Celinda grew up knowing all the stories and all the myths surrounding death and the curious along the border.

As a child she was too intrigued; often catching herself pretending on the dry and dusty cactus-ridden byways of old El Paso. She imagined the famed Texas Rangers making their runs and taking prisoners of those brave souls trying to cross into America to start a better life. Such a conflicting heart lay within a tender-aged Celinda Sanchez whose family had migrated into the United States long before she or her siblings were born. When others described the area as a *"herida abierta"* or an open wound, she couldn't relate completely. Her life had not been necessarily idyllic but she had experienced good natured souls who wanted her to be educated and trained alongside those whose families had long been established on the U.S. side of the big river.

"Start with the Cimmaron. Tell me if Tawny Crawford married Ken Cunningham and if the wedding was a big as I can only imagine it would be." Celinda pressed.

When Lacey had settled into her work routine, plying her medical education and craft to the first of several horses, and one mule, it was determined of course, that she would then work her fingers along the backs, shoulders and hips of both the older couple. It had been years as Celinda had mentioned, but she nor Hector would have dreamed allowing anyone else to move them about in such twisted release.

"OK, but remember, I don't like any of the Crawfords and only some of the Cunninghams. If it wasn't for their extensive herd needing help so often, Aaron and I wouldn't show up, but they call him at least twice a month to either take their daughters and horses to Dallas, or even further south. They've been competing in Austin with the big dogs." She stated.

When Dr. Lacey got on a tale, it was sure to be a dosey. She hadn't mentioned any of the rumors coming out of Texas, as she knew Celinda was more or less interested in more local gossip. With all the mischief being thrown about at Cimmaron Stables, be it with sisters sleeping with their in-laws or one or the other of them taking a few weeks off to go skiing, traveling, or meditating, it was no wonder Celinda's smile broadened over the varied sordid details.

"Denne and her brother-in-law on the other side, the one with the half-sister she swears is her dad's youngest, had their affair and as you can guess she had his baby. That was last year. Of all the Crawfords Denne is the only one worth giving a penny to if she needed it. I've always liked her. She didn't run off to Colorado to get an abortion like her sister Kimi did. I don't remember if it was 2018 or 2019, but she too got pregnant by the same guy, must be a favorite at family reunions with those people. I don't know, but when Kimi took off on the 'spiritual retreat' in the spring early that year, thinkin' now it was 2019, because it was before we all got locked down, but after the flood in Ft. Smith. Yeah, it was 2019; when she took off for Colorado Springs it wasn't to watch the sunrises or the sunsets. She had an abortion and the doctor there nearly killed her. I don't know if you knew that or not."

She continued, as Celinda shook her head, and stared with wider eyes.

To hear the ladies talk, one horse right after the other, a person would have to ask themselves why anyone would be in the horse world in the first place. To be a fly on the wall, or as Dr. Lacey was privileged to be, a doctor in the house, more and more mischief, bad dealings, and mayhem seemed to creep out from every dusty corner of every hired barn; be it a regal mess like the Cimmaron, or an unknown hole in the mound squatters haven like the one she had just left before coming to Bay Sorrel Ranch.

"If you remember anyone Celinda, you have to recall Emily Whitcomb, the old lady who was murdered in her home just outside of Mountain View; do you remember her? She was in her nineties and one of her grandsons strangled her for her EBT card. Bless his heart, he's been released from prison already because the judge said there wasn't enough evidence to convict him at his second trial.

"That boy was messed up when he was born, always sneaking around at the Baptist Youth Camp down there in Davis and exposing himself to whoever would take a look. He was Fourteen when he was arrested the first time for stealing the boarders' horses and selling them there at the Mountain View auction. Old man Zolfe didn't give a damn if he knew or didn't know they had been stolen. Everyone knew it. That one was a branded Standardbred. Do you remember that?" the doctor asked.

Celinda nodded of course, though she had only read the stories in the papers when papers were being printed. *"I can't get a paper now Lacey. We have to turn on the television to hear what they choose to tell us. Hector and I, we don't think the news tells the full truth anymore. When we were growing up whatever the anchors told us could be taken to the bank; now you have to stuff a pound of salt in with it if you think you're getting the real story."*

Lacey agreed for both political and personal reasons. Being a conservative in her politics, she had been called a conspiracy theorist by some of her clients and one of her patients. The difference between the two was she could walk away from a client, but a patient carried an entirely different oath; one the good doctor took seriously.

"Don't have to tell me. If you think about it, we've not been told the truth since I was in college. I voted the first time in 2004 just barely making the cut that year for registering. I've not been happy really with our choices, but the news should be a place everyone can trust." She reiterated her friend's concerns.

"Oh, before you get the mule for me, let me tell you about the fire at the Hidey-Hole in Noble. Did you hear about it?"

She asked, realizing everyone in the world had heard about it if they were into horses at all.

"Every last horse was spared, right? Tell me that's not insurance. Tell me they didn't know what they were doing."

She said, as she described what she had been told by one of the local ladies who she occasionally popped in to buy feed or grain from.

Apparently, several people in the area had heard shouting, gun fire, and even backfires from trucks and tractors before seeing the blaze from whichever vantage point they had. At length the moon held his face from the night owls whose necks craned a bit to see what was taking place as smoke began to billow and twist itself into blackened vipers of the night sky. Both the barn and outbuilding where the hay and grain were stored were encased completely in fire; the smell of a strong agent perhaps gasoline or sweet kerosene could be caught on every other breeze passing from the fields and over through the wooded fortress.

When the roof of the large barn fell, all hope was lost in the hearts of those looking on as to saving any of the 30 or 40 horses known to be stalled at night. For as small a place as it seemed to be the Hidey-Hole boasted over 60 acres, mostly wooded. Still, if there were enough blades of grass to store so many horses to board, Dale Ellis was the one to do it. His cheap and cheating ways were nefarious and well known about Cleveland county. Sheriffs and lawmen had been trying to catch Ellis growing pot years before it became legal to do so; this wasn't his first attempt at running the insurance game to fund whatever his illegal schemes seemed to muster. For any boarder to think they got their money's worth at his barn was foolish at best, but there he was every month advertising on Craigslist that he not only had openings, but he sold off any horse if the owners couldn't pay board or wouldn't pay it when he indiscriminately raised their fees; at times, Ellis simply sold a horse to sell it.

"Rumor, and yes, it's only rumor has it that Dale sold off Kate Carnison's grey stallion that she used for her Andalusian breeding program. She had

him kept up at the HH for about six months out of each year, bringing him back to Denton, just outside of Dallas you know; it's past the Rose Quarter Horses on I-35, just where you make the decision to go east or west. Her place has that big grey horse statue on top of the barn there; the one with the teal blue roofs.

Anyway, Ellis sold off her prize stallion through a Craigslist ad, but she did manage to get it back after calling in the FBI because she lived in Texas and he was in Oklahoma. I don't know if it went all that far, I don't think he was arrested or anything, but after this last stunt he should be. Every last horse was saved and there was evidence that they had not ever been stalled that night. You know him and his rules. If you don't stall your horse he claims a pack of coyotes got it, and he's off selling it in another ad in another area such as what you get down in the bayou of Louisiana. That place is crazy."

She stated, shaking her head.

About the time Dr. Lacey was putting pressure on the newest mule to come into her life's practice, Steve Mueller came around the last wash rack tossing a bottle of Dawn liquid soap into the air before catching it behind his back; showing off a bit for the ladies. He'd met Dr. Lacey before, but hadn't seen her in a minute, and not at the Bay Sorrel, maybe back at the ranches in and around his old work haunt in Bethany.

"Say Steve, I've got something for you." Dr. Lacey teased, before reaching into her bag of supplies just out of reach of the mule's back feet.

"It's a new can of WD-40. I hear it's good for loosening up tight nuts and rusty tools that haven't been used in a while. They say it gives better penetration and everything."

Her toothy grin couldn't be any cheekier if she'd rehearsed the impromptu gest a 100 times.

"Don't worry, your secret is safe with me. Jule and I go way back; I'm just happy someone's getting through that gate, if you know what I mean."

21

Another fire had broken out a few nights before Lacey Hoel had visited the Bay Sorrel. This one, a bit closer to home, and though rumors flew around the air with regards to it being set for insurance or other purposes, Celinda held her tongue tightly at church, choosing only to share her thoughts with her favorite equine chiropractor.

"A lot of folks, not necessarily at our barn, but around the state don't think a horse needs a chiropractor Lacey, but let me say with impunity. I know; I know it's the best thing and you're just the best there is, even if I have to say so myself."

Celinda mentioned.

"The fire that took place last week here or rather there in Bethany was something to be shushed for sure. It didn't take off. The barn manager caught one of the girls in the act and she's been singing like a bird. She's was here at this barn, they all have at one

time or another, but with Jule now in charge it's really different."

Celinda said, looking behind her and just over her left shoulder to be sure her sweet Hector wasn't going to come up and surprise the ladies; interrupting their chatter-fest.

From what she could remember from the anchors on KFOR-TV the police and local officials were investigating the fire as an arson, but not for insurance on the part of the owners. It could have been a vicious prank gone bad. One or the other news reporters, Celinda mentioned; they were all so young these days, said that the horses were safe, all of the family members that owned the facility were safe. The barn's grain storage had been set on fire with alleged purpose of malice, the only suspect at this time was a young girl, a minor whose name was being withheld from the public. The reporter stated that the girl was possibly left at the facility by two or three others to be their scape goat, all of the people she pointed to had been interviewed and all of them had alibis for the time the police claim the fire started at the barn.

"Well of course, they're all going to say they were with each other. That's the plan you know. They do it, they slip off, leave that one poor girl there to take the wrap, and they claim they were having a party or something clear over on the other side of the county. That's a given."

Lacey stated before asking who the girl was that was caught, thinking maybe she knew her. When she heard for a second time that the girl's name was being withheld due to her age being that of only sixteen, she thought about the hundreds of girls that age in that part of Oklahoma who boarded both at English barns and at Western barns. The High Five, the barn mentioned in the second fire, was just the barn to confuse everyone in the horse world. Like the Bay Sorrel Ranch, it allowed both disciplines to ride, even boasting on their ads that they were non-discriminating about such things. It was flat amazing to the chiro just how many barns would ban anyone if they didn't ride the same way the owner did.

"I can understand having an English barn for English riders who compete and that's what the barn is, a training facility, or something like that, but to say a girl or boy can't board there because their saddle has a horn or their horse hasn't been shoed is just stupid." She mentioned.

"Tell me Celinda, is Jule's daughter Melora's Mustang training working out. I don't see any signs or advertising for it, but everyone's talking about it."

While they walked their way over past the white barn and through a few gates, Celinda felt she wouldn't be in too much of the way if she escorted Lacey through to the area where not only Melora Armstrong, but her handy side-kick apprentice Keegan Tanner could be found corralling and free lunging one or two of the wild ones in the blocked off section of a newly cut outdoor small pen of about fifty feet by fifty feet square. When Keegan's eye caught that of her favorite animal medic, she literally leaped toward the woman with her arms open to their full extent.

"Dr. Lacey! Oh my gosh, it's you, it's really you. I didn't know if I would ever see you again, not after your horse's tail was cut at the High Five last year. You got married, you moved, you went away...oh my stars, you're right here now. I love you!" cooed the girl, making heavy motioning gestures to Melora who saw the entire thing, but couldn't exactly stop what she was doing to come over the side rail. Nodding to let Hoel know she would join them soon enough, a menacing sorrel gelding whose branded neck revealed he had been fouled less than three years prior, made himself known. His thrashing, rearing, and kicking display showed his willingness to be called an exhibitionist. Such a flashy pageant of majestic power; a force to be reckoned with for sure.

"That boy's mine!" exclaimed Tanner with more than enough excitement to fill the barn.

"His name is Hercules; I liked it better than Homer. I don't why I think I only had two names to choose from, but we're reading the Odyssey in class and then I watched Hercules online so yeah, it's that. I'm a dork. You know that." She claimed throwing her arms around her friend.

"Herc can't help himself. He's out of his pen and in the bigger one. He has a friend and maybe even a girlfriend, but he's been cut. He just may not know it yet. He was probably asleep at the time."

She rattled, but didn't let up. If Lacey thought she talked a lot, she had nothing on the Tanner kid. Keegan could wrap circles around anyone where that was concerned.

Before either of them had asked, Keegan was filling them in on what all she heard on Tik Tok about the High Five and the fire. Parents and friends were called by police to check the alibis of the kids being accused of the fire; the ones who swore together that they weren't anywhere near the barn at the time that it went up in flames.

"The fire didn't destroy much because the hand grabbed a fire thing off the wall and started at the base of it. I remember in school we learned how to put out fires with those things, and yeah, you have to aim it at the base, but it depends of course on the type of fire that it is. You don't add water to a fire that starts with gasoline. The one in the barns usually have a foaming chemical for that reason, and it worked." She said.

"They grabbed a girl, and they're not saying who it is, but I know who it is because it's all over the place; it was Lily Craigstone. She and her mom are talking to my mom at the Cactus Rose to be sure and have my mom give me an alibi since Bree Morgan was trying to say I was in on it. Thing is, and you don't

know that Lacey, I live here now. I'm with Melora and Jule, only Jule moved to an apartment...anyway, they caught Lily and took her to the police, and she gave them someone's wallet. It fell out during the whole thing. She's a girl, she doesn't have a wallet, so now the police know one of the boys who was there wasn't at the party they were claiming to be at, so he's going to be talking really soon."

She nodded while reaching into her jacket pocket to pull out her buzzing cell.

"Oh my gosh. Damn...I mean heck darn jiminy cricket..." she said laughing.

"Lora says I say 'damn' too much so I have to say something else if I want ice cream. It's a joke. I don't really get deprived, she just...well, never you mind, she's like another mom. Anyway, I just got an update from Shaina, she's another boarder here. She said Lily gave the police Chase Finley's wallet and she told them that she...oh my God!" cried Tanner, before turning to Melora who had walked up to the rail to include herself in the conversation.

"Shaina said that Chase Finley is being accused of getting Jodi Williams pregnant and Lily Craigstone's mom is saying he killed Jodi to keep her quiet. Lily and I were there over at the lounge with Jodi the night she was killed." Declared Tanner.

Lacey had only heard about the Williams girl from another boarder who knew a boarder further south. Not all the news that is news makes it way to the Red River, but if it involves the murder of a young pregnant girl whose body was found in the middle of a debris-riddled pasture, any horse world person is going to hear about it somehow in some way.

"Chase wasn't on the property at all that day, not that I remember, and I would have heard his truck, it doesn't have a muffler. He's fixed it now, but not then, he got pulled over a few times for it being too loud. Lily said Chase told her that night, the night they burned the feed barn that he got Jodi pregnant and that he wanted her to run off and marry him. I guess she didn't do it or wouldn't do it and then he killed her maybe. I don't know, that could be why, but if he wasn't on the lot then it could be someone else. He could have just been telling Lily a whole pack of lies to be closer to the situation so he can be better than what he is. People say he's weird and I don't blame them. He's given me the creeps too; he can't ride I know that."

Laughing at her friend Dr. Lacey, put her arm around Keegan's shoulders before asking if riding or riding well was a requirement for being a good person. If so, she imagined that she and her husband needed to stop hauling and manipulating them and maybe get on top of one for a while so their collective reputations could shine again.

"I haven't ridden in five years kid. I just don't have time. Aaron hasn't either, and to be honest, when

we got married we thought we'd do the whole coming into the barn riding matching white horses, but no one had any to borrow, and my Paint is about as pathetic as they come you know. She's about to give it up." Lacey laughed.

"Do you still have Candy? Is she still your gal now that you have the brave Hercules to work?"

With a bit of a sorrowed furrow to her brow, and a lower hanging of her head, Keegan let her friend know that Candy had been escorted over the Rainbow Bridge by one of her favorite vets, Dr. Sid Croswald Jr., who wasn't to be confused or mistaken for his good father, Dr. Sid Croswald Sr., who was everyone's small animal vet; at least everyone she knew.

"Junior took Candy off the property about a month ago. I knew it was time to let her go, but what I didn't know was that she had a tumor in her stomach. He came out to age her since I thought she was about 30..."

her words interrupted, *"Thirty!"* cried Hoel, *"I would have never known that, you really kept her up for that age, girl, you really did. How did you know, or what made you think she was so old?"* asked the doctor.

When it was all explained to her friend, the way Candy came into her life, the deception that Hodges and others had brought about over the whole thing; it hurt Hoel to know that people do such cruel and unnecessary bidding towards other horse people, especially with kids; when a kid loves horses, you tell them all that they will encounter, engage, and go through. You don't lie or use euphoniums, you let them know that owning a horse or some cases a pony, is far more arduous than just grooming, petting, and feeding the thing. Hard and dedicated work goes into it. Difficulty at some points, and abysmal challenges at others.

At twelve Keegan had been through a few hoops. She knew the formidable burden and duties involved; Keegan Tanner was a rare and precious stone to be sure. Not every kid could understand the depth of responsibility being a horse owner could be.

"Girl, I'm so sorry to hear about that. I know you loved her, and I saw it in her eyes too. Hey, I think I have a few photos of her when I last worked with her. I know I have the one of you and her standing in the barn door with Bree Morgan's first place ribbon on Candy's bridle; when you did that I laughed so hard. I can send those to you if you want me to. God, wouldn't she had just killed if she knew you nicked it for a photo op?"

Laughed Lacey, not realizing the depth of her statement.

Stephen Mueller wore his unofficial official face when he showed his face at the office a few minutes later to speak with Jule. He wanted to let her know that with the new development in the High Five fire case, and with Chase Finley being singled out as being the boy that dropped his wallet and was now being accused of impregnating Jodi Williams, it wouldn't take the police long before coming back out to the ranch to do another once-over to see what they could find either in someone's tack box or maybe in parked car.

"If it's on the premises here Jule, it's not private property anymore. It may be their car or truck, it may be their tack box, but if it's parked here and they pay you to keep that camera rolling as it eye-balls them when they come in and leave each time, the police have a legal right to search, the camera that is. They can search all the tack boxes too, you own them. There is no right to privacy; even if they think there is.

"If you have anyone here you think could shed a few rays of light on the matter, call Mansfield and let him know, but here's the thing, it can only happen once. If he goes off and serves the warrants that one time, and only on one car or truck or tack box, then the word will be out and everyone will clean their glove boxes and trunks before driving back onto the premises. You'd have to do it when they're all here. Can you do that? Maybe call a boarders meeting?" he asked.

Jule didn't much like the idea, being a conservative herself, her political mindset cringed thinking she could be used in such a way to bring about justice as it should be, but also possibly infringing on a person's privacy at the same time. Knowing the girl was a boarder, a good person, and that the person who killed her probably knew her from being at the barn, she told Steve she could try to do something light and airy, something that wouldn't require them to be there, but if they did, they did, and yeah, if Mansfield had a few warrants to serve he could serve one to her and Melora as well, so it wouldn't look like they knew anything about it.

Mueller mentioned that was how they found the grandson's note in the Whitcomb case down near Mountain View; the kid had written his brother saying he was about to get the EBT card and they could meet at Starbucks on Main to sell it to the kid his brother had found to put up a $100 for the newly charged card. Whitcomb had been killed the day her benefits were restored in full. To think someone would murder their own grandmother for so little a reward sent shivers down the backs of both of them, virtually at the same time. Their eyes caught one another, and it was a silent hug between them that offered a prayer for a woman who neither had met, but she could have been literally anyone's loved one.

When the boarders gathered in the lounge later that next evening, Jule began her discussion as to why it was important that they gather in the first place. Starting with her ideas for a future wedding reception, she wanted to get ideas from them as to what they believed could be used for a charity event which she would use to cloak her celebrated nuptials in as well.

"We can do something like a barrel race for the Western riders, a Dressage competition or exhibition for the English riders, maybe even a few inter-discipline trades where say Shaina is a judge since she can do both styles. We can have ribbons and other prizes, maybe do a music thing in the middle or end of it to bring money to our favorite charities. Whoever wins the overall all-around gets to pick where the money goes. It's just a few ideas now, they've been beating around in my head, but I wanted to give you guys the chance to think too." Jule stated.

Jule stood at the front of the lounge and had the others facing her, she glanced out the window of the lounge; the door fully closed to keep some of the noises of the police search out of ear shot. Starting with the tack boxes made sense to everyone, as at least the police could scour them before needing to issue any warrant; entering and pretending they had just arrived. No one needed to know what if anything had been found in the boxes. Chief Mansfield gave instructions to only take photos of anything found, so that a proper more personal search warrant could be issued if necessary.

The search warrants as well as his prepared speech wasn't necessary as it turned out. When the uniformed officer entered the lounge he was greeted with handshakes, nods and good overall respect from every boarder and every one present. Mansfield asked if he could search their cars, their trucks, and he included their tack boxes, pretending he and the others had simply just arrived. None of those present gave the slightest hesitation to allow a search, asking if they could provide assistance, even going out of their way to give him details he may not have received otherwise. A feeling of relief careened through Jule's pulsing heart, her anxiety for the moment had ceased. Melora's grin had returned, where before she had held her emotions. As no one had brought Keegan Tanner in on the plan, her genuine curiosity was shown; even appreciated, as she told the police what she had been told by Shaina the day before that something may be up; she just didn't know what it could be.

22

Outlaw Henry Starr had made the news again, even after his death on February 22, 1921. The native Cherokee bank and coach robber had been celebrated by those claiming he wasn't as guilty as the papers and stories had made him. One of his distant relatives now living near the area of the barn went out of her way to find clues and evidence to clear at least some of the man's tainted reputation of being a notorious gang member whose end came after attempting to rob two banks at one time. The feat wasn't met, but it also wasn't the first time such a move had been attempted either. In October 1892, the Dalton gang had tried the same stunt up in Coffeyville, Kansas, and had met their end as well.

Though Starr wasn't gunned down right there at the site, he did die of his wounds with his second or third wife by his side along with his seventeen-year-old son whom he had named out of respect for the president at the time who had given him a full pardon, back in the day, for still more dubious and outrageous antics. President Theodore Roosevelt, the 26th President of the United States had felt a bit sorry for Starr, feeling that his upbringing and status as a Native could have played a slight role in his choices. Because of his willingness, or his stated willingness to change, Roosevelt pardoned Starr when he was not yet forty-five years of age; claiming he had half of his life ahead of him, and promising he would change for the better. For a time, he did, but of course, as many men and women do, the thrill and excitement of living on the edge and being ruthless and wild overtook the Oklahoman and he was once again back at his old tricks.

The story reminded Jule of the many times she, as an insurance agent, had run across those who had either let their policies lapse, or they hadn't remembered to pay a premium, only to ask for forgiveness. There were times when they would swear up and down that they were victims of uncontrolled circumstances, and the stories they told were so perfectly rehearsed, they even came with smidgeons of truth that could be either proven or disproven, but they begged and hoped the agent would reinstate their policies. Nine times out of ten it was a really bad decision to do; often ending up with the insurance carrier paying out a claim to someone, either the client themselves who failed to disclose a loss, or in one case she remembered, to a woman who had been struck and injured but she had agreed to say it happened the day after the coverage so she could in fact be covered.

Why she had allowed herself to fall short over and over again as a young agent was beyond her, but Armstrong had been raised to think the best in people, not the worst. Even when she competed at rodeos she never dreamed of the antics that could be perpetrated on others just because one athlete thought she could move up the ranks if she discredited another, or maimed their horse before a race. The thoughts of those kinds of tricks rarely popped their ugly heads up in reality, but that was way way back in the '80s and again in the '90s. Today, if a girl like Jodi was riding well; as well as she did, she could find herself in an invisible overwatch of sorts. She could become the nucleus of a cell of would-be harmful traitors who wanted nothing more than to rid themselves of her edge over them; rid themselves in such a permanent and drastic way.

Chief Mansfield couldn't and wouldn't say what if anything he had found but he did let Jule know that one of her boarders had a thing for another, and perhaps she could keep an eye out for that, the oppression seemed a bit less innocent and a tad more invasive than the lawmen would like to see or hear in the next news cycle.

"Keep an eye open, and if you see anything you think needs to be addressed, maybe get your daughter in on it and she can have Keegan video when the two

of them come and go from the barn. I don't like seeing sixteen or seventeen-year-old girls running around up here by themselves anyway, but we can't really stop that. You have a curfew, right?" he asked.

"The barn hours are from 7: a.m. to 10:00 p.m. every week day and they can stay until 11:00 o'clock on Friday and Saturday. She added, *"... but if someone needs to be here later, they text me or Melora to say so, and we keep the CCTV cameras running. We turn some of them off during the day to save a bit, but after hours they are all on, especially on the outside of the gate once everyone has left.*

"I wish we had had cameras out back by the north pastures earlier, but you know Chief, we had just bought the place. I just...well, I hate myself at times thinking I could have done less and I could have done more. I didn't have to traipse out there with my big ol' cloggy boots destroying any prints the police needed and I could have had more lights, more cameras, more eyes. I just can't sleep sometimes thinking about Jodi and her unborn baby." She stated.

"Oh, yeah, that." Mentioned Mansfield.

"The baby wasn't Chase Finley's. I don't have permission to tell you everything, but medically speaking, we'll say, he can't get anyone pregnant. I guess maybe he told the Craigstone girl he had so he could appear cool or something, but his own mother told me that Jodi hadn't given him the time of day. Now, that doesn't mean he didn't kill the girl, he still

could have, especially after writing her the poems and her not giving him that precious time of day.

"To be honest with you, I don't know that Jodi Williams would have even known she was pregnant. Some people don't find out for nearly a full three months. My wife was telling me that. We had our twins nine or ten months after we got married and she only carried them less than eight months. She found out she was pregnant around Christmas time, and they were in our laps that next Memorial Day, so if you do the Math on that..."

he began counting the months between late December and his wedding day in mid-August, he determined that the babies would have been in his wife's womb sometime in September, but she went another eight or so weeks before feeling strange enough to check it out.

"Horses go eleven months I'm told. That's a long time. I can tell you; Joanna Brimley Mansfield was 100% ready to get those girls out by the time Valentine's rolled around. She was already getting big then, you can't imagine how she felt by Easter."

His smile said it all, the proud father of twin girls who had just turned seven were the joy of his heart.

"*Did the dogs get their man, Chief?*" she asked.

"I know they hit on an area outside the barns where we used to keep the manure. Did they find the truck or the person they found to their noses' liking?"

She hadn't really wondered too much about it, but she knew Chase's truck hadn't been there. No one had heard it, and he never parked where the dogs had hit their mark.

"Banderoff. The truck parked out back belonged to Tucker Banderoff, but he was hundreds of miles away that night. Could be that someone else drove it, we can't get him to open up about who he may let drive his truck. His father swears no one touches a Banderoff car or truck, mainly because he sells insurance you know, and he doesn't want to add anyone to their policy. He told me he'd be adding people left and right if Tucker let everyone he knew drive his truck when he's gone. Can't seem to keep his boy in check I think...that's what it sounds like to me." Said the cop.

"You say he told you that he'd have to add people to his policy to be covered? That's odd. We're in Oklahoma. The vehicle has to be covered, as long as someone paying the policy gives a person permission to drive it, it doesn't matter who drives it. I mean, yeah, they need to have their own insurance, but he doesn't have to write anyone's name down on a policy or pay an extra premium for allowing them to drive something he's covered with his own initial policy." She thought out loud.

"I have a policy on my two cars. I have Melora on the policy as a driver, and I pay a bit more for that, but if my son Rogan or my other daughter Brooke needed to drive the car, or for that matter anyone with a valid driver's license, I don't have to call up my company and add them. I just give them permission.

"Now, Chief, that being said, if they have an accident and it turns out it is their fault, I am responsible. I mean, my policy takes the hit. I know that going in, but no, I don't have to call up the carrier and add anyone. I don't know why a veteran agent like Banderoff would tell you that. That's his business. He's not only with a carrier, he's a broker. He has access to dozens of carriers. I'm sure he has the best coverage possible. He's that guy." She concluded.

When the Chief left, the only thing on Jule's mind was to get in touch with Steve to bring him over for dinner that evening; and go over what Mansfield had just implicated without realizing he had implicated anything.

"Still the investigator, I see."

Stated Mueller, giving his angel a bit of a nudgy hug to both tease her into his arms and rib her for being such as nosey-Nellie.

"Come on Steve, someone drove the Banderoff's truck, the kid's truck. It was parked there, and it was sniffed out by the dogs. Think with me, let's go over this. Tucker is gone, his dad has access, and if his dad

had been talking to Jodi about reinstating her insurance, that could mean that he was trying to give her a means to pay off her back debt using something he wanted rather than a few hundred dollars. She was a month in arears according to the information Mansfield got from Banderoff. I mean, I could look that up on the database, but think about it, the girl is eight to ten weeks pregnant. Maybe she finds out, maybe she tells her parents, maybe they kick her out of the house and strip her of her insurance."

Jule indicated with a tilt of her head, knowing she could never do that to one of her own.

"But if she was kicked out of the house," asked Steve, *"...why would they let her keep the truck in the first place? Was it hers? Did she own it outright? She wasn't eighteen yet, so it couldn't be in her name."*

Promising themselves to take up the mantle the next day, the two headed off for a good dinner at Zio's Kitchen before returning to the apartment to rearrange furniture, making room for some of the more chosen pieces from his own place; furniture Jule had allowed him to bring over without too much of a fuss. Sharing any space after being alone was hard to do; it meant compromise, giving and taking and being nice about it. This was in fact a new-new for the author, and not something she looked forward to with a completely open heart or mind; still, she was about to marry the man.

23

Keegan couldn't compete in any event leading to the prestigious all-around due to her age; only competitors over the age of 13 could enter games and races which would qualify them for the coveted spot. Though it wasn't as if she had the money to enter either. Larissa Lowell would have been asked to fork up over fifty dollars had the pre-teen been eligible; if only because Keegan Tanner's well behaved and slightly guilty demeanor would never have allowed her to ask Melora or Jule to put of the entry fees. It was OK she told herself; next year isn't that far away, and she didn't have a horse to ride that wasn't somebody else's horse in the first place.

The middle school age range may have included pre-teen riders, but the younger set was only there to be seen in exhibitions. Several of Tanner's friends from school had entered the county line up, she hadn't participated in the events leading up to the qualifiers, giving the excuse that she was working with her new charge; Hercules, a deep chestnut Mustang gelding she had chosen over one of the shorter bays Melora found herself involved with. Most of the girls in her classes at school weren't familiar with the breed, but a boy just about her age who literally towered over anyone in the 7th grade took it upon himself to learn as much as he could from the school library before attacking the internet to find just about everything he could about the horses of the wild west so he could have a foothold in the stirrups of Keegan Tanner's life. The boy was smitten.

"Cam Learner won't leave me the heck alone, and it's bugging the crap out of me."

Complained the smiling Tanner, her heart racing all the while she pretended to be sufficiently annoyed. She motioned to Dr. Lacey, who had happily joined the Armstrongs to accompany them as well as Tanner to the events; something she remembered fondly participating in while growing up. Though she hailed from another part of the state, the county competitions in any county led to the regionals and the state competitions before too long. Lacey's favorite, as was Keegan's had always been the barrel races.

"Cameron Learner? He's twelve? Oh, I'm getting old. I babysat him when he was born!"

Hoel stated, trying to bring the girl back down from the clouds a bit.

"He had the best parents out there; they paid me full charge and gave me a tip too."

She added. With Cam sitting less than twenty-five feet to her left, Keegan purposely turned her back to him to face Lacey before asking if the boy was still watching her.

"Oh, he's watching alright..." she snickered, giving Cam and his parents a swift wave and that winning smile of hers,

"...and he's standing up, and he's...coming this way..."

and just as she started to say he's about three steps behind her, Keegan nearly jumped out of the stands to make her way to the stadium floor before tearing off through the crowd of onlookers to make her escape leaving the youth to wonder that much more about why girls even exist.

While Dr. Lacey explained to her old charge what it was about girls that made them so impossible to understand, she reiterated that Keegan may not be competing, but that she had managed to bring her Mustang Hercules to the show to get all the desensitizing he could.

"She's got him tied up out behind the red barn, on one of the posts. She's asked others not to get too close, so she's on the far end. If you really want to make an impression you'll go pick her up a Starbucks

before you go see her. I know she's been drinking everyone's coffee when she thinks we don't see her. Don't tell her I gave you the money for it OK..." she stated reaching for a few bucks,

"...just let her think you knew she liked it. She likes a lot of cream and sugar too. I tease her all the time calling her drink a dirty latte for sure. If she could, she'd swallow every grain of sugar in the container. Only use a little that way she'll have to ask you to stir it with your finger and make it sweeter." She teased.

Cameron's face turned a million shades of red, his ears nearly popping with hope. He took the money and ran off to the concession stand faster than either Lacey or his mom and dad had ever witnessed before.

"I gave him money to get something, hope that's OK." She hollered over to the Learners; again smiling. No one could resist the woman when she showed all of her pretty pearly teeth; those dimples took them all instantly.

Without mentioning her intention to do it, another girl had made her way over through the red barn to see what sort of trash Keegan Tanner had managed to drag in with her to the county competitions. Though Taylor Anderson wasn't quite out of high school, she hadn't let that stop her from entering the school-aged games, claiming she had been held back. Even if it were true, and it was, several of the parents had asked that the girl be disqualified; not because of her high school grade status, but because she would turn twenty in the fall. They didn't feel that she was a fair opponent. Judges however, made an exception for Anderson, due only to the fact that once a competitor in the state reached the age of thirteen and could fully go up against the others, all the others could be full on adults. Age wasn't an issue after that point; Anderson was on the list.

A stiff breeze and dusty winds hit them all somewhat unexpectedly. The girl racing in the arena had to deal with the uninvited gusts through her second and third barrel, trying not to eat the top layer of the arena as she made her final turn to head back to the gates. The rider gave a hoot, raising her head and fist to shout her excitement! Best time in her life, she pulled a 15.9 and hoped at least one of her friends had the withal to record it. She knew she could get a clip from the officials, but why spend the money to do that if one of her cousins or buddies had their iPads out to capture it all?

In Oklahoma, a 15.9 wouldn't do much for a qualifier hoping to move ahead in the sport, but for a county run that didn't hurt the girl's reputation any. When her name was called, and she was handed the white ribbon for hitting third place, Lauren Perkins couldn't contain herself. She had never been on the stand before; this was a first. Though the packed audience's noise was clearly given for all of the competitor's Lauren felt she had been the center of all of their attention for at least 15.9 seconds; she almost cried over the fact. Her red roan certainly stood prouder than usual.

When the left side of the arena was seen pouring out to the back area chasing what seemed to be a cacophony of sirens with blaring blue and red lights, Lacey Hoel looked at Melora for support wondering if Jule had been seen over the past several minutes or not. Having not made so much as a cough over the dust, Jule had simply disappeared during Perkin's monumental run. She had taken a text or a call according to someone in the stands beside them; and the next thing they heard or knew, ambulances were charging over the sod to meet up with whoever or whatever was going on in the back of the fairgrounds just behind the red barns.

"*Keegan!*" exclaimed Melora, only to have Dr. Lacey assure her that the girl was in good company with Cam Learner over by the concessions; they could see the two, but now that they could see them, Hoel recognized the plain look of agony or shock on the little girl's face. Cameron was actually holding her; it was more like he was rocking her. Something was clearly wrong. Catching up to the two kids, questions became statements, intel flew out of the youths as if a fire hydrant had burst on the scene.

"*Slow down! I can't get a thought in, what happened? Go slowly, start from the beginning, and sit on your hands if you need to, girl, I can't....*" Melora's calming elements were kicking in. Tanner was about to take another deep breath, Cameron squeezed her hand, looked her in the eyes and said,

"It's not your fault Keegan, she knew better, she's older and knew better."

But still, the moment was pregnant with anxiety for all of them.

"Taylor got on top of Hercules! She tried to ride him. She pushed me away and said I didn't know what I was doing, and she just jumped on him."

Keegan's lips shook while she tried to explain.

"We didn't have a second Ms. Armstrong, I swear it." Protested the boy, *"Keegan's telling the truth, the bitc...sorry...Taylor Anderson just pushed Keeg down and took two steps to jump on the horse's back. He didn't know what was going on, that's for sure, but he knew he didn't want her on him. Before she could get up onto him his back legs swung around and struck her right in the chest and maybe in the head. I don't know. I didn't see it; I was trying to help Keegan.*

"I dropped my phone in all the rush, and Keegan's isn't working so we had to keep looking for mine. I got over by Taylor and drug her to the side by her ankles to get her out his reach. He couldn't go any further, but he wouldn't even let Keegan near him to make sure he was OK. We don't know what happened except she said Keegan didn't know how to break a horse and there she went...to try, I guess."

His words explaining much more than expected.

"Who called the ambulance?" Dr. Lacey asked her husband Aaron who had just caught up with his wife at the stands. Lacey, then turning to each person beside her to see if anyone knew, glanced back at Cameron. The boy explained that they did find his phone Keegan texted Jule to tell her what happened. His guess was that Jule had called 9-1-1 and got ahold of someone because they were there in under a minute.

While Lacey sent up a quick prayer for Taylor, Melora raced to the back of the red barn trying to find her mother. What she found was a mass of onlookers, chaos in the throes of hollers, hands, voices, and threats being hurled both at the horse and at Anderson. No one wanted to blame the girl, but most wanted to at least point out that being irresponsible was something that can cost a person their life around livestock; especially around wild animals.

The wildness of the Mustang, for some, was the main issue. If the horse hadn't been present the woman wouldn't have been trying to show off, but then again, claimed others, and quite loudly with fists clenched, if the woman hadn't been trying to one-up a little girl in the first place she wouldn't have gotten hurt. Baeleigh Fite, a fair official, heard Keegan as well as Cameron Learner talking to Anderson for a few minutes before it happened. Her statement was taken by both county officials and local city police, as they filled out their reports over the incident. Keegan's main concern of course, was for Hercules. Would the authorities try to put him down for being a horse, or would they understand what really happened and send Taylor Anderson to prison for trying to either steal her property or something along those lines.

Fite mentioned that Tanner had taken the coffee from Learner, they had laughed about the amount of sugar and the fact that Dr. Lacey had told him to stir the thing with his finger. Both kids wondered out loud if that even worked, when Anderson came walking up to the couple with purpose in her step. Anderson then chided both at the same time calling them *"lame"*, *"stupid"* and other things that the witness couldn't recall at the moment, but said that when Keegan mentioned something to the effect of not being able to hear Anderson; maybe she was hearing the wind, that's when Anderson pushed her to the ground the first time and she spilled her coffee. Taylor then walked off toward the horse, but the Fite heard the boy call out to her saying he wasn't trained.

Since she had always been spoiled and unable to control her arrogant behavior, Taylor Anderson stomped on the small coffee cup to be sure it was useless before pushing Keegan a second time, and telling her that in Texas where she's from, twelve-year-olds were veterans when it came to training wild horses. She was going to show Tanner how it was done. That's when Learner leaned down to help Tanner, and the snooty waif of a being tried to run and jump onto the horse like someone might try in a western film; as if she was a stunt woman. That's how Baeleigh Fite explained it.

"That girl literally jumped up like she was in some sort of old western film and was going to break the horse while he was tied up. The horse said no, and there she went."

According to a second witness, one who had assisted Learner with finding his phone, Taylor had either screamed or let out every ounce of air in her at impact. He claimed he saw the woman bend in half, her head almost touching her knees in the air. It was all in slow motion, but he saw her land. Like Cameron, the man wasn't sure if Anderson's head was struck by the horse when he threw another pungent blow, or if she had already landed just inches from his hooves. When he and the boy pulled Taylor by her ankles, it was because she had managed to move a few feet from the horse, and they weren't able to reach her by her shoulders without placing themselves within his kicking range.

Once the dust had settled, and the crowds dispersed, Melora was asked by the county authorities to provide proof of ownership for the animal, and to show his vaccination records as well any important information they could use to straighten out the mess before them. Officially, because signs warning any and all persons on the premises that any unnecessary actions on the part of a human would not lead to any responsibility on their part, most of the discussions were shorter than would or could have been expected if the woman had been molested by a passerby or assaulted by another human on county grounds. Working with animals lends certain chances, the signs were in place for good reason; and this event was one of those reasons.

When the blue and red lights of the ambulance drove away, Anderson's mother Tammy Vaughn couldn't stop herself from spitting in the face of the youth she believed responsible for her daughter's injuries. Before she could protest the action, Steve Mueller, the former Bethany police officer, spun Vaughn around, dragging her forcibly to the ground before pulling out his cuffs from his hip pocket and containing her long enough to be taken into custody for assault and battery of a minor. He may not have been within his jurisdiction, or even within his official right, but placing a person under citizen arrest in Oklahoma was still a very real thing. Sheriff Bayless made sure to compliment the former cop for his assistance and of course taking the opportunity to tease him about not being able to leave the cuffs at home; apparently some habits die harder than others.

24

After a few weeks, the barn drama and gossip around the state had settled to its normal roar with very little to talk about other than the poor judges who didn't know their way out of any number of wet paper sacks when it came to deciding which rider won what, and most of the complaints weren't coming from the Western riders, but from the English riders who hadn't been treated fairly in all the years they had bothered to try and bring a bit of culture to the state of Oklahoma. To anyone in the world of Dressage, Cross-Country, Jumping, Hunter or simply Show, the riders, to a person, complained that the men and women chaste to give points could be paid off, could be bribed or they could be biased and poised to give less points to anyone from the Sooner State so as not to have to deal with them at higher levels. The only one truly affected at the

Bay Sorrel Ranch would have been Paul Abernathy, a rider of distinction.

Abernathy's mood remained focused. He wasn't going to allow the rumors of speculation and scandal to interfere with his plans to move up in the world of horsemanship. With his legal practice also seeing a stirring rise, he found himself in a curious predicament; enough so, to be in the mental state of realizing that the horse world brought great benefits and even a higher level of esteem and appreciation from his legal-minded colleagues. It may be time, he pondered, to bring about an accord of determination in his professional life to make his mark there; a place where he could be both daring and seen without the costumes, the innuendo of cheating. He wouldn't have to worry about or deal with the losers who simply wouldn't believe he had achieved his deserved accomplishments on his own without assistance. In the courtroom there was no one to *"judge"* the outcome, the law took care of that. He could shape his defense, employing and wielding his knowledge easier in a business suit than he could high boots, tails, and a top hat.

When Cathy Craigstone entered the back of the blue barn searching for Paul Abernathy it wasn't for another private lesson in whatever it was that others claimed she had been paying him for. She had been all but banned from the premises. Paul was in fact, a criminal lawyer, and her daughter Lily, it seemed, would need the best her mother could afford if she wanted to be free from the shackles that hung around her kid's neck for having been arrested and charged with arson a month before. Lily, though only sixteen, was being tried as an adult. Abernathy had suggested to the mother early in the incident to convince her daughter to talk, squeal, spill out any and everything she could against the others who were not only there, but had participated in the pouring of the kerosene, and the setting of the blaze before driving off and leaving Lily to take the wrap by herself. Abernathy mentioned that anything Lily could give cops as a way of leveraging her own guilt, she should take the opportunity to do so.

When Lily was first arrested, she had adhered to every word of advice given to her by Paul Abernathy, who though he wasn't officially her attorney of record, had agreed to do a few meetings pro bono, or at least he wasn't being paid in cash. There was no retainer set, no receipt given. When Cathy sought the man at the barn that morning, she had found him lounging with Helene and others, sipping coffee and eating what was left of the gingered bread pudding left on the main table for all to enjoy. Melora had a thing about cooking at random times; mostly to reduce any stress she had built up within her mind from dealing with the obstinate animals she had chosen to gentle.

"Paul, I need your help. Lily just told the police all about Chase Finley again, but this time she told him something I didn't know. She said Chase told her someone he knew had followed Jodi that night, that they had tried to talk to her and that she resisted. He

didn't say who, Paul, he said they were older. He swore he didn't have anything to do with it, but I think he was just trying to impress Lily, he's been stalking her on Facebook for over three months and it's a little too creepy if you know what I mean. If he killed Jodi or even if he's telling the truth about getting her pregnant, for God's sake, I don't want him hanging around my daughter!"

Her words whispered, but with excitement, and others tried to listen. For some, the barn walls had ears, but for others they weren't thin enough. Most tried to get information from those who were either washing horse, grooming, or tacking up when someone spoke in the actual barn itself. In the arena, there was next to no hope of overhearing anything, which is why Paul Abernathy walked his "*client*" into the open space.

"Cathy, you know your daughter is not a virgin, right? I mean, that's why we're together now, isn't it? You and I? She was a bit of tease and I was a bit drunk, but since you were so...so kind,"

he mentioned, while running his fingers down her arms, taking her into his hold to calm her before continuing,

"...since you didn't have me arrested, I can only tell you that you have yourself a minx and if Chase Finley, Tucker Banderoff, or even that clerk at Tractor Supply, that Thom Sutherland whose been eye-balling her for the past several months, if he wanted her,

they'd all have her. She's not the innocent child you make her out to be."

He cooed, silently wondering to himself what realm the woman usually chose to live in. Perhaps her fantasies were better orchestrated than those of his own; it was worth exploring now that he wasn't facing a criminal charge of pedophilia, but could conquer mother-vixen whenever his throbbing hormones preferred.

"I know she's active, Paul, I'm fully aware of that. She's on birth control, we've talked about it, but if Finley knows who got Jodi pregnant and he's saying knows, that person was the killer. If we can get something like on recording or in writing to give the police, maybe they'll let Lily go on the fire charges. Can you help me?"

She asked, without much hope in her voice.

Melora's baking extended to cooking if she were at home in her own kitchen; something Keegan was apt to brag about whenever she did have a chance to speak to one of her older brothers. With Mitch and Brant off at college and Miles thinking of breaking all the family traditions to head up North for his formal education after he graduated, Larissa Lowell couldn't keep up with her family duties with any means of being consistent. About the only thing she could do to make all of her ends meet was to pull an extra shift or two at the bar, and then try not to spend it once she had taken the money from the till in an advance on what she may have been paid if she hadn't already borrowed against it.

"Lora can you make that stuff you made in the crockpot the other day. The one with the creamed sauce over chicken and peppers?"

the girl asked. The dish was officially known as *"Marry Me Chicken"*, but since the cook never used the types of whole peppers required, she just called it something else; usually creamed chicken and rice, something benign like that. Melora agreed to whip up the dish.

Whatever it was, it served two or three purposes, not just one. For starters the meal itself, when finished, couldn't be beat. Hot steaming spicy thick chicken breast pieces smothered in hot thickened cream cheesy white gravy with several colorful spices, poured over a bed or rice was great, but when you added a topping of parmesan cheese to it, and drank it down with that southern woman's sweet tea, it was good enough to rave about to just about anyone, brothers included.

Secondly, once the meal was finished and the left overs put away, Keegan could count on what she called *"debris fries"* the next day. The dish was made famous in Louisiana she knew that, but didn't know when or how.

"What you do, Miles,"

she bragged to her brother once he finally answered the phone,

"...is you get those frozen fries, or you can make them from real potatoes if you want, too. You heat them up or fry them in the deep frier thing, and then you dump a bunch of cheese and this stuff on top of them, and it's so good. It's better than nachos and you know I love my nachos."

She laughed, remember a time she and her brothers got literally sick from eating them just about every Saturday morning. Her mother wasn't worth much to any of them, but she managed to nick quite a few big backs of corn tortilla chips from the bar every Friday night before she came home.

"Miles, I've not eaten this good in my entire life. If you want you can come over for Thanksgiving this year because Lora and Jule are doing a whole family thing for the barn. There's a lot of boarders who either don't go home for it or they don't really have other family so Jule decided to make it a yearly thing. She's even doing a summer thing next year for the Fourth. We don't have time to plan it this year, but she'll bring in singers and we'll do races and the English people will show off their skills for jumping, and Dressage. I asked her if we could set a fox loose to chase around but she said no."

the girl laughed.

Her older brother congratulated her on the win; having nabbed a place at a real table for life rather than having to admit to everyone what white trash he felt he had been brought up to know. In his gut he envied his little sister in a few ways; not only did she have money coming to her when she turned of age, but she was being cared for now. When he was twelve he never saw his mom, and he was saddled with babysitting his brothers and the baby through her toddler and tender years. He couldn't imagine not having a sister to love, but was absolutely satisfied that she had somehow made strides he could only dream about.

"When I go to my classes each day I think about you sis. I think how you're going to become a famous rider, maybe not even go to college, but just step into the big time with your money and all your talent. I don't know anyone luckier than you, but you think you're a burden. You're not a burden kid, you're a blessing. If mom ever tries to say otherwise, just let me, Mitch or Brant know. Mitch is actually getting one of those DNA tests so he can prove his father is Cody Traywick. He figures if he can put enough pressure on Traywick's family one way or the other he can get a settlement. I'm all for it, but I can't even begin to think to know who my dad is. Mom wasn't exactly up front about it any time I got around to asking. I don't think she knows."

He said, letting his heart sink, but lifting his voice to add just how proud again he was of his only true fan before hanging up the phone and thinking about the debris fries Keegan talked about. They sounded really really good.

When she detailed the conversation later to Jule, Steve, and Melora, Keegan made such a big deal out of the hot savory fries that Steve had to request the first meal too, just to get to the point where he could later pour the remnants over some homemade deep-fried fries; he couldn't wait. Melora shook her head saying she was better than being known for only making one meal, but before she finished her thoughts she stated, or rather almost blurted the word *"debris"* in a somewhat questionable way.

"Mom, it's debris, that's what the police called that pile of rubble out in the pasture where they found Jodi. They called it debris. If you think about it, it's not matched up with anything, none of it was. It was all just construction crap that Brian Scott's maintenance friend in the city dumped out that way, and then the neighbors said they'd go through it now and again to get the metal scraps to sell off; leaving the fiberglass, the drywall, and the rolls of carpet. I think Scott was thinking he could open up a dump site where people could do a sort of landfill from all the apartment make readies that were supposed to be built this way.

"That's what Joan Morrison and her husband Keith were saying. They own the lot next to us, but when Keith died in January Joan sold it to Canadian County and now they're going to do that on that

property. They'll allow it to be filled with debris and trash, and either do a monthly burn or take out all the bigger pieces that can't be crushed. She was telling me since I had the Mustangs. Believe me, when I tell you that the city council didn't give a damn about my Mustangs, but Joan did. Now, because of the ranch being up and running, they can't do the whole fire thing or the burn thing, but they can do more crushing and more controlled fires as long as they only last an hour or so, and they have a fire marshal present. God, I love Joan; I loved Keith too. He was funny. Did you know..."

she continued before being interrupted by Mueller,

"Melora...wait...did you say Brian's friend who was in construction dumped all that stuff, the debris onto the property? That could only be one man, and you know him. He used to be in construction he and his dad, but now he's that insurance idiot on television with the loud and stupid commercials. He's that...that guy, you know him honey, Kurt something."

Steve said, motioning with his arms.

"Banderoff?" asked Jule with a tinge of surprise.

"Yeah! He's Tucker's dad, the one Jodi Williams was dating, I think..." Steve stated, he continued,

"... he tells the story that he and his dad were in construction and when the roof fell in on his dad and

hurt him badly, he got out of that line of work and into insurance when the insurance claim paid to the claimant didn't include covering the costs of his dad's medical bills. I guess the old guy never had his own insurance because he was said to be buried later in a pauper's grave through the Oklahoma County fund for that a few years later."

Jule thought about it, and she remembered the newspaper story about Kurt's dad.

"I only remember that because my parent's house was built by the same crew that the older Banderoff worked for; the Wright Way Construction Company. That actually makes sense because Kurt left the business after he got married and was having their first, that would be Tucker. He's had those family-wearing-the-same-lame-clothes photographs in his advertisements for umpteen years, but yeah, he makes sure everyone knows what happened to his dad and how important it is to have your health and final expenses covered." Jule stated.

When they put their heads to it, thinking about the debris, how it got there, and who knew what was left of it, Jule decided to place a quiet call to Chief Mansfield to see if he could ask the people who took the pieces to test them for fingerprints and to try and match them with both Jodi Williams and Kurt Banderoff. Since Tucker wasn't in the area that night, and he no doubt hadn't been out to that part of the north pasture ever in his life, his fingerprints wouldn't be found.

Another week passed before Chief Mansfield called to thank Jule for her insight, without letting her know anything had been done and without confirming or denying anything had been found.

Steve wanted to know the results of what all happened with Taylor Anderson, and whether or not the authorities had planned on euthanizing Hercules, who had since the incident been penned up in an area of smaller confinement should they be forced to give him up. Having found just that morning that Herc was again being lunged and worked by his favorite gal, Mueller mentioned that he could sort of put two-and-two together, but wanted to hear it from, well, *"...the horse's mouth if possible"*.

Jule gladly deferred the question to the manager of the barn, asking Melora to fill her fiancé in on the details while she tied up a few loose ends of their wedding plans; plans that would take place in a quaint chapel downtown in Oklahoma City rather than kicking up dust and getting her new and very expensive dress dirty. She agreed that a reception for the couple could be, and would be held in the white barn arena following their vows and a change of clothes. Anyone at the barn willing or wanting to attend the actual ceremony needed to *R.S.V.P.* because the little chapel only held up to twenty people total, and anyone after that had to stand in the back throughout the service.

"When Sheriff Bayless called this morning to let us know that Herc was free to work and he wouldn't

be put down, I woke Keegan up and told her she didn't need to worry about anything, and all of her bad dreams were just that, dreams. She hasn't had a good night's sleep since then, Steve, and you know, Taylor and her family haven't even tried to take any responsibility for it, but the other good news is, she was rejected from enrolling at Cashion and Chesterfield because of her age.

"She'll either have to get a G.E.D., which I think she's going to do, or she can try and apply at other schools. She can get into a junior college with a G.E.D., and maybe others, I don't know. She brags so much about her love of Texas, maybe the Lone Star State will have her back, unless they're sick of the trash carrying itself around too. I'd go on about her, but you know my mom, and know how I was raised. I can't say much without tainting her good training, now, can I? I'll just say 'bless her heart' and be done with it." she smirked.

"Well then, I guess it's my turn for rumors, gossips, and half-truths, and I don't mind telling you ladies I have zero basis for which to hang my hat on, but from what I hear off the grapevines that are growing in and around Norman, Oklahoma City, Bethany, Warr Acres, and out this way,"

started Mueller, bringing his arms around the two Armstrong women to seat them in front of himself before continuing his tales,

"...Lily Craigstone was picked up again for questioning. She all but laid the finger on Chase Finley

for impregnating Jodi Williams, but his family protested saying he was given medicine for a sort of rare thing when he was younger, and his T-levels are just about at zero; and they won't get any better as he gets older. She went on to blame Bree Morgan, Sam Banderoff, Tucker's younger brother, and a girl named Shelly something for the fire at the High Five, but she did say Chase was there too, he drove the truck, his truck.

"Lily mentioned again how Bree had wanted to cause a scene, make it look like a disgruntled boarder had burned the place, and when Trish Bellows collected the claim for it, Bree was going to demand at least half of it saying she knew who did it and that she could talk them out of doing it again to the other side of the facility; the one where the horses are kept. What do you want to bet she would manage to get all of her stuff out first?"

he asked, raising his eyebrows, and tipping his imaginary hat towards the ladies, while simultaneously taking a low bow.

"Oh my, quite the chaos! I hope no one gets an idea to do that here at Bay Sorrel, maybe I need to call up ol' Banderoff and get another policy in place that has a really big payoff, that way he can have his little minions do the dirty work and try and bully me with the check being paid but made out to the both of us if I wanted to see any of it."

Jule laughed. Her writer's mind had triggered a thought in Steve's police head which could have then trickled into his mouth forming the next sentence that no one in the room could audibly understand. Before he had finished thinking, his cell was stuffed into his pocket, and he was walking Jule and Melora out to the front of the lounge area to see if they could see anything being parked over to the side where the manure pile once sat.

"*Stay right here.*" He directed, asking Melora to position herself as if she were walking into the building.

"*Jule, you go into the lounge, pull up the 2nd blind, the one Keegan said was broken, but she could see through it. Pull it up all the way to the top, giving you the best possible angle there is.*"

He guided, adding that he would take his truck, enter from the south gate rather than the one on the east where everyone usually comes through, and he would park his truck, headlights off, even though it was morning, he made a point to mention they would be switched off. He'd pull his truck to the side of the building to see if they could see or hear him approach.

When he had successfully managed to slip past them, using the long trail of a drive that led to the larger house rather than the main road and gate, they collectively looked at one another and knew that essentially anyone who knew the house had not been sold yet, could open the front gate to the big house, then drive to the back of it, open the gate leading to the barns and drive right up the path that the hay guys and the guy dumping the sawdust would drive, or used to drive before they were asked to take the same route as everyone else.

The murder had happened before the closing of the big house. The fence lines hadn't been taken down or reconstructed. The paths were still there, they were narrow, rather steep and dark if someone had turned off their headlights as Steve had claimed, but there it was...proof that anyone who knew the place well enough could do it. If a man, a man who had once dumped endless loads of debris, paraphernalia, and construction materials using his friend's backyard paths to get to the gates so he didn't have to carry his load by hand, knew about the narrow roads, he could drive them and park anywhere to the west of the lounge after hours and never be seen by people, or by cameras that hadn't been set up at that time.

Because the big house had no occupants, and the smaller house wasn't even on the same side of the property, no one who may be in either lounge, or out of a blue barn could have seen him park his truck. The man had to know Jodi would be at the blue barn because the white barn was off limits. He also had to know when she was going to leave the barn if he had made arrangements for her to meet with him. The only man they could think of who knew both would be the man who was going to possibly reinstate her insurance and that man was none other than Tucker Banderoff's father, Kurtis David Banderoff, former construction man, who was once asked to testify at the coroner's inquisition for his father's case as to whether or not he had been present when the fire that broke out at the house they were working had been set intentionally or if it was in fact an actual accident.

25

When the verdict came in a few weeks later, convicting all of the teens involved in the fire at the High Five, as well as loosening up information regarding other mishaps and accidents taking place from one barn to the next, everyone knew that the teens couldn't stop talking as each hoped to blame the others seeking plea bargains. They begged their respective legal counsels to beg the courts for every leniency they could muster claiming the teens were normal, average kids who though full perhaps of angst and attitude, who really meant to do no harm. For the most part the various jurors came back with precise and valued sentences once the cases were complete and the sentencing for each teen began.

Bree Morgan, the instigator of most of the events was given the most stringent sentence of eleven years behind bars, without hope for parole until she had completed at least six of those years. At just over seventeen years old, coming short of her eighteenth birthday by mere weeks, she would be at least twenty-four before she could hope to breathe free air again. This sentence, of all of them, seemed to hit the hardest with Jule, as she remembered dealing with Bree's father on a couple of occasions where board and payment for missing items came into play. The man seemed to rally for his daughter right up to the point where he couldn't use her, and when she eventually ran up a tab that he would be required to pay, he took a hike. David Morgan hadn't been seen on the scene for nearly four months.

When Steve, Jule, and Keegan all said the word *"karma"* at the same time, no one spoke for a few seconds, and then they all did, again, simultaneously expressing their respective opinions on the matter. Not every one's sentence was as harsh, apparently there had been a local farrier named Jesse Cotton who had known about the scheme and rather than telling Bellows about it, or calling the police, he made the kids swear they'd call him when they needed work done on their horses. He may have been an accomplice, but it wasn't necessarily after the fact; not one of them called the man when they needed their horses trimmed. He was given a fine of a $1000 and 500 hours of community service to be served at the Sheriff's stables until the last hour was worked off.

By contrast to Bree Morgan's sentence, Lily Craigstone, and mostly because of the good work performed by the king of Dressage himself, faced her upcoming senior year with doing community service to the tune of 1000 hours; taking her out of any real time to compete in the barns or for any school activities. Her heart made heavier because of it, she realized she had dodged an incredible bullet, but because she was labeled a snitch by all the others, their parents, and even school administrators who enjoyed their rumoring, the Craigstone family decided a move would be best. County officials let the family know they would be in touch with the county authorities where they finally landed, with Abernathy going the extra mile to ensure the courts couldn't leak that location into the public for any reason.

When she thought about it, and she thought about it quite often, Jule Armstrong had wanted to become a barn owner to get away from the world and the stress it put upon her as a renowned author who was expected to better her last book by producing another and then another. Her world of working as a corporate insurance investigator had been plain and simple compared to the rigamarole she was exposed to as a sole-proprietor to the newly christened Bay Sorrel Ranch. With the new book's success and the upcoming expectations being put upon her, Jule wondered if it wouldn't serve her and her new husband Steve to either sell or lease the property fully to Melora, but she couldn't see herself doing that without being equally equitable to her other kids. She hadn't truly given the ranch the whole *rest-of-my-life* thought when she bought into it. It was a new hobby almost; something she was already regretting.

Knowing Melora couldn't afford the place on her own, she decided to keep it, but to charge Melora officially for rent space to board the others, and to train and flip her Mustangs. It wouldn't be much of course, but if she could break even, and have the place out from under her feet for a while, Steve and she could complete their plans of selling his condo down in Norman, the one he bought so he could be closer to her, and they could ride out the lease on her apartment before getting their own place, maybe a short drive from the barn. It made sense to her, she could keep control, be the owner, make decisions about gatherings, parties, charity events, and such, and at the same time let Melora handle all the headaches, backstabbing, and crazy horse nonsense that somehow seemed to follow anyone and everyone at each and every horse barn around the world. She had said it before, but would say it until her dying day, the best thing about horse people is their dogs!

"Mom, I know you don't like drama, and this isn't something we can control, but you have to hear about it."

Melora mentioned to Jule, dragging her minion Keegan into the office behind her and looking rather lost for reasoning.

"*I don't even know where to start, but there's a guy at the back fence line with a big ten-horse trailer, and he's taking all of Darrell Hodges' horses. He hasn't proven to me that he's Darrell's brother, but he says he is, and I've called the police, who told me to call the sheriff instead, apparently, it's a county issue. I've placed a call to Bayless, but he's out of town, so another one is on the way to take a report. The man says Darrell died unexpectedly last week, and they're burying him in Arkansas tomorrow, but that he's taking the horses to give to his own kids who live in Siloam Springs on the Arkansas side, and West Siloam here in Oklahoma. I don't know Mom, Darrell hadn't paid board in two months and I can't really make this man pay it, but can't we sell those horses ourselves and make up the money?*" she asked.

"*Makes sense to me, what did the sheriff say? Was he apt to listen to the protest or was he thinking the man has the right to take the herd? Did you ask?*" Jule inquired.

"*He said he's coming to check it out. Keegan locked the south gate that doesn't even belong to us now, but the guy came through it, so I guess he convinced the new owner of the big house, that since Darrell used the back pasture and his rig was too big to turn around, it would be OK. I can't see through it, and I can't understand why people just open their arms out and let people trek through their land to get to ours. We need another fence line there, one that *doesn't have a gate and won't break if someone thinks they can plough through it. It's not his land; he can't just let people onto our property."*

Melora Complained.

"If you want, I can go meet the sheriff's deputy, he's pulling through the front gate now." Spoke Keegan, before heading out the front door of the office to do just that.

As the latest *brother-taking-what's-rightfully-his* situation only put the icing on the cake concerning her choice of career paths being that of an author more than that of a barn entrepreneur, Jule reiterated her thoughts to her daughter. Melora both understood and promised to do more in terms of letting her level of responsibly grow as quickly as it possibly could to remedy this and future situations. Darrell Hodges hadn't been sick, but since no one was fluttering up to the office to spill the latest beans on the matter, Jule just assumed he had suffered a heart attack and moved on from any thoughts other than what she and Steve could do to make the best of their future.

"If I find out Chase Finley got that man pregnant and then killed him last week, I don't think I can take it." Jule admitted with a teasing grin.

When the Dressage world qualifiers came around to the state arenas, making the news on both Tik Tok and other social media outlets, Jule and others wondered why they hadn't seen or heard of Paul

Abernathy's involvement. Why he hadn't been a part of it this year hadn't really entered their minds until it entered their minds that he hadn't been making a fuss, making demands, or making anything really since his stint at helping Lily Craigstone with her punishment arrangements. No doubt, Jule mentioned to all within earshot, since she wasn't apt to speak openly about such things in the lounge for everyone's ears, Paul had done something along the same line as she had done; he had made a choice to stop straddling the fence between two major paths which couldn't be fully appreciated if they were split, but if by choosing one side over the other marks could be made, then that was the better choice in the matter. Paul was spending more time at his downtown law firm, doing what he could to become a partner of Rainey, Riddle, Moss and Moss. It was a good call.

To tie up the morning chores, Dr. Lacey Hoel presented herself again but this time without her usual bulky tackle box. With her she brought a portable table, one she could unhook and stand up just about anywhere with a good flat floor, and have a makeshift work table for her human patients to lay on while she cracked, popped, and labored on that patient's body parts. The good doctor wasn't alone with herself either, she had brought along a feisty black and white fluffy friend, who she claimed was a shoe-in for the barn.

The pup was a registered *AKC* Border Collie she had taken in trade rather than forcing the new young client of hers to pay what he and his wife couldn't pay after being told the price only after Dr. Hoel had trekked the eighty miles one way to adjust their cute pony. What's a dog in trade she thought? He was worth something, maybe even more than her standard rate; he was registered and he was the epitome of both a good obnoxious and that *only-his-mother-could-love-him* obnoxious that manifested itself naturally every time Lacey took two steps in a direction the dog felt was the wrong direction.

"Dammit, I'm telling you, these dogs are born with it. He herds me every time I leave the truck. He won't let me go where I know I need to go. He wants me to go where he thinks I need to go."

She complained, while reaching down showing her dominant side by picking the thing up to give him a good kiss on the face.

"God I love this dog, but I don't need one. Do you need one Jule, I'll make you a good deal on him." She said.

Thinking about it, and thinking about how he would work out at the barn for Melora both as an emotional support dog and a good barn dog, a deal was struck. When Steve and she had been twisted to the point they couldn't stand up straight again, Jule asked what the total price would be including the dog. When the price given was the same as if the dog hadn't been a part of it, Lacey let Jule in on the secret that she really hadn't driven eighty miles one way to fix a pony, that was her cover story to give Steve the time needed to feel Jule out to see what the verdict of his conniving had bring to fruition. Afterall, a good dog is good to find, and a good emotional support pup, well, that was the only thing he needed to hear when he agreed to pay the pony's fare in exchange for the runt of the litter if they could spare it for $125 horse adjustment. They could.

The dog *"Chess"* had been named for the distinctive pattern of coloring on his face. The dog's entire face had been split perfectly down the middle by an imaginary line separating a completely black left side and a completely white right side. The black saddle on his back was the only tell-tale sign of his breed other than the natural instincts he carried while hunching and crawling his way through each barn upon seeing something new for the first time. Cats, people, a random goose, all made his pretense and fantastic herding dog brain kick into overdrive. When he wasn't menacing his way through each stall to check out the hocks and hooves of every horse that tried their best to end his life, he would dart through the barn at speeds no one had witnessed before; not of a pup as young as he was.

"That dog is either going to be killed or he's going to take over, one or the other love, and Merry Christmas, he's yours."

Jule mentioned, thinking November was close enough to spring an early present from Steve and herself.

"You're calling him 'Chess', that's brilliant! He'll learn to play that game well here with the livestock not knowing his next move."

Steve mentioned, congratulating his stepdaughter on her more recent success with one of her Mustangs finding its way into a new home just that very morning.

"When did he ship off? Was he any trouble, or did he just walk right into the trailer like you had hoped?" he asked.

Keegan Tanner's head on a swivel couldn't help herself when she stated that not only had the horse marched into the stall, he was the only bay Mustang that either she or Melora had managed to find a home for. It seemed a little easier to find homes for the sorrels and the chestnut horses. If a horse had to be flashy to be useful than in Keegan's mind only about fifteen out of a hundred horses would ever be useful. She was all about the name of the ranch at this point, saying that more people needed to stop being so concerned about color and pay attention to the horse's eyes if they wanted a good horse to ride.

She wasn't wrong; Melora had not been able to even catch one of the other bays, a mare who simply would not behave herself or allow others in the herd to do so. Armstong was on the verge of calling Gary at the *Bureau* in Pauls Valley to make arrangements to bring him back, before she realized she had purchased the horse through the sales authority, and not through any program. The mare was hers, and she either had to deal with her, sell her, or send her off to someone she felt would more than likely ship the horse to Mexico to be slaughtered.

"Most people don't realize that when you eat a horse that comes from America it could have poison running through it."

Keegan stated bluntly, and seeming out of thin air. She did that, she often just said whatever was on her mind, but if the subject of her outbursts had something to do with horses, you could bet the girl knew what she was talking about.

"You're going to have to explain that one to me."

Spoke Steve, untying the cord around his hoodie jacket to release his head to let it breathe. He had been raking copious mounds of leaves out in the pastures to make piles for the kids to jump in if they chose to do so. He had always loved to do it as a kid, and thought why not bring some of that pure and unabridged joy back to the barn boarders today who couldn't stop staring at their cell phones long enough to give anyone an ounce of attention.

Keegan raised her left eye-brow after hearing Steve's reasoning for raking, before going through the process of what happens when a horse in America has a certain disorder or medical condition requiring it to have insulin shots, antibiotics for this or that injury, or just if it's being shot up with things to make it perform better during shows or races, if the horse has been treated, then it's sold or sent to slaughter through an auction, that horse could potentially poison someone if they ate it.

It was more or less apt to be more serious if a human ate the meat, but it has been the reason that several dogs had died in the past and no one figured it out until they figured it out, and then when the laws went into place for auctions and others to disclose any treatments it didn't do much to detour anyone from simply not disclosing it. Animals and people still got sick, they still died, but unless and until they could point out exactly which horse it was that killed them, there wasn't much anyone could do about it. Facts are facts whether anyone believed them or not.

"Yep! That's another brick in the wall for me!" Jule said.

"She's done it again; I just can't even keep up with this kid. She knows too much. You're not twelve, you're 456 and you have been breeding horses the entire time. What's your secret?" she asked,

"Is it collagen, is that it? Do you bathe in milk? Do you drink lemon water? What are you doing to be so damned smart and so young all at the same time?"

Jule teased Tanner, as the two hugged for the first time in a long time.

"Hey, there is something I need to ask you though; something important." Jule mentioned, as she

stepped back from Keegan to pick up a letter from the corner of her desk in the office.

"I got this letter from my attorney today, it's a follow up to the letter and correspondence your mom sent to me about three maybe four months ago, right after the barn celebration thing in July. Do you remember? Your brother Mitch had done the DNA thing, and was attempting to get some help from the cowboy he believes, well, now he know is his father."

She questioned, waiting for the obligatory nod that Keegan was apt to give while not wanting to say anything out loud. It was a habit she formed when she wasn't sure what she wanted to say.

"Well, this is a form, a letter that can be given to you in a week or so when you turn thirteen. I can let you read it, but you can't sign it yet until you're of legal age according to what was recommended by Dr. Cheney. The psychologist you spoke with last spring and again last month. She has recommended to the courts that you will be mature enough at age thirteen to make your own decision about who you want to live with, but you are also needing to understand that with the decision no one has any right whatsoever to the control of your future estate. I can't help you get it, Melora can't help you get it any sooner. You have exactly five more years and what, two weeks, until you get that money put into a bank account unless you'd rather keep it in a trust and just start living off the

interest. We can give you advice, but we'll wait on that, that's for another day.

"For now, the decision to be made if you even want to make it, is to either stay in the same situation you are in now, living with Melora and having visits to and from your mom, or you can choose to move back in with her, because she said with the boys gone off to college the place gets rather lonely and she could use you there. The other choice, and this one is a big one, one you need to think about really hard, is to allow Melora to adopt you; as her actual child, but again, that would have no bearing on..."

Before she could finish the sentence, Keegan had jumped from the edge of the counter where she had been sitting in the lounge, and into the arms of an unsuspecting Melora Armstrong, who had just walked through the open door of the room.

Knocking the two of them to the ground, Keegan began crying saying she loved Melora more than anything or anyone on the Earth. She wanted *option C*, she called it, the third one. She wanted Melora to be her mom. Jule had a little explaining to do, before giving Keegan the letter, as she hadn't exactly spoken with Melora about the third option, it was something she had thrown out as a potential option to Dr. Cheney and her attorney Anetta Sanders once they had agreed to a Zoom meeting on Halloween afternoon.

It was only a thought, a passing option, but when Larissa Lowell realized that she wasn't going to be able to have any control over the estate even if she housed the child, Anetta had suggested removing the mom as she felt she could be a potential threat to her well-being, and she wanted to give Keegan every chance possible at having a better life now; right up to her eighteenth birthday.

Melora's eyes met those of her mom, questioning the questions that were being asked by Keegan regarding the possibility of it all being more realistic than she could have even imagined. Feeling upset with herself again, and instantly regretting her forward actions before even having a conversation with her daughter about the matter, Jule's heart raced within her chest just before it caught in her throat and she was unable to say a word.

"I choose C. I want Lora!"

Keegan repeated, and with her emphatic insistence Melora's heart leapt completely out of place as well. She hadn't been so needed, so loved, or so wanted in all of her life. The past several months with Keegan by her side training and being someone she could show emotions to, someone to talk things out with, it was more than she had ever had with her own little sister who had always been at odds with her, and who grown to love her, but not in a deep and meaningful way. The word "*Mom*" was a little ominous; it scared her to the core, but she wondered if she could get used to it, or maybe if they just kept it between them; telling the world that maybe Melora was her permanent guardian, maybe that would help.

Keegan Tanner would have nothing of it. Stating that she wanted to go to school and tell the world through her postings as well, that she was being adopted by the best mother in the world, and that when it was all said and done, Melora, *her Lora*, would be a much better parent than she had ever remembered. She believed in her heart of hearts that her dad would have approved and if he were alive now he would be her only parent. She had never felt comfortable, safe, or even cared for under Lowell's care, but with Lora, there was no question.

"Please. Please say you will. I'll sign it on December 2, and I'll stay up past midnight to do it, I'll sign it the second I turn thirteen. You'll be my mom! I can't think of a better birthday present ever!"

She cried, but tried not to choke herself on her own tears.

"Well, it won't be immediate Keegan,"

warned Jule, who by this time, having seen her daughter's face knew she would be absolutely forgiven for being so bold,

"...there's a hearing, and your mom has a chance to try and talk the judge into not letting it happen, but we'll do our best to make sure it does. Again, let me say it clearly, the money will not be a

factor. I don't want you thinking you have to give that to her if you don't live with your mom, OK?"

Keegan's nod was different this time. It was just as silent as the last time, but with her arms so tightly clasped about Melora's neck, she couldn't speak even if she had to.

26

An unexpected flock of Canada geese flew frantically through the wide-open giant metal back door of the blue barn causing quite a stir with both horses and riders. Some riders were dumped to the ground from the rearing of their mounts, while another two or three managed to withstand the interruption. Crissy Harroz had been one of the first to hit the ground, but the buoyant and study six-year-old never let the upset turn her smile into a frown; she was there that day to learn to jump and nothing was going to stand in her way, not even a manic pony who must have felt the world had finally come to an abrupt and panicked end. Crissy stood her ground, picked up the little pink crop whip she had been holding, and thoroughly without hesitating, began disciplining the little Cob mare until she had returned herself to her station and become the obedient mount the little girl required.

"Crissy Harroz!" exclaimed Keegan at the same time the little girl's mother had entered the training circle to be whatever help she could be before realizing her oldest daughter had managed to keep herself and her horse in check.

"That's how you do it, girl. You tell that pony! You don't take guff from her, not now you don't."

Keegan continued to encourage and give respect where she knew respect was deserved. As their training continued, with Keegan being one of the class attendees rather than a trainer this time, Deb Robbins found her way to the back of the now opened circle to find out what she could from Tanner as to why she was walking her horse and not riding it.

"Well Deb..." laughed Keegan, whose smile seemed to beam from one end of the barn to the other,

"Hercules here is basically still pretty wild. I've been on his back a few times, and he's been OK with it, but I don't want to push him in here with all the noise and all the distractions. We're just going to watch, wait, and see what happens. He's pretty chill right now, but last month I couldn't have even dreamed about walking him into this arena with so many people getting lessons. He's doing great. I think he may even end up being a dual horse; both English and Western if I can find a saddle that will fit his high wither; he's a monster up there."

She added before removing her hand from his shoulder, moving back his double-mane of thick flaxen hair to reveal a larger than average bony hump; one of genetic design possibly indicating that he had a bit of the Andalusian horse in his blood.

"Mustangs are mutts you know, they come from specific areas and managed herds. The Bureau of Land Management tries to keep good records on all the major studs on each site, but this guy has a little dance horse in him and if he's naturally interested in becoming a show horse or jumper maybe, that's the route we'll take. I just need to get him desensitized to the sounds, the smells, the people, the energy - - he's learning."

She stated with pride.

"By the time we have our birthday cake next week or so, I'm hoping he'll let me ride long enough to at least take photos of it; I don't like making quick getaways off him when I have my phone on me, so I've not had the guts to carry it, but I'm hoping when we do a little more of this stuff he'll get the idea and realize we're not all out there trying to eat him."

Deb laughed at her younger friend, saying she hoped turning the *Big 13* didn't hurt much. It was after all, the next really big step for a kid. Deb couldn't help but remember a time when she was Keegan's age when she too wanted nothing more than to be given a horse for her birthday; and it was probably either her 12th or 13th. Sandra Robbins, a single mom trying her best to make the ends at least pretend to come together, worked two jobs, one of which was that of an adjunct professor at Oklahoma City Community College on the south side of Oklahoma City. Just making the drive from the barn to go to work or come from it to pick Deb up took nearly an hour when traffic was heavy. Deb knew the sacrifices her mother made and appreciated every one of them. Having her own car meant the world to the girl, even if she couldn't pull a trailer with her Honda.

From the front of the line, closing in on the back end, Melora Armstrong followed Paul Abernathy's instructions to the letter. His involvement that morning was perhaps his last, and he wanted to find a replacement if possible. Feeling that Shaina Cleveland or Amber Pickett had been most likely to take over, he began allowing them the freedom to make choices and lead the next steps of the training. Since Shaina would be picked up sooner than later by her longtime boyfriend De'Shawn, Amber was given the task to lead the next session. De'Shawn came early on some days to watch his girl giving lessons and looking as commanding as she did. Wearing her high-knee boots, her hair pulled up into her helmet, and that crop whip firmly swishing in her less dominant hand gave him chills. He was a hard-working student as well; seeing Shaina in her element gave him something to smile about, she was his life's highlight for sure.

Melora's phone rang just as Amber's request for her to step forward and try to align herself and her horse with the others.

"Sorry, no disrespect, I promise." Stated the pupil,

"...but I have to get this call, it's John Wilson, the singer from Scotland whose coming over to do the show next summer. He's...well, no disrespect, I have to take the call."

With that she left the circle as well as the barn, talking to John, letting him know that she was choosing to whisper so as not to disturb the next instruction from Amber Pickett to the others.

To her surprise, John Wilson hadn't been calling from Scotland, but from Dallas, where he had been playing for the past few days and recording a few tracks for several other Christian artists who had requested his accompaniment when they had booked their sessions. Popular as he was with other studio artists, he was a foreigner, whose presence in the United States required a work visa from time to time. He had mentioned to Melora last spring that he had missed out on being there for the wedding and reception because of it, but wanted to let her know that the reinstatement of his documents meant that he could book the 4th of July gig now if she was willing to have him, and if he and she could agree that he wouldn't accept any actual payment. He would be happy to open his guitar case for any charitable contributions; but his gift to Jule and Steve, he said, was to play well and give them the set he had wanted to play when they had first exchanged their vows.

All is well, Melora let the singer know, before handing the phone to her mother with a quick update on the situation with Hercules and Keegan being in the crowded busy arena. Jule's eyebrows lifted, her lips forming an *"O"* to show her shock and amusement at the same time, before thanking John for being so patient. Their conversation lasted a little over fifteen minutes; long enough for her to go over the plans she was creating for both the 4th of July party and to invite the man to the barn if he were coming up to Oklahoma on his way out of the southern states before heading off to New York where he had planned the end of his *"American Tour"* at Central Park and just outside Battery Park where he had previously opened his case and come out with over two thousand U.S. Dollars on his way to Dallas to begin the two-city *"tour"*.

Wilson liked to tell the people back in Scotland that he was going on tour so that he could feel that much more important when he needed to give himself a boost. He had battled a bit in the past with low self-esteem. His counselors had assured him, as well as his mother's insistence as well, that saying he was on tour couldn't hurt, and could only help. His daughters volunteered unsuccessfully, to be his personal assistants.

"I cood make a trip up if you had a whee to bring me bawk so I cood fly oot in a cupple of days."

He stated, knowing that he never had to actually ask permission.

"Good!" Jule explained, saying Rogan was at the USO just by the section of the DFW airport where the soldiers gathered for gaming and recreation before flying in or out of the airport.

"He's at B11 inside the airport now, I'll call him and have him meet you wherever you need him to be. He was planning on coming back to Norman, where he lives, anyway. He can bring you up. If he doesn't I won't make him Pop's Stew tonight like I promised. He'll bring you. He'll drive to Houston to pick you up if he thinks I'll make him a vat of the stuff. You can stay here if you want in the lounge; one of the couch's folds out. There's a shower, a water closet as you call it, and a little kitchen to boot....to boot, that's another American thing. I keep forgetting you probably only pick up eighty-four percent of what we say over on this side of the pond." She laughed.

"It's nae you, I assure you, it's me." He explained.

"I'll start talkin' an' sayin' things an' nae one understands me. It's enough for me to stop an' try an' speak a bit slewer, but it's nae tha', it's the words I uss.

311

I pull out a word we uss to say something, joost wonderin' why they're starin' at me. It finally hits me an' I hove a good laugh on mysef before tryin' to think of the bet-er way to explain what I need to say."

John's accent could send Jule into a tailspin. It didn't matter if she was married, she fell in love every time the man spoke. It was fair to say however, that if Stephen Mueller could ever grasp the rolling of his tongue to the point that he said words like *"praa-eer"* for *"prayer"* or *"nae"* for *"no"* and oh, when John said *"tu-maud-row"* it just went through her.

Mentally slapping herself, and forcing her eyes to open, so she could pull herself out from the fantasy she was creating, she managed to end the conversation by letting John know he would be forever welcome, she would put out the word that he'd be playing at the barn the next day for two separate sessions, and though entry would be free to anyone and everyone, donations would be welcomed, if not actually expected. Giving back to the humbled songsmith for all he did was an easy task to undertake.

No one felt the same after hearing him sing his own songs as well as the old gospel hymns he had bridged with a some of the most amazing lyrics and riffs. He was in deed a master; a very humbled master in fact, who hadn't quite made the connection that his value and worth outshone his current choice of occupation. Jule felt if he had the right promoter, John Wilson's name would be a household word, but then again, John Wilson aptly mentioned at least once before, that the limelight wasn't where he ever hoped to shine. He was content in his work; quiet and humbled as it was.

Keegan walked her mount out of the blue barn and through the corridors of it to again desensitize him and let him understand that there were more things to life than just being out in the pastures watching the other Mustangs. Cars were a real thing. Trucks and trailers weren't all that scary and he'd soon need to be able to withstand all of the strange and bewildering sensations. Their engines and their diesel smells, if he was going to be hauled and driven all over the freaking countryside, would need to be recognized, as well as accepted. While his ears perked at every new sound, his eyes fixated on anything he couldn't immediately understand. Walking him in and out of the two barns, past people, past moving and stationary vehicles, as well as letting Herc sniff and strike at whatever he thought he needed to within reason, Keegan herself became aware of something being discussed privately; she could only hear whispers.

Taking the time to seem nonchalant and completely uninterested in what she surmised was more important than not, the girl lingered in the door of the blue barn a few minutes before taking Herc to be tied up outside the office. Walking into Jule's private space and closing the door behind her, she asked.

"Did you hear about Leslie Merriweather's son?"

asked Tanner, maybe a little too excited, before pulling the door completely, to give the latest bit of rumor to the Armstrongs while glancing out the window to be sure her horse was still standing still enough to not be worried about.

"Dean Stovich and him, Andy, Andrew, I can't remember, I think she may even call him Drew, but anyway, they were arrested." She stumbled over her own words.

"Well, Drew was arrested and then Dean was questioned because Dean said he and Chase went back to the High Five the day after the fire and they found something that belonged to Drew from years ago; it was his high school rodeo buckle. He had given it to Jodi Williams. She had it on her the night she was here when she died, she called someone and said it would be at the barn. She took it off before she left the lounge and laid it on the shelf there..."

Tanner pointed to the shelf on the wall just inside of the door leading to the lounge.

"She left it right there and then the next day it was gone or at least I didn't see it and everyone was thinking I took it. I didn't take it!" she promised.

Jule questioned Keegan with the same eagle-eyed squint she would have given to Melora, Rogan, or

Brooke if they had withheld such important information about having seen Jodi set a buckle down on the night she was murdered. She couldn't imagine what Mansfield or even Steve would say about it; but she knew she needed to drill the kid a bit further before she lost all of her enthusiasm.

"But there it was at the High Five in the dirt and Dean had been there with Bree she said before asking Drew what she wanted him to do." Keegan blurted.

"Who? Who asked Drew what to do?" Jule questioned.

"Leslie Merriweather, Drew's mom. She didn't know if Drew was at the fire or if he was with Jodi; she was asking him what he wanted her to do because he's in custody now and his mom is about to die. She's in the arena now, getting off the phone with him. I heard him tell her to say he was at her house that night, both nights, but really he was with Kurt Banderoff when Jodi was killed."

Keegan stated, before turning and exiting the office to back her horse up from getting too close to glass windows.

"Wait, Keegan, this is what, happening right now? In real time? Did you say Leslie is on the phone with Drew now?" asked Jule, now standing on the patio of the office.

"How do you know that? Could you hear them talking?" She wondering, knowing that very little that

315

happened anywhere near the barn got past the ears or eyes of Keegan Tanner. Did Leslie have the phone on speaker? How could Keegan '*hear*' what Drew said to his mom otherwise?

If the buckle had anything to do with Jodi's murder, and Drew was asking for an alibi, then yeah, something was up; something she felt she needed to inform Steve about. Had Jodi broken up with Drew? Was that it? Was he the father of her unknown baby? He was at least in his mid-thirties if not older. There hadn't been any real talk about it, but Jule could put two and two together. Maybe Jodi wasn't with Tucker Banderoff at all, maybe all this time she was with his dad's cousin Drew Merriweather.

If Drew had been with Kurt Banderoff the night of the murder riding around in Kurt's truck, and the dogs were hitting on the truck, maybe they were hitting on Drew as well. Mansfield kept everything close to the breast regarding what the dogs had found. Leslie's son hadn't been on the premises at least as long as she had owned it, but that didn't mean anything. He could have been at the BSO with his mom or with Banderoff since Kurt's own son Tucker was a boarder in the past. Drew's picture was up on the walls at the Red Feather Tack and Feed Store for being employee of the month a few times. He was well known and well liked; maybe a little too liked by some the younger girls.

Murders, suicides, middle-aged men getting younger girls pregnant. It was all just a bit too much right now, thought Armstrong-Mueller, deciding in her head to go ahead with the name change as Steve had asked her to do; even if it meant redesigning the front and back cover of her books moving forward. She hadn't always been too keen on being too traditional. When she married the girl's father, Lance Beall, he had insisted on her changing her name, which is one reason she decided not to. He remained a Beall, she remained an Armstrong. Nearly every day following their nuptials, Jule had regretted her hasty decision to marry her neighbor, a man she knew but didn't love; but everyone kept harping on her that Rogan would need a good father figure. He would be lost without a man in his life; they insisted. Damn, how she hated herself for listening to them.

Rogan's father had never been concerned about what she called herself as long as the two of them were joined at the hip and would never be separated. Their marriage took place at the county court house a week before he shipped off to the Gulf to take his place in formation to protect them all. He never returned; they married to give him a sense of purpose, something to come back to when the war ended. Rogan's appearance though a surprise to her, had been a blessing she had God to thank for; he was her promise of a new life. Joy would be restored through the deepest of sorrows.

"I don't want to seem harsh, mean, or nasty, Steve, but you know you can take my name too, if you

want. We can be non-traditionalists and both be hyphenated."

She suggested, but in doing so reaped what she knew would be a tilt of his eyes, and a lowering of his reading glasses with that crooked smile of his. He laughed a little, made a face resembling that of a Christmas elf who had just been asked to change the order of some kid he was creating something very special for, before mentioning he had plans for them both; she'd just have to wait and see what they may be.

"*Oh, Jules. I almost forgot,*" the man said, popping the top off a Fanta orange soda; his favorite among favorites in deed.

"*Angie whatshername, the woman who bought all the tractor equipment, the tiller, and harvester pieces, remember her?*" he asked,

"*She's was caught red-handed; speaking of murder.*"

Jule stepped back at his words, they had seemed so carefree, so nonchalant in fact, almost callous.

"*She's not really murdering, I mean, she's possibly allowing them to die, but she's been arrested and charged in Logan as well as Lincoln counties with several charges of animal cruelty. She's been selling live animals as grade when they have papers, and then finding carcasses or using dead horses on her farm and others who she purports to haul off to bury* somewhere. She took the dead horses and claimed they were the horses with papers. She photographed them before she cremated their remains, and then filed for the insurance coverage. The insurance guys finally caught onto her and staged a pick up either in Guthrie or Coyle, I can't remember where, but one horse was from Coyle. Mom told me."

He continued.

"When Angie and her boyfriend Donny were caught she claimed to not even own the more than 600 acres out between Luther and Wellston somewhere. She says she only leased the property from horsewoman Linda Perleston; the one who owns all the good thoroughbreds in the world it seems. Angie subleases the property, and I guess with Linda's permission, I don't know.

"She leases it to hay growers and cattlemen who pay her to leave their livestock. She feeds the animals for more money and lets them know when the animals need vet care. Turns out a horse or two died that were left out there and she then turned around and tried to pick up the insurance on a few horses that she claims she owns...Perleston owns them, I'm sure. She had to be forging Linda's name as well, I guess.

"Maybe she got greedy, maybe too many thoroughbreds died too close to the same day, I don't know, but Radner Race track out east has a few shady characters literally giving away papered horses that don't show, place, or win. It's a gambit; we're in the *wrong business woman! We could be hanging out at the horse retirement homes, pull up with the trailer, drag off a few bones and give them fancy papers so we can get paid the windfall ourselves."*

He chuckled to her, doing his best to stand up and buckle the side of his new kilt; one he knew would turn a few smiles later that evening.

"I picked this one on Amazon. It's not real, but it'll work for now. Do you like it?"

He asked, swishing his hips from side to side to let the pleats open and fly about his thighs. Jule had already started to unbuckle the garment while he finished telling her about the woman she never really cared to meet, who had seemed to never keep a rule or follow an order if it didn't seem to suit her needs. It didn't surprise Jule that Angie Banner had been behind more than just wanting to till the ground to plant something.

Bending over to show her he could flex his upper back muscles repeatedly and only a little obnoxiously, while tying his black boot, he cooed to her,

"Oh...sweetness, I'm practicing my Scottish accent. I want to be able to sweep you off your feet and throw you into the hay out there in the barn tonight so we can have a really good romp of it."

He managed to get out before laughing and spitting his way through a few attempts at saying words he felt would send her to the next realm.

"You know, Mr. Armstrong-Mueller, if you wanted to, you could also wear or not wear that little hunter kilt of yours tonight when you're lifting me off the ground where I'll be, looking straight up the pleats and folds of it to see what all I can see."

Her words tapered off before he kissed her and gave her another reason to say she was his; all his. Jule closed her eyes and whispered to her lover, *"Say tu-maud-row"*.

27

Before they pulled into the driveway of the house shared by Melora and Keegan, Rogan Armstrong informed his Scottish companion that the food would not only knock his argyle socks off, but they'd have a go at untying his dirty black boots as well. *Pop's Stew* was something to be framed if it were a painting. It was something to behold both by sight, and by smell, but when a man dipped his spoon into it, and drew out the soupy goodness of the mashup of hamburger balls, chunked potatoes, corn, peas, and mushrooms, maybe some carrots, all swimming in the thick and rich juiciness of the tomato-based spicy peppered soup; there was nothing on the Earth that could pull a man away from the table; nothing on Earth.

"If my Pop himself called an audible and came down from Heaven and told me my time was up, that I had to go with him then and there, I'd tell him he had

to wait. Mom makes Pop's Stew just as good as he ever did, and to be even more on point, since Brooke and her family are in the huddle tonight to meet you, she's making the cornbread. Mom won't take a knee and put sugar in her own cornbread, that's why we all stand around waiting for the two-minute warning for Brooke's skillet to come out of the oven, and not Mom's.

"If Brooke's here and I see Braydon's SUV now; you know she's got the ball and she's making cornbread. It's her way of kicking it into overtime, and sticking it to Mom when she can. That, her potato salad and her deviled eggs will stop the clock. Mom will even punt to the 'little one' as we still call her, when it comes to those three sides; but yeah, Mom has the game won. She doesn't mind if her opponent scores or even if she comes close, but she'll get the last field goal every time....game over. Let the crowd roar."

He animated while the Scotsman simply stared at him trying to figure out what he meant exactly.

When everyone was gathered it was typical for the gossip to fly, so Brooke's husband Braydon Stark, a massive six-foot five man carrying a full face of bearded glory, started things off by asking if they had arrested anyone in the murder case. Not really understanding that the body had been found on the very property he was visiting, John Wilson nearly choked on his first bite of stew, before apologizing and then again sharing a stare with Rogan to say he was right about it. Nothing could pull him away at that moment, he wanted to hear the whole mess. Buttering his first slice of cornbread before being shown by Ariel just how to dip it into the soup part of the meal, John's eyes fell to whomever had a bit more to add to the story at hand.

"We'll get to the case in a minute. We're also making plans to go back to Texas this week to go to the Dowd auction, so if you wanted to wait a day or two before you go back to Scotland John, we can take you there as well. The auction has been in the Dowd family for at least four generations, but the man who owns it now is a cousin or an uncle, and he's right out of Dublin.

"He's the new owner, but most of the workers and employees remained with him. Some of them have been in the same job or job set for over thirty, thirty-five years. They buy horses from other auctions assess them, and resell them. They also take in donated horses that the owners don't want to send off to slaughter and the assess those and sell them to people for much less than they could get online through an ad or through a vet's office.

"If you've never been to an authentic cowboy auction you'll love it. They start off with selling tack and equipment, we won't bother with that, but while they are selling that stuff Melora and I, and you guys too, if you want to go..."

stated Jule, looking around the table at the rest of her family, before continuing,

"...we look at the inventory, go through it with the sheet they give you that explains each 'hip' or number, and you take notes. You write out what you want to know about that horse, or maybe you do what I do, strike through the number and only circle the ones you're willing to actually consider. If you don't do that, there'll be over 400 horses to write notes about. I typically find six to ten that I would put a bid on, and Melora is only interested in the Mustangs. Since most auctions don't have Mustangs, she usually ends up going through the pens to see if I missed something. I tend to miss a lot because I'm not really buying these days."

She explained, as Melora and Keegan both jumped up to add their two cents about what they thought would be a great idea. Both wanted to blurt more, but Melora, being a bit more mature gave her *"talking stick privileges"* to Keegan for the time being.

"We think", giving a full emphasis on the word 'We', *"...that Jule should get a lot of horses and resell them, but only the good ones. You can get a horse for just two or three hundred dollars while they do the free runs, and if no one bids on them Dowd keeps them and then sells them the next week for something like a $1000 if he or his nephew ride them even for a minute to see if the horse is sound. They're good about not saying they're broke, but they lie all the time when it comes to whether a horse is broke broke or just green broke. If it's just been sat on it's not even green, it's just been sat on, but they'll say it's green to sell it for more.*

I hate that, especially after what we saw today with Crissy being thrown by Little Lady."

Keegan half-way mentioned to the shocked face of the insurance-paying barn owner who suddenly began ringing up enormous premiums in her head for no reason at all.

"Mom, there are literally signs all over the barn with the Oklahoma statutes clearly marked on them stating you are not responsible for any injuries occurring at this or any barn unless you or the barn was personally negligent, and we were not. The horse is her horse, it is not your horse, and when the geese flew into the barn Little Lady decided she was their next meal. She only took a hop anyway, and what was it, two or three feet, she's only 11 hands tall Mom, Crissy is fine."

Melora's words coming in for the landing just as John's last gulp of soupy stew was consumed and Rogan seemed to automatically understand the need to fill up his guest's bowl.

"Do you joost buy the horses an' they're delivered?" asked the singer.

"No, no, that's not how it works exactly. I have to take the trailer down with me if I think I'm going to buy something. I wouldn't want to count on someone from the auction bringing them to me. They charge about $400 now to drop a horse this far from that part of the world. When you drive to or from the airport

you see an exit that says I-35E and I-35W, it's like a little fork there, and if you take the East exit you end up in Denton, but if you take the West exit you end up in Corral City. That's where Dowd's is; just outside of it I guess. Not all roads have names down that way. I'd say you pass a few Sonics but that may not make a lot of sense to you." Jule laughed.

"You see, whatcha do is..." teased Brooke using her best backwoods hillbilly accent, *"...is you hunker down a bit in your seat cause you're gonna be there a minute. You pass the first Dolla' Generill and hang a Louie for about a mile, then you pass the other Dolla' Generill and do the same. When you hit the Braum's you stop and get something, but you keep going. They have good bathrooms too, so you can take advantage of that. Before you make it to the third Dolla' Generill you want to veer right and pass the second red barn, but remember it's been painted green since they sold it back in '99. We still say the red barn down here in these parts."*

Her banter had reached its mark, and John Wilson began to nod while stuffing his third deviled egg in his mouth.

"You won't go hungry here John, that's for sure." Rogan said, as he opened the lower half of the oversized stainless-steel freezer, exposing several half-gallon containers of this favorite after meal delight.

"Speaking of ice cream, which we did when we were talking about Braum's, I see pecan brittle, sea-

salt cashew swirl, chocolate chip, and vanilla, but wait..."

his pretense of an over exaggerated scowling face turned suddenly. Rogan closed one eye to give the evil one to his older little sister,

"Who the hell bought Bryers f-ing vanilla ice cream, and then brought it into our house?"

Rogan questioned with half his mind laughing, and the other half being genuinely curious.

"This is a Braum's family. We are now, and have always been a Braum's family. Is there any reason under the gloriously shining Sun that we could, should, or would lower our standard of ice cream and buy Bryers? I need answers!" he jokingly demanded while John Wilson tried to reason within his mind why such an offense would be taken over the purchase of ice cream.

"Brother, if it's your house you can pay the mortgage."

Sassed Melora, before high-fiving her adopted child and making the bold and unheralded comment that her own daughter had been the guilty one, not realizing that the Armstrongs had literally been raised only a mile from the Braum's factory at one point in their lives.

"She'll not need to apologize, as we're going to take this opportunity to give time and experience a

chance to see if in deed Braum's is still the only choice for our extended and immediate families."

She tried before reaping the animated and overly exaggerated wrath of her older sibling. Reaching around her throat, he pretended with great enthusiasm, something akin to professional wrestling on television, to break off his sister's head and use it as an imaginary bowling ball.

"*Never!*" he proclaimed before retrieving the faked head piece and returning it to the hypothetically detached body from whence it came. Telling him he could dream all he wanted to, but her head was squarely in place and that it would always remain strong, Melora poked Rogan in his side reminding him of the times he and she fought over who controlled the remote; a contest he believed she sorely remembered.

While they ate their dessert and quibbled needlessly over the vast and minor differences between the two brands of frozen dairy delights, Steve turned to Rogan to ask him if he had found anyone to go over the dreams Jule's son had been having; the dreams that were literally keeping him up at night lately.

"*No, not really. When I was in the USO today I met with Doc. Garcia again, he goes up there if he knows I'm coming. He told me it was more or less a condition that keeps Joes up from time to time, but I can't figure out why I see carousel horses leaving the stand and running into clouds before becoming those clouds. It's not scary, I'm not having like nightmares or anything, but the horses are white most of the time, some are grey, but they're made out of air and water or something that isn't flesh. They're going around and round without poles in their backs, but they all seem to run off the stage or platform at the same time, some of them in line, but others going in different directions. They're just leaving; not hurting themselves or anyone. Doc says it's a PTSD thing."*

He finished. As he did his eyes met with Keegan Tanner who had begun imagining the same type of scene in her own mind, trying to catch the wayward beasts, but realizing they would disappear as she grasped each one.

"Maybe they're just things in your past, but not bad things. They're just stuff, or stories, or life, or something that you did or didn't do. You can't control that, you can't get them back, and you can't detain them when they decide to go. Once one goes they all go, and then you're left with the big pretty platform, and maybe the music."

Her words began to loosen and she began to freely explain what she was thinking. As she did John's mind thought of ways he could capture her words, thoughts and meaning into lyrics, while Jule wondered if she too could be inspired by them; if she could write a story in one of her new books where something like this very conversation would take place.

"At least we know you don't suffer from Equinophobia."

Mentioned the girl, who then had to explain that the word was something she had picked up from watching Animal Planet; it meant being afraid of horses.

"Bull chips!" Rogan exclaimed.

"I think the dream means I need to go hunting with Teagan and his wife next week; it's rifle time, we put the bows away last week. He's tagging in so I can pick up another one. I've got one doe so far, and I am hoping for a good-sized buck this week. If you want to join me you can."

He said, turning to Braydon before turning to Wilson, who by now had been wondering how a twelve-year-old girl knew so much. His own daughters, twins, back in Edinburgh, were just turning nine. They liked horses, he told Keegan, but listening to her go on about husbandry for the animals, and the training required to bring a Mustang to the point of being tame enough to ride and discipline just kept his mind hopping. He hoped by relating the stories to his girls he wouldn't be stepping into an enormous future expense, but he did want to bring them to the barn over the next summer *"tour"* when he'd plan to do more studio work, so he could join the Armstrongs and now the Armstrong-Muellers with their soon-to-be annual charity events hosted right there at the Bay Sorrel Ranch.

"When you bring them, Herc will be broke, but I'm not going to let them on him. He'll still be pretty new at taking riders, and I don't want them getting hurt. Maybe Jule can pick up an older horse this trip to Dowds and we can sell off the others for profit. I don't mind working them, it's all practice for me. I just want to work horses that have been worked a bit already. Mustangs are harder than I thought they would be."

She admitted before adding,

"But it's nothing I can't handle. I like it. I mean, I really do love it. Herc means the world to me, and can you pass me that last piece of cornbread? I want to shut up now and the only way I can do that is to eat something."

With that sort of an abstract statement coming from the child, they all laughed.

28

It took her a minute to fully grasp what all Chief Mansfield was saying. It could have been because of the time change between Scotland and Oklahoma, and when the law officer placed his call to her at 5:15 p.m. his time, he reached her after she and Steve had turned in for the night after a very long and turbulent series of flights with layovers, unexpected changes and the obligatory loss of one of her suitcases. This time, the one lost was the most needed, so the mood the officer found Jule in wasn't necessarily the one she would have preferred to display under the circumstances. She had been in the old country less than two hours and was fielding the Chief's latest call.

"You're saying you have news, and some of it is good, I hear you, but you mentioned the crime scene being described as brutal, ugly, and vicious at the same time. From what I remember, it was rather

contained, in fact Chief, even the crime lab mentioned to me that they hadn't seen a less bloodied body given the fact that she must have been bludgeoned by something pretty hard; like a baseball bat or what they said could have been a tire arm. Is the media trying to say it was brutal?

"Can you tell me what the good news is, please? I'm not really up to discuss the scene because, like I said, I owned the ranch only a few days when she was killed. My daughter Melora was the one who found her. It wasn't brutal and messy, I don't like that, it makes the ranch seem like a..."

As Jule sat up on her elbow to get let her lungs take in a bit more air, she asked, *"What's the good news?"*

Turning from one monitor on his desk to the other, the Chief of police opened up a couple of windows he had resting at the bottom of the screen to reveal information pertaining to the ranch and any responsibility Jule Armstrong-Mueller may carry over the entire ordeal. Mentioning that the law is clear that any accident or incident taking place on anyone's personal or business property would automatically bring about the need to consider a strict liability case from the point of view of the victim's family, Chief Mansfield mentioned that the abstract and title of the property hadn't technically been assigned to Jule until the fourth of the following month. The land or pastures portion of the property had not been inspected though the box on the form appeared to have been checked.

"What I'm saying is, the land portion of your property, where the murder took place was not under your ownership at the time of the occurrence. You won't be liable to her folks for any other damages. They'll have to seek any wrongful death case with us, with the county or even the state. It would not affect you in any way, that's the good news. The bad news, and I don't even know if you can call it that, is that we have made an arrest based on the finding of the gold belt buckle that was at one point in Jodi William's possession.

"When we got the buckle from Dean Stovich he said it suddenly appeared on the ground in front of him and Chase Finley. He said he had seen the thing before on Jodi's belt. He had asked her about it, but she wouldn't give him an answer. The buckle says 'Best All-Round 2005'. If that's a high school 2005 buckle, that puts the owner of that thing somewhere between thirty-four and thirty-seven years old now. Williams was seventeen, still underaged for somethings, but not for consensual sex if she's close enough to eighteen, which she was; no judge in the state is going to put a man behind bars for that if the girl is apt to do things she maybe aught not do.

Mansfield paused a second or two, waiting for Jule to say something. When she didn't, he continued.

"We think another person was on the premises that night, probably hiding in a stall or something hoping the fire would burn and the buckle would be found. Someone wanted to blame the Merriweather man, Andrew Bishop Merriweather. Do you know him? Do you know anyone who would hate him enough to frame him for arson?"

asked the Chief. *"And if you do, do you have any idea what the buckle has to do with it?"*

She thought long and hard about what he said about responsibility, and realized that anything she would tell him would only be hearsay; not only hearsay, but hearsay repeated by an actual minor who was somewhat ease dropping on a private or privileged telephone conversation presumably between Drew Merriweather and his mother. Nothing she could add could benefit anyone, and it could be considered prejudice if the case ever went to trial. She would be called in a witness of some sort; and because of it she only stated that she had heard that there was a buckle, that Jodi may have set it to the side that night, but she didn't see it, and she had no actual knowledge of it.

As for her knowing Drew Merriweather, Jule stated to the Chief that she had only spoken to Leslie, his mother, about him, because their sons were roughly the same age. She had never actually met the man. Pulling at the sheets to bring them a little closer to her, she spoke into the phone to alert the Chief as to where she was at the present time, and that with the time difference of six hours, he was calling her at a time that was inconvenient after such a long or in-depth conversation. She excused herself and tried to rest, but her thoughts on the entire event seemed to wrap themselves around every neuron in her brain.

There was no way of knowing it could take place. There was no way of knowing that it would or even did take place until she was alerted, and when she was alerted her first instincts were to find the girl. In doing that, she may have compromised every piece of solid evidence available; how could she not feel responsible to the family of a sweet and innocent kid who may have found herself mixed up with the wrong set of people, and in more trouble that she could have ever imagined? Jule had to find a way to distance herself from it all if she wanted to remain positive and move forward.

Mansfield mentioned that he knew that Drew Merriweather had been either with Banderoff the night of the murder or he had been with him earlier in the day. In fact, the Chief mentioned something else; that the new CCTV public camera on Covell Road had placed Drew's truck pulling into the back part of the south barns of Bay Sorrel on the day Jodi was reported missing. He didn't come from the Big House, but from the road to the east.

Also, DNA from saliva most likely coming in the form of a bottle somewhat full of tobacco spit, had been found in Kurt's truck. The men were related; but they knew the spit belonged to Drew as Kurt was tobacco free. Through a sworn affidavit Banderoff stated he had carried Drew about town that day as well as the days after because Merriweather's truck was in the shop. Kurt had picked him up at the feed store, they'd gone to dinner, watched a movie, then went driving around. He denied being anywhere near the barn that night.

Maybe Drew wanted his buckle back; that could have been a reason for them stopping at the ranch that night, but it felt like more. Banderoff wasn't telling the full truth and Jule knew it. He may have been upset with the girl after he found out she was cheating on his son with his own cousin. It could be that she was really was going to pay him to reinstate her insurance, but not with cold hard cash. Whatever the reason for the two men being on the property that night, no one had seen them pulling up and no one had seen either of them coming into the lounge to retrieve the belt ornament. Keegan had been awake; she would have remembered. Perhaps, asked Mansfield, he could talk to Keegan again to see if she had forgotten anything she had reported when they last interviewed her.

Because she knew her daughter, Jule mentioned that Keegan's legal guardian would never allow her to be interviewed again under those circumstances. The whole matter was trying for the girl after her father's death had been so sudden just a few years back. Jule knew Keegan was sleeping in the lounge that night; perhaps the cousins had seen her as well, and decided not to go in to retrieve the buckle.

Jule asked if the buckle had been fingerprinted and if so whose prints were on it. The Chief told her that information was being held tightly by police, and would not be shared. They found something; they were just tying up ends. It was obvious. Maybe it was just about to end.

"Well then, I guess I can't share more with you at this time either, Chief Mansfield. It's impossible for me to say what Keegan remembers or doesn't remember, but she'll not be questioned again unless there is a real need. If she saw it or didn't see it, wouldn't matter. Those fingerprints matter. If hers are on the buckle you have reason to talk to her. If they are not, well, you don't. She's a minor. She's been through it. She may or may not recall what you may or may not want her to recall. She gave you her statement and I believe it will have to stand."

Voiced the protector before ending the call as cordially as her tired eyes and body would allow her to do.

Squeezing her husband from behind, she closed her eyes as a soft warm tear began to well up involuntarily for Jodi. Whispering a prayer, she thanked God for not only protecting her, but for protecting her children; her son while he was at war, her daughters while they raised families and trained wild animals. The chances of one of her children ending up dead seemed just as likely if not more than with the Williams family; mourning someone's child didn't seem too far out of the question as she tried to rest and let the jet lag take her into oblivion. It may have only been 5:15 p.m. her time in her body and mind, but the day had started over twenty hours beforehand. The woman was exhausted.

With the production of yet another new book underway, and a two-week research trip now officially starting, all Jule wanted to do or think about was where she could take her new husband to show him literally everything she loved about the country of Scotland, and the cities of Edinburgh, Stirling, Melrose, Inverkeithing, and beyond. Most of her Highland romance novels were just that, novels that took place in the Highlands of Scotland. The new book she hoped would bring about an awareness of the isles out west, the very isolated areas where just about anything could happen.

There she could fully showcase the grand and glorious scenery of yesteryear, the ones that still for the most part, remains untouched in many ways. It wasn't the same for most of the states within the United States. With each new century, and then each following decade the infrastructures leading from one area or state to the next went through constant change. Nothing from their beginnings remained unless someone made their way clear up to the tops of the highest of peaks; but even looking down from them the observer was apt to see a Winn Dixie store, a Dollar General sign, or something disrupting the pristine beauty of her homeland.

This new book, her 9th, would focus on the lives of several citizens whose lives centered around the old capital city of their land; in and around the burns and bridges leading the more rural clan associates into the various worlds of law, commerce. She hoped the new book would naturally branch out again to the ends of the thistled lands, into the 10th, 11th and even her 12th book of the *Tartaned* series. They would eventually bring about a close to the saga somewhere in the late 19th century, just about the time Queen Victoria and Prince Albert's oldest son Edward VII, who was known as *"Bertie"*, was on the throne. It was never Jule's intention to create a series, but the flow and progress from one to the other seemed to take on a life of its own.

When she thought about it, the books had been her means of escaping her reality; why had she then, in her own reasoning, chosen to settle in and buy a larger piece of property that would lend itself to eventually shackle her to the very thing she wished to avoid? Bay Sorrel Ranch brought stability to her; she knew that. Owning land, owning property allowed her to diversify her income for tax reasoning, but what purpose does that serve if she felt buckled in, trapped or unable to spread her creative wings to fly? She knew she hadn't written a single chapter of the next sequel during the phrase while she looked for land to buy, settled on one, moved from her condo to be closer to it, only to move again to get out from under part of it. It had been busy work, busy time, busy everything, but not a single page had come from it; that was the real problem in her mind. Not a single real joy had been found in trying to create what she thought she needed.

The barn however, had prompted her to move from Norman, and in doing so she had asked Steve to help her. This was the catalyst she needed to start and engage in the next best chapter of her real life. Not everything about buying a ranch had turned out gloomy and disparaging. *"I'll count my blessings."* She told herself. When she had been caught being disobedient as a child, her grandmother would give her a choice; she could either be spanked with a switch that she herself would have to go find out in the yard, or she could sit at the big oak kitchen table and write out as many blessings as she could come up with. If she couldn't find at least fifty things to be thankful for, she would have been given the remaining number in switches. It didn't take long for the little girl to dig really deeply into her mind and heart to come up with good things that she could be thankful for.

Laying there with Steve beside her; knowing he could have been there her entire adult life, Jule took in a long and deep breath through her nose before blowing it out her mouth, just being thankful for all she had now, for the way things turned out, and for how they were going to turn out in the future. She saw herself as a positive more outgoing person; but over the past year or two she had either intentionally or unintentionally wrapped herself into a self-contained cocoon of sorts. She may be morphing, but into what, she asked. She knew the books were popular, but was popular what she had wanted. Remembering John Wilson's words about being content, being humble, being closer to his God and to his soul by not being well-known made a lot of sense.

29

As time does, it passes, and things become more intricately woven with each hour, with each day, with each week, and month. Discussions about the future charity events began to take place with riders and boarders changing from time to time, and with updates regarding both competitions and events either involving some of those who counted themselves among the few who had been chosen to continue boarding at the little ranch most referred to still as the "*Old BSO*"; the ranch in the corner of the counties.

Another academic year had come to a close in Oklahoma, bringing with it the heat and humid season of late spring. With her fourth round of Mustangs to train, most of which she had purchased at Dowd's rather than taking the harder to train stock from the Bureau of Land Management through their sale authority program. Melora leaned heavily on Keegan to start the morning off as she normally did with them both drinking copious amounts of coffee mixed equally with *half and half* and large dumps of sugar. If she had her way, Keegan Tanner would have resorted to plopping chunks of thick heavy sugar cubes into each cup just to see the splash she could make in doing so. After her tenth or sixtieth show of just how much of a mess she could make, the cubes were mysteriously replaced with a pink and white canister with a pour top. Not nearly as much fun, but the result in taste was virtually the same.

Walking to the dining room windows Keegan threw open each curtain before twisting and untwisting the long rod handles causing light from outside to shine through the massive wooden blinds. If there was one chore the girl thoroughly enjoyed, it was to welcome the Sun into her life before starting out to feed the horses. She rarely felt so strong and energized in the winter months due to the timing of the rising of the Sun, but in spring, she knew she could be awakened by the first lights and still have a full day of riding and working the horses ahead of her, right after she fed Chess and took him for his morning run.

Choosing to be homeschooled after recent events involving not only the ranch, but her immediate family and of course, the adoption, Keegan had been enrolled in an online education program through the state allowing her to log in when she needed to, work the scores of gradually increased intensity modules for each course, before submitting any tests or assignments given within the course itself. Finding this method of learning to be far more suited to her method of learning, not only had her grades improving, but because the logins were remote, she was never absent, never tardy, and always ready when called upon to be so. To her surprise, she had managed to complete more than fourteen percent of her next year's assignments in two classes. Her English course and her Math course for the next year's grade were already being attempted and even achieved. To say she was rather proud of herself would be quite accurate in deed.

When she had set the table and started the toast, Keegan caught her guardian's eyes meaningfully studying whatever was on the screen of her cellphone.

"What's up, Lora?" she asked, hoping for good news, but not quite getting the good news vibe as quickly as she had hoped.

"Not sure. I'll need to call Mom back, but I think I just became either a partner in the barn with my mom, or maybe she's saying that the barn will be placed in my name when she dies. I'm not sure of all the legal wording. I run horse flesh in circles for a living, I don't really do legal stuff." She reported.

"Can I look at it? Maybe I can tell you what it means."

Inquired the new teen who had been quite willing to settle any score for any reason for her best of friends and legal guardian. It didn't matter what it took;

the girl would find a way to make sense of it if she could, and if she couldn't, she would find someone who could.

"You're thirteen now, sure...why not, go ahead, you're probably better at it than I am. I think what she's saying is she'll have the lawyers call me. She and Steve may retain ownership of it, but don't want to be expected to be here other than for the charity events and maybe for the auctions she's going to allow us to do when we start that this summer."

Keegan's eyes lit up, having only heard about the rumors or the possibilities of being a seasonal auction house for the Dowd's and for Mountain View Ranch when they had an overflow of animals they couldn't take in; it was far too exciting to think about, but something Keegan couldn't actually stop thinking about.

"Just so you know, I'm not learning how to do that thing with my mouth like they do when they do the thing they do. I hate it. I think it sounds really stupid. I'll just point to someone and say 'What are you willing to pay?' and then I'll ask the next person the same thing. We could get those cards on sticks with numbers too; that's a whole lot easier than trying to stumble over whatever they're pretending to say and come up with a really weird number all garbled up in my mouth." She laughed.

"So, what makes you think you're going to be the auctioneer, exactly? I mean, you can, I don't care, but have you been pretending to do so? It seems like

something you would do." Melora added before asking if Keeg had make heads or tails of the email.

She poured her coffee before realizing it looked a bit stronger than normal. Adding less sugar but more creamer to it, Melora Armstrong sat with her hands warming on the cup. She pulled her robe a little tighter, reached down to get a tiny rock or something off the bottom of her sock and asked again, "*Have you been pretending to be an auctioneer Keegan? No judgement, I swear.*"

Without answering her at first, the girl looked up and to the right. Squinting her eyes somewhat, and then using her nose to count out something both invisible and obscure, she brought her attention back to the forefront of her own mind to look Lora in the eyes before announcing that she, Melora Ashleigh Armstrong, would be the owner by proxy, having the rights and honors to make decisions regarding the needs or requirements of the entire ranch known as *Bay Sorrel Ranch*, which of course, included lands, pastures, the trailer that Alvarez family lived in, the barns, the outbuildings, storage areas and fences. It also included the small house, which remained in Jule's name. All of the properties would be inventoried soon, and appraised for value, but would not be sold.

"*You're supposed to decide if you want to be a partner and put up the funds to keep the ranch in the future, and over the next ten years you'll take over completely, but an equal amount of money that you will pay will have to go into an escrow for Rogan and Brooke. Jule will pay that of course, not you, so they don't say you were given more. There's another amount for all the kids if she... if Jule dies or if she just wants out of the whole ownership thing. It sounds like she wants to give it all to you, but she can't because she would have to give them the same amount of money and it's over what she has at this time.*

"She thinks, it looks like, that in time the books will take off, and she can give the others more actual cash and you'll take your portion through the property values and whatever; that way you don't get money but you get the ranch. Does that make sense? I mean it does to me. She doesn't want to own it in ten years. If you haven't bought it completely, she's saying she could sell it to you for whatever is fair market instead of $10 so that the other kids get a third of whatever the fair market is at that time. That's what I get out of it." She concluded.

"To think that you are only a kid. My God, you're hella scary and remind me never to get on your bad side, chick."

Laughed the robed one who couldn't bring her mind to the forefront of anything without another cup of her sugary milky latte.

Since the two of them had not heard from Jule in a day or so, they placed a Facebook video call to be sure all that Keegan had said was somewhat or somehow possible. When she had managed to steady herself from all the legal wording coming through the screen at her, Melora nodded her head a few times indicating that she was more than willing to do what she could to bring about the closure of the transfer of the barn and she would do so sooner than in ten years if she could. The summer charity events notwithstanding, the transfer would begin in June of that year and each year in June they would take a look at what the fair market value was for the previous, present, and future year for tax purposes and for use purposes.

They decided between them that allowing boarders could and would keep the lights on, and the water running through the pipes. They could earn more by training and flipping Mustangs, but besides just having the Mustangs as a means of income, the new plans for the future auctions would need to manifest on a monthly basis, not just for the summer months. They'd go ahead with what would be considered a dry-run for now, but plan on making the event a permanent one after both Melora and Keegan had time to study up on what would be needed. Jule and Steve almost simultaneously mentioned that the two of them would of course, remain on board and in the background to be used when necessary; they wanted the whole thing to take off. They wanted success for the ranch, and of course for everyone concerned. Steve insisting that he was very much a very silent partner; he retired from the big bad ugly world, and he liked it that way.

First steps would include becoming incorporated as an auction house, and pay any and all permits and fees associated with that. They'd go to Dowd's and speak with Iain Dowd to find out what they did in the beginning of each tax year to report their income. They'd ask how to become an auction house without sounding as if they were planning to take any buyers from their friends; that wasn't the reasoning behind the new venture. They wanted to begin as an overflow venue; a place where their friends and colleagues could count on them in case too many horses, mules, or cattle were dropped off any given month. When the auditors come out and fine a barn for being overstocked, some of the animals seemed to mysteriously disappear. That wasn't what Jule or Melora wanted; it was the reason for their thinking of assisting in the past.

"Let us take your overstock. We can pay you for them. We'll be fair, and that way the animals live, and people who ordinarily would go to you will continue to do so, because we'll let them know we're an overflow facility, until we can get our feet on the ground. We're talking several years of helping you and the others out before we can make a go of it; what do you say?"

Jule asked the Irish man who had several reasons to agree with her way of thinking.

Once the paperwork was created, signed, and filed, Bay Sorrel Ranch not only became one of the premiere barns in the state with regard to having boarders, training, lessons, and a good facility for events, it was about to become an overflow auction house. The location of the ranch was optimal, many folks in Oklahoma and Kansas would much prefer to find and buy their horses online from Dowd and then allow him to deliver them to Bay Sorrel Ranch to be quarantined and picked up. The plans were made, and the balls were rolling; rolling in the same direction, and rolling with purpose as well as being potentially profitable. It sort of reminded everyone of the airy white horses on Rogan's mindful carousel; spinning without bars to hold it all in place, and taking off in all the right directions.

"A good plan is good to have, but having a plan is essential." Jule said before hanging up the phone with her accountant on the last day of June. Her plans for the 4th of July charity were not only falling into place, they were beginning to overflow. Every boarder played a part even if it seemed they could only contribute in a minor way. Crissy Harroz wanted to know if she could lead the parade in the arena; but a parade hadn't been discussed until she asked. Not wanting to throw a wet blanket onto the hopes of a little girl, Jule agreed to allow the young rider, and her sister, who had just turned five, to be the official marshals of the event if they could do so without arguing about who got to hold the flags. One girl would hold the American flag, while the other held the flag of the Great State of Oklahoma. Their mother, who was in fact an

accomplished rider herself, agreed to ride behind the two girls to keep a watchful eye, while waving her new Stetson cowgirl hat to the crowd to prompt each and every one in the stands to rise to their feet to honor Old Glory at the first chords of *"The Star-Spangled Banner"* being played by their closest Scots friend, Mr. John Spencer Wilson.

The day would prove to be full of fun, laughter, creative skits on horseback from both the English set as well as the Western boarders; all participating and engaging throughout the day in what would be regarded statewide as one of the most memorable charity and patriotic barn events ever held. Steve and Jule donned clown faces, wore silly clothes, and practiced a little skit they felt would be heartwarming and bring folks together. When Cameron Learner showed up with his own version of hilariousness, dressed almost to the *"T"* as *Ho Ho the Clown*, a very beloved Oklahoma favorite, the barn boarders went crazy with accolades, comments and more. He would certainly turn heads and melt hearts; of course, being true to his gal, the only heart he really cared to melt was sitting on a once-wild Mustang named Hercules.

On the north side of the pastures, where once a solemn and hurtful time had been created; Trinity and Bob Williams helped the Armstrongs unveil a memorial for their daughter Jodi. The four-foot bronze statue sat atop a thick marbled pedestal. The statue reflected the girl in her youth, riding bareback on her favorite mount, a smaller spotted horse known as *Buster*. They had taken the county fairgrounds by storm when she was younger. With her long blond hair flowing behind her, her smile lighting up the skies, Jodi Williams with her keen-eyed gelding welcomed every visitor to Bay Sorrel Ranch. A small plaque on the front of the statue mentioned the short story of the tragic event, but closed with asking everyone who read the words to consider love over hate, and to show kindness at all times, as we simply don't know when our last ride on this Earth will take place.

The End

Jude Stringfellow

Bay Sorrel Ranch

ABOUT THE AUTHOR

Jude Stringfellow has authored more than a dozen books and has self-published most of them. Her latest works *"Bay Sorrel Ranch"* has a unique place in her heart if only for the fact that she herself has been in and out of the horse world throughout her life. Having never owned a horse until she was an adult, Stringfellow admired the animals from afar, hoping and wishing to become a more serious rider. Her friends and some of her extended family-owned horses, and though she was allowed to ride their horses, she wanted a horse of her own so badly, she made mistakes in procuring one for herself.

It is because of some of her experiences with boarding and riding, that Jude decided to write *"Bay Sorrel Ranch"*. Some, but certainly not all of the experiences she had are detailed in the book. In all of her writings, she hopes her readers will find something they can relate to; something they like, dislike, wish to share, or keep close to their heart.

A native Oklahoman, Jude Stringfellow grew up in the suburban city of Bethany, Oklahoma, just west of the capital city. A mother, as well as a grandmother, she splits her time between her familial obligations, and gives herself time to relax and research content for her upcoming books. Jude is a born-again Christian, yet recognizes her own faults, flaws, and misgivings. It's because of her faith in Christ, she confident and strong enough to say she will be protected and provided for at all times. She has many books to write, and many stories to tell.

You can find other books by Jude Stringfellow in Amazon. She has written murder thrillers, romance, poetry, dramatic novels, biographies and children's books. Keep an eye out for anything new; you can find most posts at her blogspot: https://judestringfellow.blogspot.com

Printed in the USA
CPSIA information can be obtained
at www.ICGtesting.com
LVHW020038260124
769470LV00074B/1971